FATHER'S DAY

ALSO BY BUZZ BISSINGER

Friday Night Lights

A Prayer for the City

Three Nights in August

Shooting Stars (with LeBron James)

FATHER'S DAY

*A Journey into the Mind and Heart
of My Extraordinary Son*

BUZZ BISSINGER

AN EAMON DOLAN BOOK
Houghton Mifflin Harcourt
BOSTON   NEW YORK
2012

For information about permission to reproduce selections from this book,
write to Permissions, Houghton Mifflin Harcourt Publishing Company,
215 Park Avenue South, New York, New York 10003.

www.hmhbooks.com

Library of Congress Cataloging-in-Publication Data
Bissinger, H. G.
Father's day: a journey into the mind and heart of my extraordinary son / Buzz Bissinger.
p. cm.
ISBN 978-0-547-81656-2
1. Bissinger, H. G. 2. Bissinger, Zach, date. 3. Parents of exceptional children—
United States—Biography. 4. People with mental disabilities—United States—Biography.
5. People with mental disabilities—Family relationships—United States.
6. Fathers and sons—United States—Biography. I. Title.
HQ759.913.B57 2012
306.874'2—dc23   2012001360

Endpaper photographs by Robert L. Smith (4 strips on the left)
and Dominic Savini (2 strips on the right)

Printed in the United States of America
DOC 10 9 8 7 6 5 4 3 2 1

To Zach who trusted me with his life
To Gerry who helped me get through it
To Ari and Pete who knew I had to write it
To every parent who knows why

Contents

"You should have died, Zach. Do you know that?"

"I didn't."

Author's Note

Father's Day is a memoir, and parts of it must inevitably draw upon my memory alone. But I have tried as much as possible to base it on primary source material. All of my conversations with my son Zach during our road trip were taped; I transcribed the dialogue here verbatim. In order to capture the flow of his speech, in which he barely pauses for breath and merges each sentence or phrase immediately into the next, I present his statements without any punctuation.

In describing Zach's condition, education, and treatment, I relied on well over a thousand pages of medical and school records that I have collected since his birth.

In two chapters, I had to draw on sources other than my own records and memory. In Chapter 4, which deals with the history of premature infants, I relied on a variety of sources, including the following:

The Machine in the Nursery: Incubator Technology and the Origins of Newborn Intensive Care by Jeffrey Baker (Johns Hopkins University Press, 1996).

History and the Care and Feeding of the Premature Infant by Thomas Cone Jr. (Little Brown and Company, 1985).

"A Patron of the Preemies" by A. J. Liebling, *The New Yorker* (June 3, 1939).

When the Bough Breaks by Winifred Pinch (University Press of America, 2002).

"Reflections on Errors in Neonatology, Parts 1, 2, 3" by Alex Robertson, *Journal of Perinatology* (2003).

"Incubator-Baby Slide Shows" by William Silverman, *Pediatrics* (August 1979).

"American Characters: Martin Couney" by Richard Snow, *American Heritage* (June/July 1981).

"Baby Incubators, a Clinical Study of the Premature Infant, with Especial [sic] Reference to Incubator Institutions Conducted for Show Purposes" by John Zahorsky (Nabu Public Domain Reprints, 1905).

"2nd Son Born to Kennedys: Has Lung Illness," *New York Times* (August 8, 1963). "Kennedy Infant Dies at Hospital," *New York Times* (August 9, 1963).

Official Guidebook (to the Chicago) World's Fair 1934.

In Chapter 5 on savantism, I used these sources:

"On Some of the Mental Affections of Childhood and Youth: Being the Lettsomian Lectures Delivered Before the Medical Society of London in 1887, Together with Other Papers" by J. Langdon Down (Nabu Public Domain Reprints, 1887).

Bright Splinters of the Mind by Beate Hermelin (Jessica Kingsley Publishers, 2001).

The Real Rain Man by Fran Peek (Harkness Publishing Consultants, 1996).

"Prodigies" by Oliver Sacks, *The New Yorker* (January 9, 1995).

The Man Who Mistook His Wife for a Hat by Oliver Sacks (Touchstone, 1985).

Mental Deficiency by A. F. Tredgold (Nabu Public Domain Reprints, 1915).

Extraordinary People by Darold Treffert (Ballantine Books, 1989).

Islands of Genius by Darold Treffert (Jessica Kingsley Publishers, 2010).

"The Marvelous Musical Prodigy, Blind Tom, the Negro Pianist," Cornell University Library Digital Collections (circa 1867).

FATHER'S DAY

Chapter 1

Zach

I

I AM MEETING ZACH AT Brooks Brothers in the sodden, sullen aftermath of Christmas. He has just come from work at the supermarket where he has bagged groceries for four hours with one fifteen-minute break. I cannot imagine my son doing such work at the age of twenty-four. It shames me to think of him placing sweat-drenched jugs of milk into their proper place and learning initially, with the extensive help of a job coach, that the eggs must be placed separately in double plastic bags. He has been doing the same job for four years, and he will do the same job for the rest of his life. My son's professional destiny is paper or plastic.

Except for brief lapses in which he pesters fellow employees like a seven-year-old, following them and calling out their names in a purposely aggravating singsong voice when they are trying to work, he does his job well. He limits his conversations with customers, although by nature he is ebullient and friendly. He no longer interjects his views, as he did several years ago when he was working at K-Mart one summer stocking supplies. When a customer asked where to find work gloves, he announced that he found it an odd request: "What do you need gloves for? It's the summer." It defied his sense of logic; gloves are for cold, not hot, and Zach just wanted to make sure the customer understood the order of things.

He is well liked. Female cashiers call him "my guy" and "my baby" and treat him with protectiveness. He calls them by their first names, as if they all served in the trenches of World War I together. But he lacks the dexterity, or maybe the confidence, to handle a register or work the deli section. He fears change, because routine is the GPS that guides him. He orders the same entrée virtually every time we go out for dinner: salmon. He occasionally ventures out into the uncharted territory of a Cajun chicken wrap or even a crab cake, but it is the pink flesh of salmon, even if it is more gray than pink and flaking off in dry chunks, that safely brings him home. He leans back in the La-Z-Boy I once gave him for his birthday and often watches the ten o'clock news on Fox, not because he wants to keep up on current events, but because he takes comfort in seeing the usual television newsmakers like the mayor and the police chief and the indicted city official proclaiming innocence although the payoff money was found inside his pants. He also liked learning the names of the anchors and the weatherman. The world by its nature is chaotic and unpredictable, but Zach always narrows it down to a reliably straight line.

Because of trace brain damage at birth, his comprehension skills at the age of twenty-four are roughly those of an eight- or nine-year-old, although he is quite verbal. He can read, but he doesn't understand many of the sentences. He has basic math skills, although he is still prone to using his fingers. He understands money to a certain degree. Because his mother, Debra, and I encourage independence, he is allowed to use public transportation to go to Philadelphia where his other job is, stocking supplies at a law firm, and where his brother lives. The train stops at 8th Street and Market. He is supposed to walk the rest of the way if it is daylight — about seven blocks. But sometimes he sneaks in a cab ride. The fare is ten dollars. He dutifully pays the meter but then he leaves a five-dollar tip, making him a favorite among Philadelphia cabdrivers who otherwise drive in silent misery.

He can't add a hundred plus a hundred, although he does know the result is "a lot," which is close enough when you think about it. He goes to movies, but the action and plot don't filter down to him; he seizes on images that he has seen before. I took him to see *Spartacus* once, when he was eight, and, after a blood-flowing scene at a Roman villa where Kirk Douglas single-handedly kills two million buffed-up soldiers with a plastic knife, he turned to me and said, "Look Dad! A pool!" He has always loved pools. In his early teens, he belonged to a swim club that competed against other clubs. He swam the fifty-yard freestyle. He finished far behind the other contestants, but it didn't matter. He still finished, every stroke like swimming against a frothing high tide. To this day, I don't know how he did it. It is the most monumental athletic feat I have ever seen.

His IQ, which has been measured far too many times, is about 70, with verbal scores in the normal range of 90, but with performance skills of about 50. I love my son deeply, but I do not feel I know him nor do I think I ever will. His mind is not simple. It is limited to a degree that profoundly frustrates me, but it is also inexplicably wondrous at certain moments. I have dedicated my life trying to fathom its inner workings. I can make educated guesses, some of which I think are accurate. I'm not a psychologist or psychiatrist, but I have spent nearly a quarter century trying to pinpoint the best learning and life strategies for Zach, so I am far more confident of my conclusions about him than theirs, some of them so haphazard they might as well have been made during the fourteenth hole on Maui before the convention luau.

It is strange to love someone so much who is still so fundamentally mysterious to you after all these years. *Strange* is a lousy word, meaning nothing. It is the most terrible pain of my life. As much as I try to engage Zach, figure out how to make the flower germinate because there is a seed, I also run. I run out of guilt. I run because he was robbed and I feel I was robbed. I run because of my shame. I am not proud to feel or say this. But I think these things, not all the time, but too many times, which only increases the cycle of my shame. This is *my* child. How can I look at him this way?

Because I do. Because I think we all do when confronted with difference, reality versus expectation never at peace or even truce.

· · ·

As his father, I should go to watch him work at the grocery store every now and then. I should offer support and encouragement because he is my son. I did go once. Zach was in one of the aisles on a break, and he didn't know I was there. I saw a coworker approach him. I thought they were friends. It made me feel better. The coworker spoke with rapid excitement.

— Hey, Zach!

— Oh hey Brian!!

— Hey, Zach, you know the woman with the big tits? She wants you, Zach! When you gonna put the move on her?

— Yeah.

— She's waitin' for you, Zach! You better do it soon!

— Okay Brian okay!

Brian knew Zach was different. He knew from the way Zach talked aloud to himself. He knew from the way Zach paced and took in breaths like he was gasping for air. He knew from the sudden tics that sometimes overcame his arms and torso. He knew from the way Zach walked, slightly hunched and Chaplinesque, one foot toward the east and the other toward the west. He knew from the way Zach had difficulty understanding. He preyed on Zach with leering joy. He laughed at Zach and walked away. But that wasn't what hurt me most. What hurt me most was how Zach welcomed the attention. He yearned to please Brian. He yearned for Brian's acceptance, although he did stop short of seeking out the woman with the big tits.

And that still wasn't the most painful part. I should have grabbed Brian by the neck. I just ran.

I am forever running. I am still running from that moment I first saw him through the window of a hospital operating room on a suffocating August day in Philadelphia in 1983. Doctors and nurses surrounded him in a tight circle. He was a bloody quiver in their hands, born thirteen and a half weeks too soon and weighing one pound and eleven ounces. They held him with their arms high and outstretched almost as if they were offering him as a sacrifice. They held him ever so gently as if he might break into a thousand pieces or just crumble into dust.

His skin was almost translucent. His arms could snap in two like a wishbone. His fingers could break like the point of a pencil. His legs were tissue paper. They knew the odds of his survival were very low. I also knew that if he survived, he would not remotely be the son I imagined. Which is a nicer way of saying he would not remotely be the son I wanted. I had little clue about medicine, but it was irrelevant to the obvious: any baby born so many weeks prematurely, with immediate difficulty breathing, looking the way he did like a weightless feather, would suffer long-term effects.

Debra and I were married at the time. She had been on bed rest in the hospital for nearly two months. I was on my way to visit her. It was a Saturday. I was dressed in a polo shirt and shorts and loafers without socks. I'd stopped at a convenience store and bought a can of Diet Coke and a bag of chips. I had no idea she would be in labor by the time I arrived. All I wanted to do was drink that can of Diet Coke and eat those chips as I watched Zach glow with blood in the bright bath of lights in the operating room. I felt like eating because I felt like a stranger. I felt I was just there by coincidence, wandering into the wrong room and seeing through the glass a woman I did not know giving birth. None of this made the slightest sense. None of this matched fatherhood. I didn't feel like crying. I just felt like walking away. And this was only half of what had already happened.

Another bloody quiver had already been taken from the womb by the time I got there. It was Zach's twin brother named Gerry. He weighed three ounces more. He had been born three minutes earlier. Because of those three minutes, and his positioning in the womb, his lungs were more developed than Zach's. He could not breathe on his own, but there was enough oxygen flowing through him initially to protect his brain from harm. Zach's lungs were not developed enough to give his brain the oxygen it needed in those crucial first moments.

Brain damage settled like a patchy mist, some places forever abandoned, and yet some places heightened and magnified. Zach would eventually be able to walk and talk. Remarkably, he would suffer no physical side effects from his birth. He loves to communicate in simple snippets, mostly by asking questions. He can be unwittingly funny because he tells only the truth of his feelings. But his IQ places him on the borderline of mental retardation. Why sugarcoat it? My son is mentally retarded.

You can boil an egg in three minutes. You can fetch the morning paper in three minutes. You can empty the dishwasher in three minutes. You can reheat the leftovers in three minutes. You can call for Chinese takeout in three minutes. You can eat Chinese takeout in three minutes. You can determine the very course of a life in three minutes.

It was Gerry who was able to breathe on his own after a month. It was Zach who fought for his life in the neonatal intensive care unit, his tiny chest pumping up and down, never at peace, the frantic pulse of wanting to live and the frantic pulse of not wanting to die, always on supplemental oxygen with the green tube taped across his lips so it would not slip from his nostrils. Gerry who left the hospital after two and a half months plump and mirthy. Zach who stayed there for seven and a half months, intubated dozens of times, which like all medical terms has a clinical beauty to it that purposely hides what it really means — shoving a plastic tube down Zach's trachea into his airways so he could breathe as his tiny body shook with the tearless cries of pain that is equal to that of an adult if not more so. Gerry who made the benchmarks of sitting and standing and walking. Zach who remained tethered to supplemental oxygen for another year and a half after he came home, with the canister always beside the crib and the alarm monitor on in case his breathing and heart rate perilously diminished.

Gerry went to the fine Quaker private high school in the shadow of the Philadelphia Art Museum and then college. Now he was getting his master's degree at the University of Pennsylvania Graduate School of Education. Zach went to the private school for children with severe educational handicaps and then the self-contained program at the high school where he learned vocational skills and basic hygiene such as remembering to brush his teeth and use deodorant every day. Gerry deserved all of what he got because of his sheer will to live, and Zach deserved none of it despite his sheer will to live.

Debra and I threw a graduation party for Zach after he got his high school diploma, a symbolic milestone since he hadn't fulfilled any of the normal requirements. It was a grand occasion. Nearly a hundred people came from all over the country because he was and always will be truly beloved. I got up from the head table to give a toast. "Today Zach is a high school graduate!" I yelled. The cheers rose into a standing ovation. He received dozens of gifts that night, piled up on a table like a bonfire. He was the epicenter of the galaxy. I wondered if he would ever have a moment like this again since there would be no wedding or birth of a child or golden anniversary. I knew Gerry's future would include all of that. I knew Zach's future would always include bagging groceries.

II

Zach is already inside Brooks Brothers on Walnut Street in Philadelphia when I get there. He is tired from work. The stacks of shirts and the cold-cut platters of striped and solid ties on circular tables and the racks of khakis and flannels pleated and unpleated and cuffed and uncuffed overwhelm him. He bends down to touch a tie. He has always fixated on ties. When he was a little boy he insisted on picking ones out for his grandfather and uncle, deliberating between one covered with little whales and a classic striped. Later on he asked for ties every Christmas. He has gotten so many, he still has some he has never touched a decade after receiving them. Now, among questions he uses every time to communicate with someone new, he asks whether he wears a tie to work. The other four basic questions he asks in his rote way are: "Where do you live?" "Where do you work?" "Do you drive to work?" "What is your birthday?" He never forgets the answers to these questions. Throughout the year he calls dozens of people, some of whom he hasn't seen in twenty years, to wish them a happy birthday. He is the Birthday King, and many now call him to make sure they haven't missed one that could lead to unwanted trouble. He is always right. They don't even try to remember anymore.

Zach acts like he's happy to see me. Since Zach does not know the meaning of acting, he really does welcome my presence. I am not like him. I have always been terrified of making an ass of myself, hyper-self-conscious, sometimes social but often beset by anxiety and depression and the downside of mild bipolarity: a morning cocktail of Klonopin, Effexor, Wellbutrin, and Lamictal that my wife Lisa makes sure I have taken, terrified of medicated-less consequences.

— Oh hi Dad!

— Hey, Zach. How was work?

— Pretty good.

— Did you bag a lot of groceries?

— I did.

— Did you talk to any customers?

— I didn't know anyone there anyway it was a Friday people I know don't come until Saturday like around two because that's when my shift starts maybe Sunday after church sometimes.

— Remember you are there to work. You can't talk to them very long.

— I know.

— Did you pay attention?

— Yup.

— Did you bug anyone?

— Nope.

— Did you break any eggs?

— Oh Dad . . .

— Are you ready to spend your gift certificates? You have five hundred dollars' worth.

— I'm ready.

— Do you know what you want?

— A tie maybe.

— You have a hundred ties, most of which you have never worn.

— Oh.

— I think you need to get some other things.

— Like what?

— Maybe a sports coat.

— Maybe a sports coat.

— Maybe new pants.
— Maybe new pants.

The smell of the new clothing in Brooks Brothers is aromatherapy. It takes me back to the once-a-year pilgrimage with my father in the 1960s to the flagship store on Madison Avenue and 44th Street in New York to get clothes for school. I can still see the button-down shirts and flannels and khakis we'd chosen piled high on a table. I can remember my father looking at my haul and saying, "Maybe we should throw in a blue blazer." After we threw in a blue blazer another suggestion followed: "Let's just take a little peek at the men's section." So we went to the men's section. "Can I help you with anything?" the salesman always said. "Just looking," my father always said. "Let me know if I can be of help," the salesman always said. "You got it," my father always said. He went through the racks of clothing twice. He made a move to the elevators. "You should get something, Dad!" I always told him. He always returned to a certain jacket on one of the racks. "Let's just see how it fits," he always said. "Of course," the salesman always said. He always bought two. Then he always bought a couple of shirts and a couple of ties and a couple of pairs of socks and a couple of pairs of underwear.

"Well, Buzzer, we had a pretty good day," he always said after we'd left the store and crammed ourselves inside a taxi with all our shopping bags. The one thing he never said was that we were the only two people in the entire world at the moment. But I knew anyway.

I am all too aware of what I am doing with Zach so many years later at Brooks Brothers on Walnut Street. I am trying to dress him into myself when I was a boy with my father. I am trying to make him into something he isn't. Zach tries on a pair of classic gray flannels. I am anxious that they fit him well. He goes to the dressing room.
— Everything okay in there?
— I'm fine.
— How do they look?
— Pretty good.

He comes out of the dressing room. The pants cannot make it over his protruding stomach. The legs billow like the jib of a sailboat in a dead wind. I silently rail against the cruelty of his metabolism that in a few years has made his midsection mushroom after being stick thin throughout his youth. The salesman knows I am trying to dress this man-child in Brooks Brothers from head to toe. He intuits my need to keep alive some fantasy that my son must have gray flannels because he works as a lawyer or hedge fund trader.

The salesman steps in and tries to deflect the tension of my frustration. He calls Zach "Hey, buddy" with familial intimacy. We move to the rack of blazers, five-hundred-dollar coats selling for forty percent off. I pick one out for Zach. The blazer fits Zach in the shoulders but there is no way he'll ever be able to button it. It is the best we are going to do. My frustration becomes agitation. My agitation becomes bitchy admonishment.

— You eat too much, Zach.

— Okay.

— How many times do you stop for a Kit Kat?

— Sometimes during grocery breaks.

— No more Kit Kats. No more cheese. No more fried foods. Your stomach is getting enormous. It is hard to find you clothes that fit.

— I'm sorry Dad.

— How many times have we told you you need to eat less?

— A lot.

— What has Doctor Runfola told you?

— I need to lose weight.

— Do you know why you need to lose weight?

— Because maybe it's bad for you?

— Do you know why it's bad for you?

— Because you kind of look big?

— Eating too much can affect your heart. Also because you have high blood pressure. So no more Kit Kats. You understand? This is serious.

— I'm sorry Dad.

I don't think he truly understands the medical implications of obesity and high blood pressure. He will try to lose weight because I have told him to and his mother has told him to and his doctor has told him to. But he cannot grasp basic principles of good health. This worries me, but it has nothing to do with why I'm so agitated now. The promise of a new Brooks Brothers wardrobe is just an illusion. What I experienced as a son with my father I will not experience as a father with my son. He is not a hedge fund trader. I should have known that by now. I will never know that by now. I can't.

We purchase the blazer, which Zach is still wearing. He asks the salesman if they have a pocket square he could put into the breast pocket because that's what *my uncle wears and maybe it would be nice maybe to look like my uncle yeah yeah Dad don't you think it would be nice to maybe look like him?*

The salesman finds a pocket square. He slides it into the breast pocket with the peak sticking out. Zach looks regal. He looks transformed. I never knew he noticed such touches. He is not an abstract thinker; he does not pick up on aesthetic details. It is a common blind spot for people like Zach who harbor aspects of autism, although his diagnosis is not nearly as tidy as that. Yet it *was* an abstract and aesthetic notion for Zach to see the pocket square in his uncle's breast pocket and want it for his own as a sartorial touch. It surprises me. It gives me the necessary elixir of hope.

Which is when I first get the idea.

III

We celebrate shopping success by visiting the Barnes & Noble several blocks up Walnut Street. Zach goes directly to the map section. He always goes there. I have never seen him go anyplace else in a bookstore.

He picks up a map of Philadelphia, but since he has about a dozen maps of Philadelphia and has memorized virtually every street in the city without trying to memorize them, he moves on. He considers a map of one of the surrounding counties, maybe Montgomery, maybe Delaware, maybe Bucks, but he has plenty of maps from these areas as well, and he feels like traveling. He settles on a map of Kansas City since he has recently met someone from Kansas City. He takes the

Kansas City map and unfolds it. He holds it high with one hand as if he's looking for just the right angle of wind so he can fly. He buries his head in the interstices of streets and avenues and parkways and boulevards. He pinpoints the street he is looking for, the address of the person he has met from Kansas City. He looks at it once more, touches it with a finger from his free hand. He will remember it forever after.

I watch at a distance as if I'm observing some otherworldly phenomenon, the pelicanlike presence of him with that one hand held high as if he's barely balancing, his face so deeply buried inside the map that his nose almost touches it. I like that he is unaffected by the thought of how he looks, the idiosyncrasy of it. And since I'm a parent, and all parents live through their children whether they admit to it or not, I probably love most of all that my son, *my son,* can do something that so few can do. Nobody can read a map like Zach does.

I poke about in the adjacent guidebook section. I thumb through Frommer's guides to Turkey and India and Spain. I move to a different section and pick up a book called *1000 Places to See in the United States and Canada Before You Die.* I have been to many of them. I have visited forty-nine of the fifty states. I have driven across the country four times. I love the lonely roads where your thoughts come to you with such clarity, as if you are living in them, touching them. I crave the truck stop junk food, even the whiplike lengths of "beef" jerky that settle in your stomach only after stubborn reluctance. I make peace with the burned coffee and the whitener that becomes more and more popular the deeper you go into the heartland. I find pleasant mystery in the funky off-the-exit-ramp motels whose polyester bedspreads smell of sex and Juicy Fruit and hairspray.

My father taps me on the shoulder again. It's inevitable that thoughts of your own childhood crowd around you as you raise your own children. Still, given the forever horror that happened at the end with my dad, I am surprised he keeps appearing. But he does, prompting me to remember the road trips we once took together.

When I was ten we drove from New York to Hanover and Dartmouth College, where my father had gone to college. In the recollection I carry with me, probably not quite true and yet as true as it should be, there wasn't another car on the road once we hit New Hampshire. Just me and my dad kicking it through the night.

Dartmouth football was in its heyday in the 1960s. He had become a fanatic, and I followed in his wake to show solidarity. If you're bleeding Big Green, Dad, so am I. I always cried when Dartmouth lost to Yale. He put his arm around my shoulder in the pothole of the Yale Bowl and did not say a word, his acknowledgment that any pain is legitimate if you love something. He certified me, even though he knew he had on his hands a clinically oversensitive child who feared too much of the world. It was like the fireworks show every July Fourth on the Jetties Beach in Nantucket where we owned a house. I loved the spectacle but I was terrified by the sound. My father anguished for me and plotted a solution. He brought along two huge pillows that he held over my ears so I wouldn't freak out. I looked ridiculous, but he didn't care. So I didn't either.

It was after midnight as we neared Hanover. "Look, Buzzer," he said, as he pointed to the speedometer. The needle had hit a hundred. It had to be the coolest thing any father anywhere had ever done. Even if he did risk losing control of the car and killing both of us instantly. "Don't tell your mom," he said. My father trusted me with a secret! We were confidantes.

We drove to Saratoga Springs one summer to see the horseraces. The trip had been planned hastily. He had found a motel on the outskirts. There was a reason it was on the outskirts, slowly giving in to dereliction. But the bed in his room had Magic Fingers. It supplied instant amusement as you plunked the quarters into the metal box next to the bed, then felt rolls of pain grinding into your back and wondered who had been clever enough to invent something so worthless that someone still used.

We went to the historic racetrack but the only tickets we could get were in the grandstand. The beautiful people of Saratoga in their silk and ascots and wide-brimmed hats flitted about with languid arrogance in a separate section. I caught occasional glimpses of them. I envied them. I wanted to wear an ascot. I wanted to flit with arrogance.

My father sensed it. "They're all a bunch of stuck-up fucking assholes," he said. Even more thrilling than going a hundred miles an hour: his first profanity to me.

Many more millions would follow.

At the Barnes & Noble, I continue to thumb through the guidebook. I thought I knew the country, had picked it clean, but there is still so much to see. Zach puts the map of Kansas City back and plucks another one. Enough. I am impatient. It is his bookstore routine, but we have repeated it dozens of times now, and the over and over and over is gnawing at me.

—Zach, you ready to go?

—I'm ready.

—Did you find a map you wanted?

—Yeah.

—What is it?

—A new map of Philadelphia.

—You have a dozen maps of Philadelphia. Why do you need another one?

—I don't know I just do.

We go to leave. We stop. We are like the film *Groundhog Day* except nothing ever changes. Until now.

—Hey, Zach. You and I are going to drive cross-country this summer!

Zach scans his memory.

—Uncle Bobo drove to Texas once he got hit by a deer.

—I'll be more careful than Uncle Bobo.

—It wrecked his car I think.

—Zach, what about the trip?

—Will Gerry go?

—Nope. Just the two of us.

—Oh.

—You don't seem very excited.

—No no no I'm very excited how will we get there?

—We'll rent a car and we'll drive.

—To where?

— To California.

— Hey Dad I have an idea I think you'll really like yeah yeah yeah I think you'll really like it.

— What is it?

— Maybe we can fly.

IV

I ask Debra what she thinks. Her optimism was always in direct proportion to my pessimism, so our marriage lasted the predictable length of about four years. Or maybe three. She is reticent about the trip. She rightly worries about Zach sitting still in a car for long stretches no matter how hard he tries to rein in his body. She also points out that Zach is interested in neither hiking nor walking nor nature nor sightseeing. She and her husband, Paul, and their two children and Zach and Gerry had gone to Yellowstone National Park a few summers earlier. Zach was not only resistant to this journey but angry about it. When a dizzying flurry of bats flew over the trees during a nighttime walk to appreciative "oohs" and "aahs," he complained, "It's not even Halloween yet." In Zach's mind there is a precise slot for everything, and he balks at any departure from his precision. Bats are for Halloween. Gloves are for winter. Why is it so difficult for everybody to understand that?

Gerry's response to my idea is typically terse and direct.

— Two weeks in a car with Zach is a very long time.

Zach's mother frets that Zach will be unbearably uncomfortable. Zach's brother wonders what Zach and I will talk about. I worry that I'll be subjecting Zach to something he is doing solely for my sake. Zach wants to fly.

The notion of the trip becomes even more precarious when such typical attractions as the Badlands and Mount Rushmore and Wall Drug and Bryce Canyon and Yosemite and the Pacific Coast Highway must be avoided since I have seen them and Zach has never heard of them and has no interest in ever seeing them even if he did.

If we go at all, I have to figure out a route that has resonance for

Zach. That is not so easy. The idea is beginning to seem impulsive and implausible, spawned in a giddy flash on a cold and brittle day. It is maybe a well-meaning notion. More likely it is a selfish one, a father forcing his imprint on his son and creating an experience that becomes memorable only because both parties spend a lifetime unsuccessfully trying to forget it.

I am not going to expose Zach to something he silently hates. But I still think about the trip. I wonder if there is a way to structure it, not to treasure the country's epic attractions but to give rebirth to his past, go back to the present because of the way his mind works. I still think about the moment on the ground floor of Brooks Brothers in the after-Christmas emptiness when he asked the salesman for a pocket square so he could look like his unfortunately named Uncle Winkie. I always will see it neatly folded into the breast pocket like a church spire.

There was a spark inside Zach at that moment. Maybe it is a spark that rises like a busted firework, only to drain thinly back down to earth with a diminishing whistle. Or maybe I waved the surrender flag too long ago on my son, gave in because it was easier to give in.

Zach and I are driving across country.

Chapter 2

═══════════

Bon Voyage

I

WHEN ZACH WAS YOUNG and still living with Gerry and me during the week so he could attend the specialized private school in the area, I sometimes stood in his room in the dark and watched him sleep. His body teetered to the side, and his mouth curled open. I wished that I could crawl inside him without him ever waking and reach into the marbled matter of the brain to re-attach a wire here and a wire there, a couple of broken strands that just needed splicing, red to red, yellow to yellow, blue to blue.

He had his memory that was beyond remarkable. He had his no-nonsense style of interrogation with adults. Whatever else ticked inside him, there was an unlimited hard drive that saved every answer. I saw these give-and-takes as tiny ships of hope on the darkened sea, beacons of promise that would one day spread over the water until you could see the shore. He would make it to the island of normalcy, even though there is no such thing. All it would take was a simple re-arranging of those wires. He seemed so impenetrable, but then came moments when he redacted what was important in the world to its essence.

— What are you thinking about, Zachary?
— I'm just thinking about things.
— What things?
— Just things.
— Are you okay?
— I'm okay.
— Are you happy?
— I'm happy.
— Do you love me?
— I love you.
— How do you know you love me?
— Because I love you.
— Do you know what love is?
— It's love.

I began to wonder if there was more to my son than I ever knew or wanted to know. Debra and I had hovered over Zach all his life regardless of the freedom we granted him inch by inch. There was no other choice because of his limitations. Do you have your shirt for ShopRite? Did you forget anything? Do you have money? You can walk around the block twice but you have to be home in ten minutes. You can't have dessert. You can have dessert.

We had been appointed his legal guardians for life when he turned twenty-one. That too was a necessity. But we refused to make him a shut-in. He needed to work, whatever the work. Because he was so good at map reading, giving him the freedom to use the transit system became a potentially great opportunity: he craved freedom, we all crave freedom, and this was a way to give it to him.

Debra and I gave him a cell phone and taught him how to use it. I raised hypotheticals with Zach.

— What do you do when a stranger comes up to you?
— You walk away from them?
— That's right. What if they ask for your wallet?
— You give them your wallet.

— What if they ask for your money?

— You keep it because you need the money to get on the train to go downtown?

— No, you give it to them.

— What if I don't have any money I don't carry so much.

— You should always have money. We will give it to you. What else do you do?

— Call you or my stepdad or my mom?

— That's a good idea but the first thing you do is call nine-one-one. That's the police.

— I call nine-one-one.

— Let's practice. I'm a stranger. I come up to you. I ask you if you want to go somewhere or take a ride. What do you do?

— Call nine-one-one.

Perhaps he was ready.

The first trip was nerve-racking, like a baby taking his first steps. Would he wobble and fall? Would he need rescue? But he called when he got to the appointed stop — the corner of 15th and Locust streets in downtown Philadelphia. On his own without telling anyone, he started getting on the train a little early. He went to the Reading Terminal Market downtown to get Chinese food where the proprietors knew him because he introduced himself and asked their names. He went to the Barnes & Noble and branched out to maps of foreign countries. He began to meet me for dinner around the city, sitting at the bar sipping a Shirley Temple before I arrived. The only thing missing was a cigarette and a blond with his own patented pickup line: "Hey, baby, when's your birthday?"

Zach had a way of looking at the world that wasn't haphazard or accidental. The more independence he got, the more independence he desired. He loved taking the train to work. There were many people he knew. He always sat next to one of them, firing away with his questions and remembering the answers. They embraced him with understanding and tolerance and delight at his uncensored innocence, except for one man who told Zach after a single trip that he didn't want to sit with him anymore. Perhaps the man was being callous. Or perhaps he was just startled that after more than twenty years of not seeing Zach, my son still recognized him and knew his address. Or wanted to know his birthday. Or the names of the people who swam in his pool, even though Zach had never been to his house. The man liked riding the train alone because it was his quiet time, and Zach's inquisitions ruptured that quiet.

Zach told me he wasn't upset by the reaction. He never said he was upset, although I think he was in this instance. It confused him why somebody he knew, however tangentially, wouldn't want to talk to him since he was just trying to be friendly. Not all people are the same, I told Zach. Some people just like to be left alone.

— I shouldn't sit with him anymore?

— Zach, you know the answer to that. You shouldn't sit with him anymore.

— What if I see him at the station can I say hi?

— You just need to leave him alone. It isn't that he doesn't like you. It's just that he is busy with other things.

I could feel the wheels of Zach's brain slowly start to produce an answer that made sense to him.

— I guess he's private.

He figured it out. Just like he figured out that love is love.

It appeared that Zach observed tiny decorations of life, carefully storing them away on the hard drive of his mind and then incorporating them for future use. He had a *valid* sense of logic, even if most people failed to see it. Or maybe all he had on a sustained basis was a determination to find a good restaurant for the next meal to satiate his very expensive gourmand tendencies, no McDonald's in his particular playbook. It was always hard to tell how much of Zach was the result of deliberate effort and how much was just the result of his wiring. Actually it was impossible. He had never expressed himself with deep introspection, and he never would.

All my life I had yearned for conversation with my son. A conversation making him aware of his own reality. I had never told him what had happened when he was born. I never mentioned the term *brain damage*. I never mentioned the reason he went to special schools. Did he know he would never marry or have a family of his own? Did he know what sex was? Did he know who I really was like Gerry did, like my youngest son, Caleb, did?

Why had we never discussed, even in the broadest terms, his long-term future, no matter how wrenching the subject might be? Maybe because I wasn't sure how much he would understand. Or maybe because I couldn't bear to think about it. Because when I did, the same image always appeared:

I am gone and his mother is gone and Zach is old now, in his sixties, stooped and scraggly, his brown eyes more dark and furrowed than ever, his voice raspier than ever when he talks to himself, still doing with dutiful duty what he started forty years ago, bagging groceries. I see him walking the streets, on the way to some group home with his hands in his pockets, warding off the wind. I see his head cocked at that forty-five-degree angle as he talks in his self-chastising way, and passersby edge away because this guy is on the edge. Through windows filled with greasy fingerprints, I see my son sitting on a bed beneath a ceiling lamp spitting out freezing light. I see him quiet on that bed with his hands clasped in front of him. And then I see him talking aloud to himself some more, which no one tries to silence because no one else is there.

II

I had never told Zach about himself because I thought I was protecting him. I began to think I was not protecting him at all. Zach had to know the truth. Or maybe I felt the time had come for his father to tell him the truth. As long as I concealed Zach from himself the bond between us would never seem right. There would be love, but there would not be complete connection. The truth had also become his right. He deserved to know who he was. He deserved to know who I was.

I couldn't predict how much Zach would understand. While his vocabulary was rapidly expanding, his knowledge of what words meant was not keeping pace. When I tried to give a definition, or more important to explain the ramifications of certain actions in life like the need for good health, he *tried* to understand. I could literally feel him sifting through that hard drive with all those millions of data points. But his thought process was like using any steppingstone he could find to get across the water. The hard drive did not help him with the concept of preventive health, or terrorism, or racism, or civil liberties. He did not know who Osama bin Laden was. He did not know about Islam or the Middle East or the Holocaust or World War II. He had some vague idea of what 9-11 was: he knew something terrible had happened, but when the anniversary came he called to wish me a "happy 9-11!"

Our relationship for most of our lives had been largely predicated on games. He loved goofy hypotheticals of what would happen if he did something I told him he could not do. When I kissed him good night, he invariably asked me if there was a certain word or name he could not say after I turned out the lights.

— What can't I say?

— You can't say Rick Lyman.

— What happens if I say Rick Lyman?

— I will have to come back upstairs.

Dressed in his usual garb of T-shirt and gym shorts, the bedspread and the top sheet kicked down like unwanted rags in preparation for the tickling war we referred to as "cuddies," he began to giggle. Then giggle some more.

— What happens Dad if you come back upstairs?

— I will have to give you a cuddie.

— No no no.

— Then just don't say Rick Lyman.

— I can't say Rick Lyman?

— You can say anything else but not Rick Lyman.

— Not Rick Lyman?

— What did I just say?

— Not Rick Lyman.

— You can say Rick. You can say Lyman. But not Rick Lyman. Okay?

— Okay.

— Okay?

— Okay.

— Good night, Zach.

— Good night.

— Good night.

— Good night.

In previous lives, we had obviously both appeared in *Waiting for Godot*. And perhaps written it.

I walked down the stairs and waited at the second-floor landing. He was plotting strategy.

— RICK!

I said nothing.

— RICK!!

— I said nothing.

— RICK L!!!!!

I said nothing.

— RICK LY!!!!!!!

I said nothing.

— RICK LYMAN!!!!!!!!!!!!

I ran back upstairs and banged open the door. Between giggles, he pleaded false innocence.

— Dad come on Dad.

I came closer to the bed.

— What did I tell you NOT to say?

He stood on the mattress in final preparation.

— Dad seriously Dad I need to get to bed.

It was on.

He squirmed with surprising strength, accidentally kicking me in the head and scratching me with his long fingernails. He jumped out of bed and I began chasing him around the room. I threw pillows at him. He threw pillows at me. I got ahold of him and tickled again. He kicked me in the head again. I chased him around the room again. I became exhausted and finally had to stop. He seemed exhausted as well. I rolled the top sheet over him and kissed him good night. I shut the door to his room. I went back downstairs into my room. From above I could hear a pulsating drum getting louder and louder.

— Rick Lyman. . . . RICK Lyman. . . . RICK LYMAN! RICK LYMAN!!!

He could have gone on forever. At any time. At any age. But when he turned twenty-one, after nearly fifteen straight years of doing it,

I decided it had to stop. I was ambivalent about giving up this tra-
dition, though. What else could we do together that brought him so
much pleasure? But I could not stand it anymore. It only reaffirmed
our frozenness. Could we not move on to something else? Anything
else? Now, when I put him to bed, there were no tickle wars.

— Zach, you're twenty-one now. Not six. This is what six-year-olds
do. I can't do it anymore.

— Sorry Dad.

— There is nothing to be sorry about. You're just too old. You're
twenty-one. What happens when you are twenty-one?

— You're not supposed to do things like that anymore.

— That's right. Do you understand why?

— I'm twenty-one I'm kinda too old for this now.

I closed the door to his room. I stood right outside. I burst back
through the door.

— Just don't say "good night."

It was on again.

I knew it was the one thing he loved about being with me. I was
scared of losing it.

If I was going to talk to Zach with a directness and intimacy I had never
approached before, the setting itself had to be a place of intimacy. For
the past decade he had been living primarily with his mother and her
family in New Jersey, half an hour away from my home in Philadelphia. I saw him every weekend and sometimes more. But the longest I
had ever spent alone with him was a week. We needed time together.
We needed to once again fall in love.

We *needed* to drive across country. No matter how many times I
had done it, the road was always fresh. Like a precious inheritance,
I wanted to pass that experience on to Zach and have him seize it as
much as I did in my own life. My expectations *were* high.

A wise friend tells me I am dooming myself from the start by raising
the bar far too high. She tells me to just let the trip flow. She tells me
not to go searching for epiphanies and revelations. She tells me to take
the natural bends as they come. It is sage advice, and a shield against
the deflation of expectations. If you deliberately look for surprises and

significance in life, all you find is an old box of cassettes by America and Heart and Peter Frampton you bought when you were alone and very drunk, and nobody else was watching. But I still want to seek out epiphanies and revelations with Zach beyond the only one I've ever had, the day he was born. I so hungered to crack through the surface into his soul and have him do the same with me.

The trip must engage Zach. The passenger seat must be more than torture rack. Scenic attractions are clearly out. Yet I still think initially it should be a trip to expand Zach's horizons and let the wonder of the country at last course through him. Then I recall the experience of Yellowstone. In addition to his fury over the ill-timed bats, he found Old Faithful woefully lacking as a water slide compared to Hershey Park. And there wasn't a taco concession in sight.

Zach is interested in people. It doesn't matter whether he last saw them twenty minutes ago or twenty years ago. The route becomes self-evident. We will travel across country in ten days, stopping at all the places we've lived before or know well — Chicago; Milwaukee; Odessa, Texas; Los Angeles. Branson, Missouri, the evangelical antidote to Las Vegas, is an add-on because I have always wondered what happened to Yakov Smirnoff. The real Las Vegas is on the itinerary as well.

Las Vegas will be the highlight. I am sure of that. By the time we get there a new understanding and bond will have developed between Zach and me. I will speak the truth to him; there will be catharsis. I know Zach gets overwhelmed with too much sensory stimulus. But I am convinced the kinky kinetic kaleidoscope of Las Vegas will dazzle him much like fireworks dazzle him. He won't be able to take his eyes off the lights that ignite the universe. Zach himself has already taken to Las Vegas. He calls it "Vegas," as if he just joined the Rat Pack.

No scientific research is required to know that this is, by any ordinary standard, the worst cross-country route ever contemplated. There is literally nothing to see in terms of sights or natural beauty. The hills and mountains of western Pennsylvania have beauty, but the rest is an amalgam of tarmac, concrete, grass, dust, dirt, blown-out little towns with nothing open except the pawnshop, mesquite bushes, bugs smeared against the windshield like frosting. The stretch in particular from Milwaukee to Odessa, which we are probably the first human beings to ever undertake voluntarily, is without redemption.

We sit at the kitchen counter together half a dozen times to plan. Zach needs to be involved in every decision, so that the trip becomes a truly shared experience. Mutual agreement on where to stay. Where we should eat. How many miles we need to drive in a day to keep to our schedule. Where to stop at night in between our primary destinations. I promise Zach that we will try to go to an amusement park every day since he loves speed-of-light rides.

At this, he displays mild interest.

I buy him a new Rand McNally atlas of the United States.

No interest.

I purchase an octagonal gadget from a truck stop that gives the distances between every city in the United States: 1,433 miles from Yakima to Yuma, 876 miles from Vicksburg to Van Horn, 963 miles from Altoona to Albert Lea, 1,315 miles from Milwaukee to Odessa.

Definitely no interest.

I purchase guidebooks of the United States that describe interesting places off the usual path.

Less than no interest.

— Hey, Zach, what about Metropolis?!

— Where is it?

— It's in Illinois.

— Remember when we went to that basketball game in Illinois in 1991?

— Metropolis is the home of Superman.

— That would be nice.

— Have you ever been to any of the Superman movies?

— My cousin Nick lives in Chicago in Illinois we're going to see him.

— What about the Superman movies? Have you seen any?

— No not really.

— Do you really want to visit Metropolis?

— I remember the building where you worked in Chicago it was the *Tribune* building and remember Dad I used to go up there sometimes and see Barry Temkin.

— Do you know who Superman is?

— Not really.

— I think maybe we should skip Metropolis.

I ask him what kind of car we should rent.

He suggests a Cadillac.

His mother tells me he's getting more excited the closer we approach the July departure. I hear him tell people that "I am driving cross-country with my dad." His acknowledgment encourages me. But Zach's lack of engagement is worrisome. Perhaps the whole thing *is* too overwhelming for him. Perhaps the divergence from routine *is* just too radical. He seems more distant than ever. But then I figure it out. There is a precise motivation behind Zach's detachment.

He really does hate being in the car.

He really does want to fly.

III

On a Sunday afternoon in the third week of July, the twins and I are standing in the second-floor study of Gerry's apartment. Zach and I are leaving the next day and have come to share an early farewell dinner. On the far wall, held together by yellowed Scotch tape, is a paper map of the United States. I never noticed it before, and I gravitate toward it. Gerry watches from a few steps behind me. He understands better than anyone the tangled stitching of the journey I am about to take with his brother. He knows I am apprehensive. He also knows the importance I have attached to it. He knows me better than anyone, since we lived together from his birth until his graduation from high school. He also knows his brother better than anyone. He understands how tightly Zach clings to the lifeline of his literal landscape, next meal, next train ride, next ice-cream cone, next quesadilla with extra sour cream, next Kit Kat bar if nobody is looking.

I am glad Gerry is here with me. He plays off my overreaching one-liners, chuckling in the right spots like a dutiful laugh track. He is responding to me even though it is Zach's attention I am bidding for. Zach's affect is dulled; he looks far away into some pinpoint of space that only he can see. I believe he does see something, hear something, know something that cannot be touched by others.

— Zach, show the route; where are we going? Where are we now?

He points to New Mexico on the map. It is a strange and uncharacteristic error given his gifts.

— Is that where we are?

— No we're in Pennsylvania.

— Where?

— We're in Philadelphia.

— So where are we going?

Zach traces a tentative line with his forefinger. He speaks each word slowly. He is fearful of making a mistake. His eyes rise up to look at me. Then roll back down.

— I guess we would go out to Pittsburgh . . .

We have been over the route a dozen times, yet it has not sunk in. His look reminds me of the psychological and mental aptitude tests he took when he was young and turned to me in bewilderment, trying to make sense of the instructions when it was all a nightmarish blur of square pegs and round holes. He is overwhelmed because he is scared; any step away from the Routine is a frightening leap for him. We normally spend a week in Nantucket with my sister, Annie, every summer. She is kind and loving and hilarious. She talks more than anyone I have ever met, but a lot of it is to offset the fact that I don't talk very much. When we're there, we see the same people, we eat at the same restaurants. He always walks downtown to Kevin Dale's office and drinks a bottle of water. He goes out on Michael O'Mara's boat. He visits Billy Einstein. It is his zone of comfort. It is where he wants to be going now. He will not tell me that. He hates to disappoint me. The day is supposed to be celebratory. *Waiter, shots of tequila for me and my boys here!* Instead, it seems weighted by the heat that presses down. The liquid air reminds me of when the boys were born, the last thing I wanted to be reminded of right now, the last thing I ever want to be reminded of.

We leave the apartment and walk to a restaurant called the New Wave. We sit outside to the dull clank of silverware and the transit buses headed to downtown Philadelphia in trailing burps of gray exhaust and the speedy gossip of women in unrequited love coping with men who act like broken traffic lights — on again, off again. I order the grilled hanger steak salad. Gerry has the flatbread pizza. Zach has the shredded lamb taco because there is no salmon on the menu. Gerry offers advice to Zach.

— Have a good time. You'll have fun. Don't be against doing new stuff. Sometimes you're hesitant about that. You know what I mean about that?

— What do you mean?

— You like to have your routine. You like to wake up in the morning. Eat breakfast. Read your e-mails. Get ready for work. It'll be different now.

— Yeah.

Silence . . .

Gerry fills the hole with talk about the courses he's taking for his master's degree — school and society, a social studies methods course, student teaching at an inner-city elementary school. Penn has one of the finest schools of education in the country. The work is arduous and sophisticated. I am enormously proud of Gerry. So is Gerry, who never ever thought there would come a day when he would attend an Ivy League school.

I glance over at Zach. How can they be twins? Sometimes I wonder if they are even related. My pride in Gerry tamps down because of the guilt I feel for Zach. The goddamn guilt. The scrap-metal weight shackled to my ankle. It is always there.

— You look lost in thought, Zach.

— Yeah.

— What are you thinking about?

— Nothing.

The food comes. More silence. Forget what Zach and I are going to talk about for *two weeks* in a car. What are we going to talk about for *ten minutes*? Gerry again fills the space.

— Hey, Zach, is that lamb?

— At the July Fourth block party on the Fourth of July they made lamb I sat with Jay he's a member of a golf course.

It is a typical string of non sequiturs connected by disparate strands of memory. The plates are taken away. We wait for the check. I look at the mottled sidewalk and see blotches of blood and vomit and tiny bits of glass. I glance again at Zach. His head is cocked at an angle. He is staring inside his space. We need to get out of here.

We walk back around the corner to Gerry's apartment and go inside to fetch Zach's red suitcase. Then we come back outside. I have my black camera bag with me. I insist that they pose in front of the apartment door for a final picture before we leave. I like to be reminded they still are twins.

In my study is a photograph of Gerry and Zach taken when they were six years old. I was living with my second wife, Sarah, at the time in a suburb of Milwaukee. She took the picture.

They stand in front of the house we rented, wearing black jeans, white socks, and striped shirts, Gerry blue and Zachary green. They are holding each other's hands. Gerry looks straight ahead, and Zachary gazes at Gerry with adoration. They look like what you always hope twins will look like, in the uniqueness of their love.

I try to get them to imitate the posture of the picture taken almost twenty years ago. I am trying to replicate the possibilities that existed then, that moment between the two of them, my belief that it would all somehow work out even though I knew it would not. Zach was beautiful back then, with marble-smooth skin and eyelashes as long as a wedding train. I thought that this beauty would last into eternity and somehow shield him. It was an irrational thought. So what? Any parent who has a child that is different has a right to be irrational. It is how we cope. It is how we pray.

Gerry tells Zach to stand up straight as I fire off photos. He drapes his arm around him. He coos into his ear. Zach bursts with laughter. Their fingers intertwine. Then untangle.

— I'll miss you, Zach.

— I love you.

— Make sure you call me, let me know what you're doing.

— I will.

Zach and I walk back up the steps to the street. Gerry yells.
— AND TRY NEW THINGS!

IV

Zach and I go home from Gerry's apartment. We are leaving early to-morrow morning. Zach has packed by himself with economy, tight balls of clothing inserted into his red suitcase and a blue knapsack con-taining the Fort Knox of all his private possessions. I have packed the opposite, an enormous black soft cloth bag of clothing for different parts of the country. A hanging bag. A computer bag. A camera bag. There is also a green duffel bag that weighs fifty pounds and contains virtually every photo taken of Zach and Gerry from the worst mo-ments to the best. Each night we will pull out a fistful of pictures and Zach will fill in the names and places that I have long forgotten. An-other blending experience.

All our bags are neatly in a row by the side door, a joyless line of at-tention. They are sick of waiting. So am I.

— I think we should go tonight because I'm kind of excited.

— Yeah.

— Just the two of us. Are we going to learn a lot about each other?

— Yeah.

— What are we going to learn?

— A lot.

— What do you think it's going to be like being with me for two weeks?

— Different.

— Different? That's interesting. Why different?

— Because I'll be away from my other family.

— You gonna miss them?

— Yeah I'll probably call them a lot of people want me to call them.

I feel another uptick of self-doubt, but I move on. I grill him to make sure he has everything. He assures me he does. I am tempted to open the suitcase and see for myself. The razor he says he brought particularly concerns me, because the blade is usually two years old and rusted. The shaving cream he says he brought is a tiny can of Gillette Foamy, which I thought was discontinued after World War I. I have no idea where he got it. I let it go. I let all of it go. He does not like being treated like a child, and as much as I can I don't want to treat him like a child; his suitcase is his suitcase.

I go up to his room on the third floor to fetch a pillow and blanket so he can sleep in the minivan I've rented for the trip. To call this space Zach's room is a misnomer. It is simply the place where he sleeps when he stays with me. I should have done more to fill it with his possessions. I'm not sure why I did not, maybe because he never seemed to be here for very long.

I don't turn a light on. I don't want to be reminded of the sterility. A single bed with a drab brown bedspread is wedged into the corner. *Sports Illustrated* etchings of Ted Williams and Eddie Arcaro that came from my own childhood hang on the walls. He has no idea who these men were. The square eye of a television he never watches stares from the back wall. His only remnants lie on top of the chest of drawers. They are business cards from restaurants. Some are from restaurants where he has eaten. Others are from restaurants where he has never eaten but walks in and asks if he can take a card. He keeps all of them in a plastic box. There are hundreds. He has memorized the addresses.

I hate this room. It has nothing of Zach in it. It reminds me of the point in his life and mine when he was a young teenager and I let him go. I grab the pillow and blanket and rush downstairs. I am suddenly hungry although I have just eaten. It indicates stress. I rip open a package of processed turkey from the refrigerator and shove several pieces into my mouth. It actually indicates both stress *and* gluttony.

I go outside and pack up the minivan.

— Off we go, Zach. What do you think, pretty crazy?

— Yeah.

— Exciting, different. Are you nervous?

— No.

— Are you feeling anything?

No answer.

The motor kicks up. The minivan shakes only moderately, reminding me of the Magic Fingers at the motel room in Saratoga Springs with my father.

— What's going through your head?

— Nothing.

— Nothing? Are you ready?

— I'm ready.

— Here we go, Zach!

— Oh wait wait!

He has obviously left something behind despite all my interrogation. All I've ever done with Zach is sweep up after him. He is an eight-year-old in a twenty-four-year-old body.

— What did you forget? I asked you over and over if you had everything.

— Hey Dad is there stuff on top of the Taurus?

— What are you talking about?

— There.

— Where?

— I don't see anything.

— Right there.

I move closer to the windshield and squint at the Taurus station wagon parked next to the minivan. There *is* something on the hood of the Taurus.

— Oops, I forgot to put the turkey away. I guess I took it outside when I was packing up the car and left it there.

— That's okay Dad.

Zach gets out and retrieves the package from the hood of the Taurus. He gently places it between the two front seats of the minivan.

— Pretty stupid of me, huh?

— Yeah.

Chapter 3

———————

Blue Box

I

WE POKE THROUGH the tunnels bisecting the Allegheny
Mountains of Pennsylvania, the light inside watery and
yellowed as if lit by flickering candles. The tunnels are out
of another time, converted from railroad underpasses built by a Vanderbilt before he went broke in the 1880s. He was trying to be an indus-
trial visionary in uniting Pittsburgh with Philadelphia, but a parochial
unwillingness among the populace made the idea a frivolous pursuit.

The more you move forward in Pennsylvania the more you move
backward; the farther west from Philadelphia the deeper into the time
lock of block-long family-owned appliance stores selling televisions
and mattresses and La-Z-Boys, the descendants of Slovakia with fingers the size of shotgun shells and three-masted backs walking into
some beer-and-a-shot joint at the top of a hill drinking in silence because there's no point saying anything anymore after the coal mines
and the steel mills severed your spirit and spit black into your lungs,
smoking stubby nonfilters down to the last orange glow.

You think about the past as you roll through the night. You wait for the unknown. With each mile you gain more space from the suffocating trappings of daily life—the strip underneath the gutters that must be repainted, the landscaping bills that cost more than the house itself did, the rooms you don't need, the parties you haven't been invited to, the white wine that brings you hangovers, the crap you accrue that you never use, the crap you would use had you not misplaced it, the bills as plentiful as shells on the shore, the car insurance payment you never remember, the private school bill you always remember, the floor that the dog has destroyed, the only truly peaceful moment of the day of sitting on the john and realizing that the last roll of toilet paper is down in the basement, the refrigerator containing six different bottles of chicken marinade, the awareness that the kind of chances you took twenty years ago when you lived light you would never take now because you have submerged yourself.

As Zach and I move into the western fringe of the Pennsylvania Turnpike, I already feel, just like I felt with my father, that we are the only ones on the road. Up ahead the only thing you see are the lights of the last wagon train in America, the tractor-trailers. You come up on them and wonder if anyone has ever called the number on the back to report an erratic driver. You peek into the cabs and wonder if the little perches where the drivers sleep have sufficient porno. You try to figure how many bottles of speed they have already taken. You steal a glance at them in your minivan and wonder if they are friendly or friendly fire. You press pedal to the metal and still you can't get around the damn things. You feel glorious anyway.

— Zach, think we'll ever come back?

— Yeah we will.

— Why?

— 'Cause we'll have to.

— Why?

— 'Cause I'll have to go to work when I come back.

— Then let's just keep going forever.

He has a map in his hands in the seat next to me. He holds one wherever he goes. They have become a part of him, an obsession the origins of which no one quite knows. Some he keeps out in public; others he secretes in his blue knapsack. I respect his knapsack as much as any parent does, so I peek inside when he is using the men's room at a gas station and figure out why it weighs so much: there are dozens of maps inside. When we left the house earlier tonight, his map of choice was of New Hampshire, because he knew someone who had once run in a cross-country meet at Dartmouth. Now he is holding a map of Montgomery County although we aren't in Montgomery County.

The map-holding looks odd. It is odd. I ask him why he does it. He says with a giggle that he doesn't know. But I can tell that holding the map reassures him and gives him peace. Zach first gravitated to maps when he was seven or eight. He found clarity in them; they leave nothing to chance. He can lose himself in a map and find himself; it also becomes a special source of social capital. When he meets someone for the first time in a place he has never been to, he can regale them with his knowledge of streets and how to get to where they live from anywhere. They look stunned and think of him as a mad genius, the human GPS. The map becomes an extension of him, a badge of who he is and what he can do.

This is all guesswork on my part. It is always guesswork with a child like Zach. I have been through the circuit. All of us have been through the circuit with children with mental or physical or emotional disabilities, or autism or Asperger's or a thousand other behavioral differences that distinguish them from the Normals, the labels irrelevant. We have placed our children before enough psychologists and psychiatrists to fill the Nile. Some spend hours to find a diagnosis. Some spend ten minutes and just pluck one out of thin air. Too many of them are childhood developmental speculators relying on instant-oatmeal observations and strangely crafted tests we all would flunk. But we listen. We listen because it provides the balm of explanation. We all have the same repository at home or some variation of it.

Mine is in a blue box.

II

My blue box is a file drawer filled to capacity with neatly typed pages and impressively exhaustive summaries of Zach's condition dating from his birth onward. At first, I believed the blue box would be a cure-all. It would contain an answer and a solution to the answer. I rode the special-needs circuit to the neurologist and the psychiatrist and the psychologist and the speech pathologist and the psychopharmacologist and the battalion of special-education experts. I read all of their reports, or as much as I could before I couldn't take it anymore. The summary of Zach's incapacitations at birth seemed too monumental for any single human being to bear: yellow jaundice, constant blood transfusions, the "blue baby" syndrome, stiff to the touch, difficulties in sucking and feeding and swallowing and crying.

The blue box also documented all the missed milestones: not walking until he was nearly two; not speaking his first word until he was nearly three; unable to use language for conversation when he was five and difficult to understand when he did speak, a performance IQ in the .1 percentile. From one report alone written when he was eight: *"highly distractible," "hyperactive," "unusual preoccupations," "tends to shriek," "assuming the role of clown," "perseverative behaviors," "echolalia," "difficulties with tactile discrimination," "visual and fine motor deficits," "quite delayed," "borderline range of intellectual function," "capacity for empathy, social understanding, genuine social interaction is minimal."* From another report when he was nine: *"severely learning disabled," "poor social skills and judgment," "wandered aimlessly around the classroom," "looked out the window while he ate his snack for approximately fifteen minutes."* His reading skills then were at a kindergarten level, his verbal comprehension skills in the 8th percentile, his perceptual organization skills in the .1 percentile.

He was not easy to diagnose. Some said he was autistic. He had aspects but it was not a clear-cut diagnosis. Some said he might be having mini seizures. Wrong. One said he had Tourette's. Ludicrous. Those who tested him saw a little boy who was charming and beautiful, with a prodigious memory that baffled them given his other debilities. They saw moments when he became suddenly engaged for reasons they couldn't quite explain. He receded into emotional flatness and I have never seen him cry. Wrote Dr. Martha Benoff, when he was ten, in the best summation of him, "[He is] a child who defies simplification and clear-cut diagnosis."

So I ran with it all into his early teens, found the Vanguard School, and fought to get the city and state to pay for it because it is their legal obligation although they do their best not to pay for it and insist your son or daughter is just fine in a regular school where there is none of the educational support they need if they are to have any chance in later life to become productive citizens instead of closeted.

Each year I dutifully went to so-called IEPs, Individual Educational Plan meetings. I sat there in a circle surrounded by the lead special-education teacher, the speech pathologist, the occupational therapist, the physical therapist, the school psychologist, and several others who were a mystery to me. They talked as if they knew my child. A few of them did, but most of them did not. I knew they meant well, but their good intentions were often of little help to Zach except for those who saw their mission as a calling. As I sat quietly in that circle, I listened to them set goals for him that I knew he could never meet but which they promoted to fulfill bureaucratic requirements — completing open-ended sentences eight of ten times, answering questions about a story eight of ten times, adding or subtracting two-digit numbers with a calculator. There were dozens of them, all equally absurd. I remember once getting in the car to go to an IEP meeting, convincing myself on the way there that I had left the coffeepot on at home and had to turn around in order to avert a fire. I knew the coffeepot had been turned off. I had conjured it up so I could have an excuse for missing the meeting. I simply could not go anymore.

I largely stopped making the circuit of doctors. I stopped the testing because there were just so many times I could read that my son scored in the .1 percentile on something. When Zach was about ten years old, Debra and I found a neurologist at the Children's Hospital of Philadelphia named Larry Brown who realized that parents needed treatment as much as their children and gently tried to convince us, and especially me, to accept Zach for who he is. Dr. Brown saw a boy who had made remarkable progress from birth. To underscore the up-side of Zach's situation, he described some of the other cases he saw in his work, like the set of self-mutilating twins who had to wear muzzles because they bit so savagely. The nominal diagnosis for Zach was pervasive developmental disorder, but Brown acknowledged it was a meaningless tag because of Zach's high functioning in certain areas accompanied by "very severe learning disability, attention deficit disorder and borderline cognitive functioning." He was the first doctor who refused to slot Zach into some neat medical compartment. As he told Debra and me at one point, your son is a "mishgosh" of behaviors.

I stopped searching for miracles because I was making him a guinea pig, fodder for arrogant or clueless doctors. I stopped because I grew tired of looking for answers that would never come. I stopped because of prescriptions given for drugs whose names I could not pronounce without any real idea of what they did.

The most cursory and misguided examination was done by Dr. Joseph Biederman, affiliated with Harvard Medical School and Massachusetts General Hospital and a world-renowned child psychiatrist. He saw Zach when he was five, largely as a favor to my second wife. He examined Zach for roughly ten minutes, proclaimed he had Tourette's, presumably on the basis of Zach's tics, and prescribed a patch of clonidine to be placed on his thigh. I was shocked he had made the diagnosis so quickly. But he was *world-renowned* in his field. I obviously was not. Who was I to question him? All the patch did was cause an ugly rash on Zach's thigh that he could not help but scratch. As for Tourette's, at least three physicians said he did not have it. "Tourette's syndrome is not a viable diagnosis in the absence of chronic, multiple motor and verbal tics," Larry Brown wrote in an evaluation. Also, Tourette's is believed to be largely inherited, and none of Zach's relatives had it. So I was not terribly surprised when Biederman was found to have accepted roughly $1.5 million from drug companies between 2000 and 2008 without disclosing this income. In one case, Biederman took money from Eli Lilly while also being paid by the National Institutes of Health to examine the effects of an Eli Lilly drug.

Zach's problem was in the brain, and I began to realize that the brain, however unfathomable, is driven by what Oliver Sacks calls the "the coherent self that exists in all of us." It was an inspiring description. I began to envision Zach creating his own coherent self at his own pace. But I still struggled to accept who he was. I was still ashamed.

I wanted bragging rights to my son. My parents, and my mother in particular, had lived for bragging rights to their kids. And I had always lived to provide them.

III

I grew up in a milieu where admission to the academic elite was presumed. My father had gone to Dartmouth. My mother to Smith. My grandfather to Harvard. My uncle and two of his children to Princeton and the other to Stanford. I graduated from Andover in 1972, where 60 kids out of a class of 260 went to Harvard, Yale, or Princeton. And that was an off-year. I went to Penn, then considered a safety school by fellow classmates for those desperate to get into an Ivy.

My parents had a house in Nantucket, which they filled with guests every summer. I welcomed all of them except the *Bernsteins* because the *Bernsteins* were perfect. The *Bernsteins* could hold their own against anyone with a combination of humor and intellect. The *Bernsteins* were even friendly and funny and kind. The *Bernsteins* scared the shit out of me. Father Bob had gone to Harvard and was the head of Random House. The two Bernstein sons I knew best, Tommy and Peter, set a new standard for precocious accomplishment. Tommy Bernstein went to Yale and it was assumed that he would become either a major politician or very rich. Peter Bernstein was the editor of the Brown University *Daily Herald* and had spent a semester as the only white at an all-black college at a time when race relations were both tenuous and tense. Everybody in the family read the *New York Times* from cover to cover. They watched the Watergate coverage on television for hours a day and then spent further hours debating its legal and social and political ramifications. I tried to watch the Watergate coverage but found myself bored beyond death except for trying to understand the thick southern drawl of Sam Ervin.

I felt great relief when the *Bernsteins* left. They were too intelligent, more current than the current events themselves. I went back to delivering newspapers on my bicycle at ten in the morning since the papers in those days came by the midmorning boat. I stopped taking *The*

Sunlight Dialogues by John Gardner to the beach, which was not only incomprehensible to me but very heavy. It was an intuition, and it may well have had as much to do with my compulsive desire to please as it did with Mother's desire to have me please, but I was convinced she felt disappointed in me after the *Bernsteins* left. She adored that I was going to Andover, but I had no chance of getting into Yale or Brown because of my inconsistent grades, exemplary in English and history and abysmal in math and science, the worst dissection of a frog in the history of biology. I was not going to be superrich given my misunderstanding of most things financial. I was never going to spend a mind-expanding semester at an all-black school in the Deep South.

My mother was not comfortable being a mother. She got dramatically better at it once my sister and I were out of the house. But when we were toddlers, she never cooked a meal for us. If she did hold me, I have no memory of it, whereas I do with my father. As she saw it, children were placed on earth to perform, just like she had performed for her own mother, who had gone to law school in the early 1900s and started a firm on Wall Street in the 1930s with her husband. My grandmother believed that work was the only reason for living. My mother was the same way, finding a full-time job in the late 1950s when I was three, ultimately leaving us in the hands of a hired woman named Dottie, who cooked and cleaned and helped with homework and gave me maternal love and what little sense of true self-worth I was able to muster.

I was scared of my mother. I never wanted to set her off. She became frustrated easily, her zero-to-sixty temper, her phrase "So help me Hannah!" code red for start running your ass off. The only way to gain her heart was through achievement. Failure was not an option in my mind. When I was in elementary school and moved from the top-tier math class into one that might be easier for me, she marched to the school and furiously demanded I be transferred back. When I arrived at Andover in 1968 at the age of thirteen, my father hugged me on the front steps of my dorm; he felt like crying because I looked so alone. My mother's only comment was that I'd slouched and mumbled when I met the headmaster and made a mediocre impression.

I was determined not to subject any of my children to the same pressures I had felt growing up. Love came easily to me; few moments in life are more peaceful or more intimate than rocking a baby back to sleep in the shadowy dark of the wee hours of the morning, hearing the little gurgles as he downs the bottle of formula like a drunken sailor, feeling the soft skin in the nape of his neck drenched in the pungent blossom of baby powder, gently placing him back in the crib, until he wakes up after thirty seconds and wails and you rouse your spouse and say, "It's your turn."

I vowed that my children would never have to dance for me. But I did want them to succeed. I wanted them to make me proud. Like grandmother, like mother, like son, the rituals of inherited behavior could not be entirely eradicated. Until the traumatic birth of the twins put an end to those projections.

When my friends sent their kids off to the Ivy League, and then told me how great it was that Zach was bagging groceries, I hated what I perceived as their patronization. I knew I was taking it the wrong way, a finely tuned habit. I knew they were genuinely happy that Zach was working, even while they silently thanked God it wasn't their own kid doing the bagging. Tragedy for most of them was Penn instead of Princeton, Bowdoin instead of Brown. It *was* a tribute to Zach's progress and his character that he was working. But grocery bagging was not a bragging right. Grocery bagging was beyond humbling for a father awash in ambition with friends equally baptized in it. At least it was better than the job he also had at Pizza Hut.

I watched him working there once. I dropped him off next to a reeking plastic garbage container in a cracked asphalt parking lot. I drove a little ways off so I could watch him without him watching me. I saw him come out of the back entrance wearing an apron and holding a broom and a dustpan. I watched him as he went around the cracked asphalt, gathering cigarette butts and shards of glass and pizza crusts into a pile, the detritus of kids who didn't give a shit and figured in some subliminal way that there would always be some retard around to clean up after them. He used the dustpan to pick up the pile and dump it into the plastic garbage container. I remember watching his face, dutiful and accepting, except for the slight curl of the nostrils when he lifted the lid off the plastic garbage container and could smell the reek and rank as if it were covering him. I stayed as long as I could bear to, about thirty seconds, before I drove off.

I could not live with that image. I could not allow my son to do that kind of work for a living, scraping sticky, stringy mozzarella off greasy plates when he wasn't picking up cigarette butts in the parking lot. I could handle his part-time job at the supermarket. I could not handle his other part-time job at Pizza Hut. He needed something else. Because I needed something else. Which is why, after years of not wanting to impose, I contacted the managing partner of the most prestigious law firm in Philadelphia, Ballard Spahr, to seek from him the biggest favor I'd ever sought from anyone. I asked Arthur Makadon, whom I'd known for about twenty years, to find a job for my son, two days a week, any job, in the mailroom, as a messenger, anything to get him away from the rank and reek of that dumpster. Anything that would give him a toehold in the world of privilege and success that was mine. Arthur knew that I was asking for myself as much as I was asking for Zach, and he didn't force me to list Zach's pros and cons, his skills and unskills, dos and don'ts. He understood the code behind my request: Please don't make me have to tell people anymore that Zach sweeps the parking lot at a Pizza Hut. He took one second to respond.

—Done.

Because of his encyclopedic knowledge of downtown Philadelphia, we hoped he could ultimately deliver mail to offices at other buildings, though he started by stocking supplies and delivering interoffice mail and filling the fax machines. But I didn't care what his job was. I cared only about being able to say that Zach was working at a *law firm,* the most *prestigious* law firm in the city. I cared only about liberating him from working with people whose sweat streaked their faces from the heat of the dishwater and whose eyes held nothing because they had gone dead long ago. They were just trying to hang on, and I didn't want my son to be a hanger-on with them. This was hard-core classism, I knew, but so is America.

It wasn't Zach's liberation. It was mine alone, since Zach made no distinction about people as long as they were decent to him. He had no concept of status so he did not care about it. I had never ever heard him speak with malice or jealousy of anyone, which had to do with his always seeing the world in the literal and concrete without the spin of his own agenda. Which does raise the question of why it takes brain damage to be kind and honest and true instead of insecure and behind-the-back vindictive as so many of us are. Why is abstract thought so inherently vicious, too often interpreting events so they tout ourselves and condemn others?

But I could look my friends in the eye now, even if I had to admit to myself that Zach didn't quite grasp the subtleties of office etiquette. He saw the place as something of a commune, and he would sit at partners' desks and use their computers while they were out at lunch. He was perfectly content but the partners were not. He repeatedly asked one back-office colleague if he could rub his bald spot. It is difficult to deny the irresistibility of bald spots. But this was a new riff on an old habit of his, which he'd started with his brother when he was four and inappropriate bugging was his only effective means of attention. Zach began to fixate on the coworker with the bald spot, or maybe just the bald spot. In any case he discovered his address, walked over to his home one day after work, and peeked in a window. He wasn't there but his wife was. She became appropriately confused and scared. Who was this kid at her doorstep unannounced? I am not sure how it transpired, but the law firm found out and called me. They were gentle but also concerned about Zach's odd sleuthing. I promised that I would teach Zach what could be tolerated in an office and what could not.

— Zach, this is a serious office where people do serious things.

— You can't ask people to rub their bald spots?

— No, you can't. You should know that.

— I was just trying to be friendly.

— It's not a good way to be friendly. How would you like it if somebody asked you to rub your bald spot?

— I wouldn't mind I guess.

Not the answer I was looking for. I replaced reason with severity.

— You are to stay away. You are not to talk to him. No more going into anybody's office. And you are never ever to go to the address of anybody.

— What about if Bill Slaughter invites me we've known each other for ages he likes me.

— Bill Slaughter is okay as long as he invites you.

— Okay.

— I mean it, Zach. You are lucky you weren't fired. Do you want to be fired?

— No.

— You want to go back to Pizza Hut and sweep up cigarette butts in the parking lot and scrape shit off plates?

— No.

— Then shape up.

I had been giving Zach such bad-cop lectures since he was a young child. I hated giving them because they scared him, but it was the only way to end his bouts of teasing and bugging and pestering. He did shape up this time, and there were no more phone calls from the firm. In fact, he became popular at Ballard Spahr — a kind of a mascot. His openness became an antidote to the preternatural grimness that surrounds lawyers in their tiny offices. As the attorney Bill Slaughter said, in a comment that revealed as much about his colleagues as it did about Zach, "The great thing about Zach is that he genuinely *is* happy to see me."

I should have been proud of him. I was proud of him. He dressed as crisply as he could and showed off his ID badge to everyone he knew. But I kept on running. Even in moments when he was happiest and I should have been happiest for him.

IV

Shortly before the cross-country trip, Debra, Lisa, and I went to a surprise birthday party for a woman who organizes social activities for young adults with severe disabilities such as Zach's. For fifteen dollars an hour, we often hire someone to take him to the mall or go to dinner or the amusement arcade, something to get him out of the house, place him among the Normals. Larger activities are also offered, such as bowling or overnight trips to Hershey Park or the Jersey shore. There seems to be no shortage of clients, the obvious reason that she is creating a social organism for a group of teenagers and adults who have no natural social organism.

There were about a dozen people at the party, the parents around the table with nothing in common but our broken sons and daughters. The forced conviviality masked the anxiety we all felt about what would become of our children who were no longer children, where they would live, how they would live, with whom they would live.

The kids were mostly in their twenties. There was a pool and they played a version of volleyball with a huge purple ball that skipped and skimmed but mostly scudded. They weren't really interested in the game. What really intrigued them was the arrival of the next guest. A car would pull into the driveway, and they climbed out of the pool en masse, and they half-hopped on tiptoes through the grass like young children in Easter egg hunts. They squealed with joy when they recognized someone they knew. They formed a lifeline to each other.

Someone took a picture of our children that day. They stood just behind the table still filled with red plastic cups and the tube of Gulden's mustard and the paper plates with remnants of cake and potato chips and half-eaten hot dogs. Some looked at the camera, and some did not. Some had impairments that were more obvious than others. Some were shy, and some were proud. Some looked physically perfect, and some looked imperfect. My son was all the way to the right, dressed in a pair of borrowed swimming trunks, with his arm stretched around the shoulder of the person next to him. Zach's face was partially obscured, but there was the crinkle of a smile that comes with a sense of total contentment about who you are, no matter who you are.

He was with friends, where he was comfortable and welcomed and loved. He called them "my friends," because they were the most precious part of his life, his private jewelry box of treasures. He was also surprised and delighted I was there, which made me realize how rare it had become for me to intersect with the real life he lived with his mother and her family. He paraded me around, telling everyone when I arrived that "my dad's here! My dad's here!" He loved the party. He knew none of my private thoughts, the sadness in the eyes of all the parents around me that no amount of cheerfulness could conceal. That was my perspective at least. When I suddenly told him that Lisa and I had to leave, his face lost its sparkle.

—Why are you going?

—Somebody is meeting us at the house to do some repairs.

—Is it Steve why is Steve coming now it's late can't he come some other time?

—No, he can't. He's busy and it's the only time he can do it.

—Oh.

He looked at me oddly because he knew, in the way he simply knows, that I had just lied to him.

Lisa knew I felt tortured by what I had just done, the ride home from the party stony and silent, the infectious spread of guilt. The next morning, as we lay in bed, we talked.

—I just know I couldn't wait to get out of there. And maybe it's my own lack of acceptance. Were you sad last night?

—No, because I accept the situation. And it's easier for me to accept it because it's the situation I walked into. I never had the hope that a young couple having babies have, and then your hopes were dashed when you realized you have an impaired child and have that reality to deal with.

—It was much easier when he was younger.

—They go out into the world and people don't look at them with love and understanding anymore. They look at them as "Boy, they're kind of creepy." People find it off-putting, but that says more about normal people than it says about Zach.

As Zach and I cross Pennsylvania, I can't stop thinking about lying to him at the party.

Why are you going?

Because sometimes I don't know what else to do.

Why are you going?

Because I have to.

Why are you going?

Because I'm ashamed.

Why are you going?

Because you should be ashamed of me.

V

Zach has crawled into the back seat to try to sleep. The seat is too small for him. He was right; we should have gotten a Cadillac with a wider back seat and a radio that plays only Frank Sinatra and Mel Tormé. His body is crumpled and contorted under a blanket, his head hanging off the edge of the seat like a rock teetering on the edge of a cliff. He somehow manages to fall asleep as we pass the exits for Allegheny Valley and then Pittsburgh. I am alone with the car radio turned low. It's the midnight-to-five A.M. show about aliens with call-ins. The show is actually kind of interesting because of how convinced these callers are that a flying saucer just landed in their sink with the dishes.

I pull into the Holiday Inn Express in Cranberry about thirty miles from the Ohio border and wake Zach. We are greeted at the front desk by a young man who suffers from the remarkable irritant of congenital perkiness. It isn't his fault because it's his job. But it isn't my fault either that it's his job. Nobody wants cheer after hours of driving and arriving late. Call me romantic, but after midnight I much prefer motels where you have to yell several times for the clerk, who then comes wandering out of the back room, bleary-eyed and mildly annoyed, with his shirt untucked, takes your credit card, and hands you your room key, all without a word.

How are you tonight, sir?

I have driven over three hundred miles by myself. I have about three thousand to go. Zach and I have already run out of conversation.

How were your travels today, sir?

I have to drive 450 miles tomorrow through Ohio and Indiana to get to Chicago. I am pretty sure Zach doesn't want to be on this trip. I'm not even sure if I want to. The cross-country romance is dissolving into reality. *Two weeks with Zach is a very long time.* I am tired.

Make sure you try the free breakfast, sir!

Please, just give me the fucking room key.

We empty the bags from the minivan. Zach handles his suitcase and his knapsack easily, while I struggle with my four bags. The camera bag keeps slipping off my shoulder. Zach gives me a wide berth: he knows I could blow at any second.

We have adjoining rooms. Zach acts like he's just been released from prison. He touches the bed with his fingers spread wide. He peers into the closet. He pokes his head in to examine the bathroom.

There is a common door between the two rooms. It automatically locks when you close it, and I warn Zach.

— If you come into my room, leave the door open. Otherwise it will lock and you can't get back into your room.

— Yeah.

— It's a pain in the ass if it locks.

— Yeah.

I go through the open door into my room. I come back into Zach's room, and I close the door. We both realize instantly . . .

— I just locked myself out of my room.

— I'm sorry Dad.

— I can't believe I just fucking did this.

Chapter 4

_____

Is That All There Is?

I

W E WAKE UP. We dress. We eat the free continental breakfast out of fear of the desk clerk. Zach finds a computer
in the lobby and checks his e-mail. His roster of contacts
is impressive and ever-expanding. It is one of the reasons he compul-
sively collects business cards, to find e-mail addresses. If that doesn't
work, he takes to the Internet with relentlessness. He has taught himself to search exhaustively, part of his intrinsic process, as Oliver Sacks
has said, to make himself whole and connected to the universe of
people he likes. Because of his prodigious memory he often knows
more about their lives than they do themselves. Waiting for the train
one day, Zach saw a reporter for the _Philadelphia Inquirer_ he had be-
friended. He asked him why he was there: it was his day off. Zach was
right. The reporter went home.

Some e-mail exchanges continue for months or longer, until Zach
cuts them off abruptly and without warning. A few gently ask if I can
find out what happened, maybe get them reinstated. I feel like the fa-

ther of the maitre d' at a hot new restaurant, whom friends ask for reservations because of my perceived pull. I have none.

He doesn't even let me read what he writes. I've only seen a small sampling that a few of his correspondents occasionally share with me. He writes in caps and always asks questions. Punctuation is optional.

DEAR ART WHEN CAN WE GO FLYING IN YOUR PLANE AGAIN HAVE YOU EVER BEEN UP TO NANTUCKET MEMORIAL AIRPORT OR TO THE NEW BEDFORD MASS AIRPORT OR TO THE HYANNIS AIRPORT

DEAR STEVE WHAT COLOR SHIRT PANTS SHOES TIE ARE YOU WEARING TODAY AND IM GOOD BY THE WAY AND WHEN ARE YOU TRAVELING NEXT FOR WORK AND WHO HAVE YOU TALKED TO FROM THE INQUIRER THESE DAYS AND DO YOU EVER TALK TO VERNON LOEB OR BILL MARIMOW OR MIKE LEARY OR PAUL MOORE OR TO JONATHAN NEUMANN

DEAR KEVIN HAPPY HAPPY BIRTHDAY AND BEST WISHES LOVE ZACH WHAT DID YOU GET FOR YOUR BIRTHDAY AND WHAT ARE YOU DOING FOR YOUR BIRTHDAY DINNER TONIGHT

I try to take a peek at his current roster. He shuts down the computer.
— How come you never let me look at your e-mails?
— I don't know because I don't.
— You like to keep them private?
— Yeah.
— They should be private. You're an adult now.
— Yeah.
— Are you happy?
— Yeah.
— Are you sad?
— I'm good.
— Did you have any dreams last night?
— No.

—Do you ever dream?

—No.

—Are you having a good time?

—Pretty good.

We find the minivan in the parking lot and climb inside. I still feel slightly blurry from driving the night before but I am determined to be upbeat.

—Ready for takeoff, captain.

—Yeah where are we going?

—*Chicago, Chicago, a helluva town, a helluva town.*

I repeat the chorus. I repeat it again, hoping in vain that Zach will sing along with me, just as I am hoping in vain that I will rejuvenate. I can't get out of the parking lot. I take lefts when I should be taking rights. Arrows only take me in circles. We have not driven one one-hundredth of a mile yet today.

—WHAT THE FUCK IS THIS? HOW THE FUCK DO YOU GET OUT OF HERE?

—There's an entrance over here yeah yeah here's the entrance.

Zach guides me like a Good Samaritan helping a blind man cross the street.

—Sorry, Zach. I shouldn't have gotten mad like that.

—Yeah.

—I love you, Zach.

—I did good didn't I Dad I helped you get out because the parking lot was you know you know Dad it was kind of hard to get out of.

—That's because your father's a moron.

—Yeah.

Up ahead a sign proclaims WELCOME TO OHIO! An opportunity to make amends. I will yell the word *Ohio* with the ending slightly varied so Zach can correct me. We started playing this game sixteen years ago when he was eight, much like the rite of cuddies. He always finds it an invigorating dose of concreteness and reacts with uproarious laughter. His giggles are like hiccups at first, intermittent and inconsistent, then they start peeling off in rolls if I seize on a word that particularly strikes him. I have tired of this, just like I have tired of cuddies, but I feel repentance is necessary for the parking lot crackup. I must do a better job of controlling emotions.

I won't.

Let the games begin:

— WELCOME TO OHIEE!

He gleefully responds.

— WELCOME TO OHIO!

Now it's war.

— OHIEE!

— OHIO!

— OHIEE!

— OHIO!

— That's enough!

Zach's voice goes soft. But he persists.

— It's Ohio not Ohiee.

— I know, Zach.

He persists.

— It's Ohio not Ohiee.

— What did I just say? That's enough!

His laughter stops. I go quiet with my own duplicity. I am the one who always starts the game and then turns it off because I can no longer stand it because of the feeling of perpetual stasis. Then the guilt.

— You're right. It is Ohio.

— Ohio.

— Yes, Zach, Ohio.

The fun has been drained out of the minivan. About seventy-five miles outside of Cleveland, Zach pulls out the Rand McNally road atlas and turns to page 91. He traces the blue line of the Ohio Turnpike in the northern tier of the state with his forefinger. The finger moves past the old iron and coal port of Ashtabula, and the Geneva-on-the-Lake amusement park with bumper boats and batting cages, and Conneaut with the four covered bridges that are always part of the annual Ashtabula County Covered Bridge Festival each fall. He notes that we are closer to Akron than we are to Cleveland. The car floods with nothingness.

I slip a disc into the CD player: Peggy Lee's "Is That All There Is?" She sings in a melancholic, tuneless voice, the music simple except for some odd circuslike refrain in the middle with noxious calliopes. It is the kind of song that the Sex Pistols would have covered with more cheer. Or Frank Sinatra in some detached croon as destructive as his rendition of "MacArthur Park." Here comes the famous refrain.

Is that all there is / If that's all there is my friends . . .

— What does it mean to you, Zach?

— What?

— When she says that's all there is my friend.

I rarely ask Zach to give his interpretation of something. It makes him nervous. His hard drive stores information only. But I vowed on this trip to probe Zach's mind, find what is there, what is not there, and what never can be. He considers the question. He starts to answer. He stops. He answers.

— That's life I guess.

For the first time I wonder if he understands on some level what he and I have been through to get here. His birth and near death, my two divorces and broken engagement. All our moving around. An ongoing earthquake of adjustment for somebody who craves stability and hates change.

That's life I guess.

I guess it is. I guess it was.

II

There is no way for a couple married a little over two years to have twins born thirteen and a half weeks prematurely, each weighing less than two pounds, and not crumble. All marriages go through a tectonic shift when a child is born. But there generally isn't constant fear if it is a term pregnancy. There isn't the reality that at any second your baby can die, those noble breaths not enough to outpace death. No matter how good the outcome, you can never ever get over what has happened. You may try to block it out as I have tried to do for much of my life. But you can't. You will still have flashbacks. You will still hear the alarms of the monitors. You will never forget holding your child with what seemed like a thousand different wires attached to him to record all the different vital signs: move an inch too far and all the connectors dislodged and the nurses came running. You will never forget the look on your child's face, beseeching you to *please, please get me the hell out of here* or at the very least to *please, please just leave me alone.* You will remember the helplessness, which was even worse than the fear, because you could do nothing but watch and wait.

It felt after several months as if Zach would never get out of the neonatal intensive care unit. He would gain momentum. A steady breathing rate. Then his chest started heaving up and down, so frantically gasping for breath you could see the exhaustion on his face, a natural act we so take for granted, breathing, not natural at all in his case, only depleting him. He would have to be re-intubated.

Neonatologists were vigilant. The nurses were even better, as much psychologists as highly skilled technicians. They exuded optimism. They never showed fear. They became friends you could laugh with and cry with. They offered eternal hope whether they believed it or not. But the isolettes still reminded me of being in the hole of solitary confinement but without any infraction of the rules. One day a baby would be there. The next day he or she would be gone without a word, because there was no need for words; everybody knew what happened. The isolette, padded with a new white blanket, awaited its next inmate. The parents dressed in the blue medical gowns, who had kept silent vigil hour after hour, vanished along with their infants. But, as routine as heartbreak was in the neonatal unit, it was a vast improvement over the hellish conditions that surrounded premature babies a century ago.

III

You may talk, ladies and gentlemen, you may cough. They will not hear you. They do not even know you are here . . . Now this little baby came in nine days ago. It weighed only one pound eleven ounces and we were afraid we might be too late. It was even bluer than that little fellow over there in the other incubator . . . Yes, ma'am, it was a premature birth . . . a little over six months.

— SIDESHOW BARKER, "Infant Incubator Babies" exhibit,
early 1900s, Luna Park, Coney Island

The history of the treatment of premature infants is one of the most abhorrent chapters in the annals of medicine. Up until the 1880s premature infants fended for themselves with no help from medical science. Unsurprisingly, their mortality rates were catastrophic — sixty-six percent and perhaps even higher. Doctors played virtually no role. Birth and care were the exclusive domain of mother and midwives.

In the early 1800s, spurred by a belief that mankind had become too weak, a popular attitude prevailed that newborns should be subjected to cold baths and cold air to make them tough and resilient. It was idiocy, but much of medicine at that time reflected the philosophies and superstitions of the era. The studies and writings of eminent Philadelphia obstetrician William Dewees beginning in the early 1800s helped to dispel this absurd ignorance. "This preposterous and cruel system of hardening . . . is in fact nothing else than an experiment to see how much an infant can bear without being injured or destroyed."

Still, medical treatments of that period often did far more harm than good. Babies born prematurely and unable to breathe on their own might be treated with a whipping to jar their organs into function, or a few drops of brandy, or an onion held under the nose. The first glimmer of hope for premature babies came in 1880, when French doctor Stéphane Tarnier invented a closed incubator that could keep an infant consistently warm, a crucial element for survival. The invention had its roots in the poultry industry; Tarnier had seen a simplified version of the machine used for the hatching of chicken eggs at an exhibition in Paris.

Tarnier's invention was not particularly sophisticated, basically an enclosed basket with water bottles at the bottom. But it made a discernible difference in lowering mortality. Other doctors made subsequent improvements to its design that helped stop premature birth from becoming a death sentence. But they couldn't prevent these tiny infants from becoming a sideshow for a public always in love with what they considered to be deformed freaks.

At the Chicago World's Fair in 1933–34, a clump of exhibits bordered the east end of the area known as the South Lagoon. A visitor could marvel at the installation from the American Radiator and Standard Sanitary Corporation with displays of plumbing, heating, and air conditioning tastefully housed in a Spanish garden with cascades, pools, shrubbery, and statuary. Nearby was the Sinclair monsters exhibit, where a forty-ton brontosaurus swung its neck, jerked its tail, and emitted a screeching grunt. It was impossible to ignore the adjacent 227-foot Havoline Thermometer, the world's tallest. A little farther east stood the Foreign Villages, what the fair guidebook described as the "quaint midget village." Resembling the Bavarian walled city of Dinkelsbühl, it contained 115 "midget inhabitants," including what was believed to be the smallest man in the world, Werner Krueger, at twenty-four inches and eighteen pounds. There were shops featuring "midget handicrafts as well as a miniature taxicab, filling station and newspaper." But in deference to its customers the "midget restaurant" did serve full-size meals.

Almost directly opposite Midget Village was the popular Ripley's Believe-It-or-Not Odditorium. It featured fifteen-month-old Betty Williams, born with four legs and three arms. She was counterbalanced by Frieda Pushnik, the so-called "little half girl" with no arms or legs. Lydia McPherson had the longest red hair in the world, extending roughly seven feet. Harry and Lillian McGregor had spent a lifetime learning how to lift weights with their eyelids. E. L. Blystone had legibly written 2,871 letters on a grain of rice. Leo Kongee, dubbed the "human pincushion," hammered nails into his cheeks, forehead, and scalp without drawing blood.

The "Infant Incubators with Living Babies" exhibit blended perfectly. It contained roughly thirty premature infants, some weighing as little as one and a half pounds. The exhibit staff included a full-time physician and a bevy of nurses and wet nurses. It was a de facto neonatology unit, and some in the medical profession argued that such public exposure would only help to advance care for premature infants. But others decried these exhibitions. As the British medical journal *Lancet* lamented in 1897, "What connection is there between this serious matter of saving human life and the bearded women, the dog-faced man, the elephants, the performing horses and pigs, and the clowns and the acrobats? . . ." Rhetorical questions like these went unanswered as crowds flocked to view the preemies, hustler subterfuge in the supposed name of science.

Thousands of gawkers, each paying twenty-five cents, passed through the portals to see what were considered to be otherworldly creatures. Many of the customers were so-called "repeaters," almost all of them childless women, who came as often as they could to follow the progress of a baby they were rooting for, much like backing an up-and-coming thoroughbred. The Incubator Babies exhibit was one of a long line of such spectacles that stretched from Berlin in 1896 until Coney Island in 1943. One of the barkers at an exhibit was a struggling actor named Archibald Leach. "Don't pass the babies by!" Leach implored prospective customers until he landed a part in a Broadway play and changed his name to Cary Grant.

In the first half of the twentieth century, incubator babies, in addition to international expositions, were exhibited at circuses like Barnum & Bailey's and resorts like Atlantic City.

Fundamental notions of hygiene were ignored in the name of enhancing the spectacle. In the early 1900s, some of the exhibits didn't even have a glass partition to separate spectators from the babies, subjecting them to coughs, colds, sneezing, and smoking. At the Louisiana Purchase Exposition in 1904, an epidemic of diarrhea ran through the preemie exhibit and half the infants there died. Electricity was shut off at night throughout the exhibition, making it impossible to give the infants the constant warmth they needed.

The patron saint of the preemie freak show was Martin Couney, a doctor from Alsace who had trained under one of the world's best pediatricians before settling in America and running the Coney Island preemie exhibit. Couney's dedication to the premature infants was equaled by his profit motive. He also liked the high life. In a 1939 profile in *The New Yorker,* A. J. Liebling detailed his various sartorial flourishes: spats, a derby, a crook-handled cane. He liked his rabbit garlicky and rare, and he spent most of his time in a house overlooking the ocean that was both overheated and comfortable, the environment of warmth "exactly like a preemie" incubator, as only Liebling could observe.

Couney dubbed the incubator a "peanut roaster," and he got letters from all over the world from parents begging him to roast their peanuts because caring for them at home was physically and psychologically draining. Once these babies grew to a normal size in his incubators, Couney hastened to reunite them with their parents, not out of kindness but because he needed to make room for more preemies. After all, who would travel to Coney Island to see a six-pound baby? He knew that any freak show exhibit needed a little bit of sleight of hand to heighten the drama. Babies were dressed in clothing that made them look smaller than they actually were. Couney's chief aide, the mysteriously named Madame Recht, wore an oversize diamond ring so she could slip it around a baby's tiny wrist.

In addition to the permanent show at Coney Island, Couney exhibited at the 1939–40 World's Fair in New York. But the fair exhibit was a financial bust: premature babies were old hat by then. The Coney Island exhibit closed in 1943, the same year that New York Hospital established its own facility to care for premature infants. "I made propaganda for the preemie. My work is done," said Couney. He also made nice money.

Moving premature babies into the medical mainstream did not appreciably improve their lot. Too often, otherwise reputable doctors touted miraculous remedies that ultimately proved worthless if not dangerous. The *New York Times* proclaimed the promise of Epsom salts enemas, which were said to reduce deadly respiratory distress syndrome by achieving the proper level of body water. Later, it was discovered that such enemas caused fatal magnesium toxicity. A machine called the Bloxsom Air Lock was supposed to simulate uterine contractions. It was ballyhooed by *Newsweek,* became popular around the country, and then was abandoned because it did not remotely work.

Most catastrophic of all was the use of supplemental oxygen. In 1942 J. Robert Wilson, the chairman of pediatrics at the University of Michigan, discovered that premature infants breathed more regularly in an environment that contained seventy percent oxygen. Wilson himself noted there was no proof that regular breathing was any better for preemies than periodic breathing. Still, the change to higher oxygen concentrations spread widely, until it was discovered in 1951 that the high doses of oxygen were causing blindness in thousands of premature infants. Physicians immediately shifted to an oxygen concentration of forty percent, roughly double the amount of oxygen in the atmosphere. The decrease lowered the incidence of blindness but led to increased mortality rates from cerebral palsy and a condition known as hyaline membrane disease. In the neonatal game of Pin the Tail on the Donkey, this wasn't close to the right solution either. It was only in the early sixties that practical safeguards were put in place to measure the correct level of oxygen, such as blood gas and saturation monitors and oxygen sensors.

President Kennedy and his wife, Jackie, had the greatest modern impact on the development of the treatment of premature infants into a medical subspecialty. The death of the Kennedys' four-pound, eleven-ounce son, Patrick Bouvier, from respiratory failure increased public awareness of the plight of premature infants. Use of ventilators became far more commonplace. Neonatology was established as a medical specialty requiring specialized training and certification in 1966. By 1983, the year Zach and Gerry were born, over 1,500 physicians were practicing neonatology in the United States, and neonatal nurse practitioners had to be certified.

Zach and Gerry were lucky to have been born at a place like Pennsylvania Hospital that had superb neonatal care. But as I watched them day after day in 1983, I had this sense that we all wore blinders, the number of advances still outweighed by the number of unknowns. I remember when the head of the unit told Debra and me that they were going to try a regimen of steroids on Zach. I remember especially well the way he said it, with a frustrated shrug of his shoulders, because neither he nor the other doctors really knew what to do to get Zach to gain weight and breathe on his own. A study later showed that certain steroids could lead to diminished brain growth and cerebral palsy. We approved the steroid treatment enthusiastically. We didn't know the

possible ramifications and, like the doctor, we were desperate for progress. We applauded every effort.

In 1990 doctors finally introduced a drug that rivaled the invention of the incubator 110 years earlier in its dramatic effect on preemies. Most infants produce a substance called surfactant that is essential to expanding their lungs so they can breathe properly. But very
small infants like Zach lacked sufficient surfactant. Giving preemies
an artificial version of the substance produced stunning results. Had it
been available for Zach, his life would have been radically different. So
would mine and Debra's.

IV

Debra and I were in the shower one night when the song "Every
Breath You Take" started playing on the radio. The daily ritual of seeing Zach in the hospital, watching for hours as he struggled to take
his own breaths, had beaten us down despite our outward stoicism.
Debra sobbed in my arms. It was one of the most intimate moments
of our short marriage. Yet at that moment I felt a shift. It was ever so
subtle, like the touch of a spare summer breeze. Her arms around me
loosened slightly; my arms around her felt out of place, suddenly as
useless as flippers. The hot, soothing water was the only mercy I felt.
It was only that tiny release of pressure from around my waist, but
she was beginning to let go. I believe now she was suggesting that the
negative narcissism and the constant fear of failure, the first cousins of
the unquenchable neediness that was embedded within me, could no
longer be given out in limitless supply.

*We have a son who may live or die. We have another son who may
have problems as well despite his progress. I don't have time anymore to
reassure you about your career. I don't care about your career. I don't
have time to reassure you about anything.*

I loved every inch of my boys. I worried twenty-four hours a day
about them. I cried when I saw Zach in the hospital with those milky
brown eyes struggling to stay open, the silent message of *I'm fighting
as hard as I can.*

But I lived inside my head and I could not get outside. Work and the pursuit of success formed my only true identity. I was terrified of what I would be without it. Now I was scared about everything — my career, my children, my notion of fatherhood that had been obliterated. I had always been scared. My self-confidence was a come-on. I hid my insecurity and fear behind a barrage of angry outbursts at editors and friends and wives and waiters. I was tender and kind on many occasions, but then darkness prevailed. Success had been the only constant in my life. It was an addiction. My drug. Until like all drugs it wore off suddenly, and I needed some more.

The birth of the twins only multiplied my sense of inadequacy and yearning for success. We knew they would be premature, but still I fantasized that they would be buoyant, healthy babies handed over to Mom and Dad in soft blue blankets. I wanted congratulations instead of condolences. I wanted the joy of new life, not the threat of sudden death. This was a disaster. This was complete fucking failure. It could have happened for only one reason. I deserved it. Without ever intending it, I lived to destroy. My pessimism had become lethal. In the heat of that shower I knew without ever knowing it that my wife and I would never last.

I guess that's life.

V

We leave Ohio and enter Indiana, making us at a minimum the one hundred millionth travelers to not notice any difference between the two. Zach and I pull into a rest stop off the Indiana Toll Road. Cars search for empty parking spots with territorial disease. A brown Soviet-style building sells potato chips and Life Savers and warm bottles of Diet Coke and compressed turkey and cheese white bread sandwiches. The bathroom is overlit. Travelers recede in slow motion, then disappear. There is only Zach and I, just like there was only my father and I, but with none of the joy of hitting a hundred on the empty night highway.

— Did the divorce make you sad, Zach?

— A little yeah.

— Was it hard going back and forth?

— A little hard yeah.

— Was it hard not being with both parents?

— A little hard yeah.

— It makes me sad. I'm sorry I did it. I'm sorry I did that to you. I cried a lot about it. Do you forgive me?

— Yeah.

— I felt very guilty. So did your mom.

— Yeah.

— You know why I think we got divorced?

— No.

— Because you guys were so sick.

— Yeah.

— The marriage changed. There was a lot of tension. You came home on oxygen. You were really sick and it was so hard. You should have died, Zach. Do you know that?

— I didn't.

I pause here. It feels like the longest pause of my life. Should I go further?

— Do you know what brain damage is?

— No.

— What do you think it is?

— When your brain isn't right?

— Do you know your brain is not a little right?

— Yeah.

— How do you know that?

— I just know from my brain.

— Does it make you sad?

— Yeah a little.

— How does it make you sad?

— Because I'm not sure how.

— Is it because of certain things you can't do?

— Yeah.

— Like what?

— Not go to school like Gerry I can't do.

It was the continued vow I made before the trip, to go with my son to emotional crevices we had never gone to before. I can tell when Zach's answers are short and truncated because he does not understand. But I can also tell when Zach's answers are short and truncated because he does understand, at least some portion, and is feeling pain.

I was not prepared for him to say that he knew his brain was not right. I was not prepared at all. It was the risk I took by asking. And yet I feel gratified. He does not always float in some ether of happy ignorance. He is aware of himself. But to have a child, your child, any child, say *my brain isn't right* is still unimaginable. I have lived with that knowledge since he was born. But how does he live with it? The words repeat and repeat in my head. *My brain isn't right.* I can't get away from them and neither can Zach. He knows his life will lack so much. But he will not succumb to self-pity. He acts the way he usually does in a situation like this: he enters the rest stop to get some Combos and maybe a Kit Kat that he can eat without me knowing and ferret out as many maps and brochures of Indiana as he can find.

Chapter 5

===

Failure to Forget

I

WE ARE BETWEEN New Carlisle and Otis on the Indiana Toll Road. But Zach's mind has already made it to Chicago. — I remember David Jackson he worked with you as a reporter at the *Chicago Tribune* I remember his desk it was near yours and another reporter there named Bob Blau you went to his wedding in Chicago on August 20 1994 his wife's name was Leah remember when you and I and Gerry and Caleb and Sarah stayed at the Ritz-Carlton it was February 7 1992 there were some awards dinner or something.

The first memory, thirteen years old, bears hardly any relation to his own experience, since he met Bob Blau once and never met his wife. The second is fifteen years old.

He drops Chicago and moves on to our next destination, Milwaukee. He hardly pauses as twenty-year-old memories pour out of him. They have never disappeared, never even decayed. Most of us, as we get older, are defined by our failure to remember. Because of the chemistry of his brain, Zach is part of a rare group defined by what one physician calls "a failure to forget." His memories form a concert without a single unifying motif, a vast collection of dissonant notes that Zach somehow gives consonance.

—I remember our cleaning ladies Mi and Liu they were those Korean cleaning ladies we used to have remember when I used to get like all those warts all the time on my hand and I would keep going to this Doctor Winston remember that ice-cream place we used to go to all the time I remember it it was called Kopp's that was a good place there was nowhere to sit I remember Dad I also remember what else do I remember from Milwaukee I remember I had some interesting bus drivers this lady my first year was Alexis also I remember I went to one of Alexis's kids Alex I went to one of Alexis's kids' birthday parties once I remember a lot of Gerry's friends from school Michael Brumley and a kid named Calder who we went to a Brewers game with his dad and he got his foot stuck in the seat it was May 11 1991 I remember a guy named Andy who worked at the JCC and was a lifeguard at Family Park and we went to a Brewers game together and he baby-sat me and Gerry once and I loved him so much I remember that movie *Wayne's World* you took me to it I remember when you and I Dad went to Milwaukee November 11 1994 when we came back to visit and we went to a Milwaukee Bucks game remember the last time we saw one of the friends we are going to see her name is Lois we saw her on August 15 2005 in New York remember Dad?

He knows I don't know. I can tell by the little crease of impishness and the upward lilt of the voice.

My kid is trying to punk me.

—Zach, I don't remember what I did yesterday.

My kid is trying to punk me again.

—Remember the names of the hospitals in the Milwaukee area Froedtert and St. Michael's and Columbia remember the name of the obstetrician who delivered Caleb named Sylvia and her son named Corey and the dad named Allen and the name of the hockey team called the Admirals and the soccer team called the Wave and the food delivery truck called Schwan's that delivered the push-up ice creams and the little sausage biscuits that were so good to eat remember that operation I had we couldn't do it when I was born why did they have to do that?

This I actually *do* remember.

— I think you were circumcised. They couldn't do it when you were born because you were too little and too sick.

— What's a circumcision?

— It's when they peel back the foreskin on your penis.

— What's a foreskin?

I can't continue.

My own groin is having flashbacks.

II

Zach is a savant. Embedded within him are the classic symptoms, a darkened cognitive landscape accompanied by remarkable skills in the area of calendaring — phenomenal recall of people's birthdays and the dates on which the most obscure events occurred, the capacity to see someone once and remember ten years later where and when he saw him, flawless recall of the street grids on maps, the ability to give you the day of the week for virtually any specific date in his lifetime.

Almost without exception, savants show their remarkable skill in one of five specific areas — calendaring, mathematics, landscape painting, innate memorization, and playing the piano. They are distinctly different from those defined as geniuses, because geniuses are not born with severe mental disabilities. The condition is rare, favors males by a ratio of six to one, and tends to occur in those with either autism or developmental disorders stemming from birth.

Virtually all savants are linked by phenomenal memory, concrete to the extreme and accompanied by what Dr. J. Langdon Down, the father of savantism, described in the 1880s as "a very great defect of reasoning . . ." Lacking the ability to interpret people's intentions or engage in other forms of abstract thought, they safe-harbor in the concrete. They navigate the world through rote and repetition and routine, much like an athlete tries to perfect muscle memory. But they do it without constant repetition and practice. It is just there. "The significance of Savant Syndrome lies in our inability to explain it," wrote physician Darold Treffert, the country's leading expert on savantism. "The savants stand as a clear reminder of our ignorance about ourselves, especially about how our brains function. For no model of brain function, particularly memory, will be complete until it can include and account for this remarkable condition." Echoing Down, Treffert points out in his book *Islands of Genius* that "whatever one names [the] form of memory, it always includes certain characteristics: it is immediate; it is literal; it is automatic; it is very deep and extensive, but it is very narrow . . ."

I was present when Mary Berryhill, a postdoctoral fellow at the Center for Cognitive Neuroscience in the department of psychology at the University of Pennsylvania, investigated firsthand Zach's memory abilities in his twenties.

She gave him a series of random dates and asked him to tell the day on which they occurred. He got every date right that occurred in the 1990s and 2000s and roughly eighty percent of those occurring in the 1980s. Chance performance is about fourteen percent. Of the dates that occurred during his lifetime, he got twenty-six out of thirty correct. The four he got wrong were due to a slip-up in recalling a leap year. She then told him a day and date (Monday the third, for example) and asked him to give the month and year on which it occurred in either the past or the present. He got all six correct.

Berryhill described Zach's abilities as a "remarkable talent" and "highly intriguing." Her goal was to try to figure out how his brain did this, whether it was an "automatic process or his brain's way of organizing time usefully." She was unable to pinpoint it because savants have trouble articulating or even understanding such abstract mental processes.

I told her of Zach's ability to hold thousands of concrete memories within his hard drive — his endless, effortless recall of the obscure dates and the street grids and the birthdays. It is common for savants to ask a new acquaintance his or her birth date; it attaches a fixed point of identity to a person whom they can't identify by features of their personality as the rest of us do — "God, is he boring," "God, is he funny," "God, is she mean," "God, is he successful. I hope he dies." What is truly unique about all the people Zach encounters is the date on which they were born. That data point easily becomes part of his constant effort to create predictable structures: everyone has a birthday and it never changes unless of course you're a Major League baseball player from Latin America or a Hollywood star. It's the same with knowing the day of the week when given a date. As Treffert notes, there is a pattern and regularity to calendaring: it too is predictable and highly structured.

For at least a decade, I have watched Zach practice his brand of practical mysticism. Being a father, I frequently test him by picking a date at random and asking him if he knows the day. He has never gotten one wrong. Over and over, I have asked him how he does it.

— I just do.

— But how? Do you remember a certain date and then use it as a base to figure out other ones?

— It's just in my head.

I know Zach's IQ is in the range of borderline mentally retarded. I know his comprehension skills in many categories are at the third-grade level. I also know I am in the presence of something spooky and weird, the closest I have ever come to believing there is a God — or at least some otherworldly presence that chose to take up residence in my son's mind.

Accounts of savantism date back to the 1700s when a man named Gottfried Mind, unable to read or write, with no concept of the value of money, was able to draw stunning, lifelike pictures of cats and other animals. His appearance was such that he was constantly teased by young children when he walked down the streets of Bern. But the quality of his portraits was such that King George IV bought one of them. Over the past century there are the twins George and Charles, unable to add simple figures but able to give the day of the week for any past or future date within a span of forty thousand years. There is Kenneth, in his late thirties with a mental age of eleven and a working vocabulary of fifty-eight words, who can give the population of every place in America with five thousand or more, as well as the names, room capacity, and location of two thousand hotels. There is Jedediah, unable to write his name, with a mental age of ten, but able, after a five-hour computation, to give the correct twenty-eight-digit answer to the following question: *In a body whose three sides are 23,145,789 yards, 5,642,732 yards, and 54,965 yards, how many cubic eighths of an inch exist?*

There is Kim Peek, the model for the Dustin Hoffman character in the film *Rain Man,* who memorized twelve thousand books. He read Tom Clancy's *The Hunt for Red October* in one hour and twenty-five minutes and four months later, when asked to name the obscure character of a Russian radio operator mentioned once, not only knew the name but the page on which he appeared. There is Steven Wiltshire from England, who is autistic with limited social skills but a brilliant landscape painter because of his memory for visual details. For a segment on him by a production company, he was taken up in a helicopter and given a panoramic view of ancient Rome for forty-five minutes. He was then placed in a room with more than five yards of sketch paper and was asked to re-create what he had seen. It took him three days to finish; he had not missed a single detail, down to the exact number of arches in the Roman Coliseum.

The public masses first became aware of the eerie twilight zone of the savant in the mid-1800s with an African American man known as Blind Tom. As incredible as the preceding examples are, Blind Tom was even more so. Like premature infants in the twentieth century, he also became a freak show exploited for great profit.

Mark Twain encountered Blind Tom on a train from Galena, Illinois, in 1869. He had no idea who he was and the initial impression was Twain and only Twain. "When he spoke he talked excitedly to himself, in an idiotic way and incoherently, but never slowed down on his imaginary express train to do it. He looked about thirty, was coarsely and slouchily dressed, and was as ungainly in build and uncomely of countenance as any half-civilized plantation slave. After I had endured his furious entertainment until I was becoming as crazy as he was and getting ready to start an opposition express on my own hook, I inquired who this barbarian was, and where he was bound for, and why he was not chained or throttled? They said it was Blind Tom, the celebrated pianist — a harmless idiot to whom all sounds were music."

Several months later Twain had an opportunity to observe Blind Tom playing the piano. He watched him one night, then a second night, and then a third, appealing to heaven for explanation, as he witnessed this dysfunctional man spinning out perfect music that he had heard only once before.

"All the schooling of a life-time could not teach a man to do this wonderful thing, I suppose — but this blind uninstructed idiot of nineteen does it without any trouble. Some archangel, cast out of upper Heaven like another Satan, inhabits this coarse casket; and he comforts himself and makes his prison beautiful with thoughts and dreams and memories of another time. It is not Blind Tom that does these wonderful things and plays this wonderful music — it is the other party."

His full name was Thomas Green Bethune. He had been born near Columbus, Georgia, in 1849 to parents who had spent most of their lives as field hands on a plantation. He was blind and helpless as a child. He could be volatile and self-abusive, fond of whipping himself and repeating the sounds his mother made when she whipped her other children. He could repeat almost anything and he was enthralled by sounds — the sounds of the corn sheller, the sounds of rain and thunderstorms and wind, and most of all the sounds of the piano. It was intriguing but initially believed to be worthless. His mother believed her son could not be taught anything, but the plantation owner believed otherwise. He compared Blind Tom to an animal: "A horse or a dog may be taught almost anything, providing you always precisely use the same terms to express the same ideas. Tom has as much sense as a horse or a dog, and I will show you that he can be taught." He was five when he composed on his own a piece he later called "Rain Storm" and played on the piano, imitating uncannily the sound of rain hitting a roof and falling off the gutters.

News of his talent spread, and by the 1860s he was traveling the world over, advertised as "the marvelous musical prodigy, the Negro boy Pianist." His concert stops included packed houses at the St. James's and Egyptian halls in London, the Salle Hertz in Paris, as well as performances in Glasgow and Edinburgh and Philadelphia and Pittsburgh, among dozens of other cities. It did not matter how complex the pieces — Gavotte in G Minor from Bach, Caprice-Valse from

Liszt, the Waltz in A-flat from Chopin, the "Pastorale" Sonata from Beethoven. He played them flawlessly from memory, even including any errors in what he had originally heard. His repertoire of pieces ultimately grew to more than five thousand. To guard against the idea that some scam was involved, audience members were invited to play any piece of music they wanted and then have Blind Tom repeat it. His rendition was always perfect. As a final flourish, he played three different melodies at the same time. At his peak he was making $100,000 a year, but shady promoters robbed him of much of it—tragic but hardly surprising given the era in which he performed.

In 1887 the English doctor Down, the physician to the Earlswood Asylum in England, coined the term *idiot savant* to explain the abilities of Blind Tom and others like him. The term reflected what he saw as "the paradox of deficiency and superiority occurring within the same patient." The term has since been scrapped and truncated to *savant*. The phenomenon itself has been exhaustively studied, in particular by Treffert, a psychiatrist and professor at the University of Wisconsin Medical School. "So many questions leap up. How can this be?" Treffert wrote in *Islands of Genius*. "How can extremely handicapped persons possess these islands of genius? What do they share in common? Why, with all of the skills in the human repertoire, do the skills of the savant fall in such constant and recurrent narrow ranges? Why does the obscure skill of calendar calculating occur in so many of the savants?"

The great majority of savants have perfectly normal brains anatomically. Take them out during autopsy, examine the sliced wafers of them under a microscope, search for discolorations and lesions and enlargements and the viscous gray of dead zones, and you find nothing at all to distinguish them structurally from typical brains.

But fascinating theories have arisen to explain why savants are so different. Researchers call the condition of savants "paradoxical functional facilitation." In plain language, a savant's brain has overdeveloped one area to offset damage that has occurred in another area. The superhuman abilities are invariably associated with the brain's right hemisphere, the area that as Treffert writes in *Islands of Genius* can be "characterized as non-symbolic, artistic, concrete and directly per-ceived." The left hemisphere in contrast is believed to be "more se-quential, logical and symbolic."

Researchers believe that the brain may compensate for the lack of left-hemisphere function with markedly increased right-hemisphere function. Some researchers theorize that the brain literally rewires it-self by recruiting unused capacity from other parts of the brain, in ef-fect appropriating areas of the left hemisphere that have been freed up since it is no longer functioning as a whole.

The exact process by which savants perform their feats is far less well understood. Some researchers believe that savants' fantastic memori-zation skills are a matter of inheritance, although the only thing I can prodigiously remember is the winner of every World Series from 1956 to 1981. I have not lived with Debra for some time, but I recall that she had a terrible memory, always in danger of setting fire to the house because she forgot she was cooking.

III

When Zach was eleven or twelve I bought a Nintendo console for the family. I assumed Zach would have no interest in playing, nor did I think he would be particularly good at it because of the variety of men-tal processes and hand-eye coordination the game required. I bought it largely for Gerry, and of course I wanted in on the action as well. At first, Zach watched us playing Super Mario Brothers with his familiar detached look, far away in his own orbit. And then suddenly he started playing on his own. I was just gratified he was doing something be-sides looking at maps or old photo albums, but one day I asked him if he wanted to play me. I was eager to find an activity we could share, and I quietly promised myself that I would be gentle with him.

He kicked the living shit out of me.

He had memorized every move and every possible eventuality be-cause the game, like calendaring, was predicated on precise, unchang-ing rules. As he played with robotic skill and focus, his tongue hung slightly out of the side of his mouth, the only indication he gave of being human. The look on his face wasn't glazed exactly, but he wasn't all there, as if he could play Super Mario Brothers without even looking at it, would know by the sounds the game made and his own internal timing exactly what to do in what sequence. He was lightning fast and machinelike, saying nothing except for a little "yea!" when he moved on to the next level. For someone who'd had terrible difficulty holding a pencil when he was younger and needed untold hours of physical and occupational therapy, his dexterity was remarkable. He knew the minute handling of all the controls, when to speed up and when to slow down to protect the rather stupid Mario, what buttons to push so Mario could jump or squash. His coordination, which he rarely showed anywhere else, was another testament to the power of his memory; it enhanced him *physically.*

I played with him a couple more times, always with the same result. I barely made it past level one, and he made it to what seemed like level four thousand. My Marios died quickly, with that hideous deflating sound and subsequent poof of disappearance. His Marios were always being feted with stars and fireworks and offers of work at Goldman Sachs. I quit. Fathers never deserve to be humiliated by their sons like this. Instead I just watched. I extolled and congratulated and told him I was proud of him. He never said a word in return or altered his expression. Until he simply got bored one day and quit altogether. But I'm convinced that if he played the game today after a ten-year absence, he would be every bit as masterful, another chunk of information stored away forever on his hard drive.

I always felt that there must be a way to use my son's savantism to further enhance his day-to-day life. Because he could read maps so well and knew every street in downtown Philadelphia, the law firm thought he would make the perfect messenger. He did it once and never wanted to do it again. He was scared of making a mistake, but the job, however well suited he was for it, was simply too far removed from the routines that had guided his life. I thought at one point that he could be a tour guide for schoolchildren to the *Philadelphia Inquirer* and *Daily News* because of his encyclopedic knowledge of the building's every nook and cranny and all the people who worked there. But he wasn't interested; again, he felt nervous about making a mistake in a job with too much flexibility and margin for error.

His memory is a wondrous parlor trick. That is worth something. A great something because he clearly draws pride from it. But that is all. His brain truly did give him something wondrous at birth, communicating to the operators in the boiler room that the right hemisphere was interested in any unused parts the left hemisphere was planning to dump. But his brain also took away interpretation and abstract thought and comprehension. If you don't have those skills in life, what do you have? Super Mario Brothers?

IV

We are in the deep meat of the Chicago highway system now, a hodge-podge heap of numbers — 57, 80, 294, 55, 94, 90. Any false turn can mean the diaspora of Calumet City or South Holland. I have brought along a GPS whose direction dispensary speaks with a calm English accent. She is unflappable. My wife Lisa is convinced I love her most of all. I do love her. She never yells. She has never abandoned me. But now she has become insistent and stubborn. I detect bitchiness beneath her cool British exterior. Personally I think she wishes we would all go back to the days of maps instead of such pathetic reliance.

Drive .1 miles. Then turn right. Turn right, then turn left.

What kind of sense does that make in .1 miles?

I punch in commands to get us back on track.

Turn left. Then take ramp left. Take ramp left. In .2 miles, keep right. Keep right. In .2 miles, turn left. Then turn left.

— Where the FUCK IS THIS TAKING ME?

Zach is quiet. He is taking joy in another meltdown. He knows I should have used him. He is punishing me with silence.

Turn left. Then turn left. Recalculating. Drive three hundred feet. Then turn right. Then turn right. Then turn right. Recalculating. Drive three hundred feet then turn right. Then turn right. Recalculating. Drive .2 miles. Then turn left.

— She's a fucking dope.

Turn left. Then turn left.

— She's a complete dope, DOPE!

Zach abandons his silence.

— What's her name?

— Sheila.

— How do you know?

— She told me.

— When did she tell you?

— She whispered it in my ear. Sheila!

— She likes me?

She sure as fuck doesn't like me.

In .2 miles, take ramp left, then keep left. Take ramp left. In .4 miles, keep left. Keep left. Drive 1.9 miles. Then keep left.

She takes us off the interstate, sends us through a roundabout of city streets, only to put us right back on the interstate. Lisa believes I am scared of her; it's true that I lack the courage to defy her and use my own sense of direction, which I don't have anymore anyway once I started using a GPS.

We finally reach Michigan Avenue in the heart of the city. I am grinding down now. I have driven over four hundred miles and I am lost in a maze of one-way streets. I have no idea where I am even though I worked in Chicago for two years and have been back numerous times. Zach knows exactly where we are. He points out the marker of the Northwestern University School of Law. He spots Northwestern Hospital. He remembers a cousin named Pat Kauffmann who went there before she died.

— We should go by her old place she was on East Chestnut remember the address?

It was twenty years ago. Why would I? Why would anybody?

I finally see the Westin Hotel where we're staying, but I can't find the entrance.

— Why did I fuck it up, goddamn it!

Zach ignores my question. He barrages me with his non sequiturs.

— When did you go over to the *Tribune* from Pat's where you stayed sometimes would you walk over why did you sometimes take a cab to the train to Milwaukee you once spent a whole day with me at the *Tribune* I remember I saw Brooks Brothers out here once.

I cannot look at Zach right now. I cannot deal right now with these memory eruptions that are his stand-in for conversation. They only make me feel more tired, more trapped in our unbreakable bubble.

We finally find the hotel and check into our adjoining rooms. Zach wants to walk to the *Tribune* building several blocks up Michigan. I need to be alone. I don't want to hear him padding about in his room opening every drawer and cabinet and closet. I don't want to hear the squeaks and squeals he makes when he is alone. So I let him go. I tell him he has to be back in forty-five minutes. I just want to sleep.

He is back exactly forty-five minutes later. He lays a little stack of pack rat paraphernalia on the bed, free maps from tour bus booths and business cards from restaurants and clothing shops. He has also gotten something else.

— Look what I got Dad!

He points to his stomach.

— You bought a belt?

— Well remember I thought I had packed one but I didn't pack one so I thought Dad I thought it would be a good idea to buy one since I don't have one.

— That's great, Zach! Where did you get it?

— The shop right downstairs they have a gift shop.

— Zach, nobody buys a belt at a hotel gift shop. How much did it cost?

— I'm not sure I charged it to the room.

V

A bottle of Pouilly-Fuissé resides within me. We have eaten dinner, and I am drunk. I needed to get drunk. The trip has not been easy. The driving is often exhausting. Zach is often exhausting. There have been moments of surprising awareness and self-awareness, like the sun peeking out between the clouds, only to be hidden by them again. I love his savantism. I hate his savantism. I feel exalted with him. I feel stuck with him. I love his memory jags. I hate his memory jags. I also know were it not for Zach, I would probably still be in that parking lot at the Holiday Inn Express in Pennsylvania, going in circles.

Thinking of the belt he bought, I'm reminded of the time in Philadelphia we went to get his passport. Normally the application requires a signature. It could be waived in Zach's case since his mother and I have guardianship; I could sign the form myself. But I suddenly felt uncomfortable; doing so would diminish him. It was his name that belonged there, written in his own hand. I showed him where he had to sign. He gripped a pen right by the nib. He started writing out his name as if chiseling in stone, most in block letters. I could tell that he had worked on this for many hours; the lines were clean and straight and strong. I was struck by the simplicity but also the sturdiness; this was not a signature but a statement.

The belt is the same as that signature: a statement of his individuality and independence. He never would have bought it had I been with him.

I must try harder to keep his individuality in mind. I promised myself before the trip that I would focus on what he can do, not on what he can't. As my head begins to sink into the eighty-five goose-down pillows that hotels now offer to quietly suffocate guests so they can free up the room at a higher rate, I wonder if I am capable of appreciating the positive. I *always* look for the negative, a guardrail against withering disappointment and emotional free fall. Since I am drunk and sweetly drowning in pillows, I won't have to wonder for long, a welcome mercy because the wondering is so painful.

Chapter 6

Embassy Suites!

I

THE SHOPPING ALONG Michigan Avenue rivals that on Fifth Avenue, except that here people smile. In New York people smile only when a kamikaze bicycle messenger is hit by a taxi being driven by someone who doesn't speak English, drives sixty miles an hour across three lanes of traffic, and asks the passenger if he knows how to get to Park Avenue. On Michigan Avenue, the tidy displays of Cartier and Johnston & Murphy and Coach beckon with glittering diamonds and glossy wallets and fine leather shoes so shiny you could shave and get a tan in their reflective glare.

Zach carries in his hand a map of Ohio and a Chicago bus schedule. He has no interest in window shopping. His only focus is on going to the *Tribune* building. The belt was an uncharacteristic splurge, plus charging it to the room is his version of a magic lantern in which money just disappears. He buys nothing with what he makes from work, except for candy bars and a gray T-shirt with the logo of SEPTA, the Philadelphia regional transit system, because that is his favored mode of transportation. He did once go into a high-toned clothing store in Philadelphia to look for a tie, a rare burst of whimsy. Zach's concept of money, while rapidly improving, is still hazy. Prices are an abstract idea, and it's hard for him to associate the value of something with its cost. But even he had sticker shock.

— You could maybe buy four or five ties maybe at Old Navy where I sometimes shop with my mom so you know you know Dad it was silly to buy just one it's just a tie you know what I mean and I already have a lot of ties.

Zach and I often go to malls together in order to break the isolating silence of being at home in our separate orbs. He likes the food court and always orders General Tso's chicken in its 30-grade sauce. I always ask him if he wants something, and he always says no unless there is a map section, and I have yet to find a clothing store that has one. When he lived with me during the week, I once went into his red set of drawers from Ikea and found dozens of Christmas gifts never used — hundreds of dollars in cash, as well as watches and shirts. As Debra points out, Zach's modus operandi is always on to the next thing. So every Christmas, once he tears open the wrappings of gifts, he completely loses interest in the contents and wants to know what's for dinner. The journey of choice is never a journey.

We enter the Gap on Michigan Avenue. The interior is tricked out in the de minimis style, mostly sanitarium white. Loud pulsating music plays. The intent is to evoke the hip atmosphere of a converted-warehouse club, but this is a clothing store, not a place to score Ecstasy and do water-cooler deeds in the bathroom. The sales clerks are in alignment with the non-atmosphere atmosphere; you ask them a question and they reluctantly nod in roughly the right direction, underscoring that they have nothing to do and that's the point of their presence. We are there to help them fetch a nonfat double-shot latte with a twist.

I ask Zach if he needs anything; as usual, he says no. I suggest a shirt and he agrees, maybe one to look suitable for work since all the lawyers look so suitable. His requirements are specific — long sleeves and a buttoned collar because Zach has carefully observed what the suitable lawyers wear. I ask him if he sees any shirts he likes. He picks up the first one on the rack, garish and multicolored, just to have it done with so we can get to the *Tribune*. I choose a more modulated one of thin red stripes that fits him well. He is pleased.

— It's nice to look good sometimes Dad isn't it that's why I need to wear a fancy shirt and shave every day.

— Sometimes you forget to shave every day.

— Those are just the days I don't.

We arrive at the intricate and eclectic magnificence of the *Tribune* building. It is the ultimate example of the edifice complex, built over three years from 1922 to 1925 by the famed owner of the *Tribune,* Colonel McCormick; it remains a towering reminder of the days when publishers were America's most powerful titans, the exclusive dispensaries of information however slanted to their own tastes, imperious, arrogant, luxuriating in their grip of public opinion. Some 120 stones were embedded into an exterior wall of the Tribune Tower; they came from such places as the Parthenon and the Taj Mahal, the suggestion that the building, like these eternal monuments, was equally eternal.

We go to fourth-floor reception and wait for Ann Marie Lipinski, my former boss at the *Chicago Tribune* and now the *Tribune's* executive editor. There is a line of framed citations on the far wall commemorating the Pulitzers the paper has won. For the first time ever, Zach asks about my newspaper career.

— Didn't you ever win a Pulitzer or win something an award I guess?

— I did. I won a Pulitzer at the *Philadelphia Inquirer.*

Zach moves on to information of more relevance to him.

— Wasn't your health club around here that you joined I guess?

— It was further up.

— It had two pools an indoor and outdoor.

— You're right.

— How many times did you go like maybe once or twice?

I think he's punked me three times now.

— That's about right.

— Why didn't you go more?

— I always planned on going. But on the way I ate M&M's so I felt sick.

I go to the men's room and return to find Zach interrogating the receptionist. He is a close talker. He likes to point when he speaks, as if he is conducting his own words. He bears in closer. He quizzes her on the location of all the different departments. Zach acts like she is holding out on him. More questions. Ann Marie shows up, at last. The receptionist is relieved.

The configuration of the newsroom has radically changed since I was there from 1989 to 1992. I am confused, but Zach has no problem finding my old desk. He sees an old colleague of mine, David Jackson.

— Hi David I remember you sat next to my dad.

I ask Zach when was the last time he saw David Jackson.

David is a superb investigative reporter. His distrust of all answers is inbred.

— Nineteen ninety-one right up here at the *Tribune* I spent the whole day here.

Swish. Zach adds that David almost came to visit us in Philadelphia in September of 1994. Swish. Zach tells him that he liked to run. Swish. Zach announces that reporter Bob Blau, who used to work at the *Tribune,* is now at the *Baltimore Sun,* that Dean Baquet, who also used to work at the *Tribune,* is now at the *Los Angeles Times,* and that John Carroll, the executive editor of the *Los Angeles Times* where Dean Baquet now works, used to work at the *Baltimore Sun* where Bob Blau works. Hat trick. Zach pops in on the sports editor, Dan McGrath, and informs him that he lived in the Philadelphia suburb of Ambler when he used to work at the *Inquirer.* He says he knows this because *Inquirer* reporter Raad Cawthon told him, noting to Dan McGrath that Cawthon himself has moved from the *Inquirer* to Pensacola in Florida. Three-pointer from thirty feet. At lunch, Zach tells Marie the date of the *Tribune* awards dinner we all attended in 1992. Buzzer-beater. Knowing Zach's interest in the physical plant of the *Tribune,* Ann Marie tells him as we finish lunch that a new gym has been built for employees. Zach perks up.

— My dad joined a gym once.

Punked number four. The impish look again. Forget it.

— Well, Zach, we need to get going to Milwaukee.

We head toward Interstate 94 on Congress Street. I am overcome with melancholia, no surprise since my eighth-grade yearbook predicted my future occupation as undertaker. I hate going back to places where I have spent significant time before. It is not an ironclad rule, but when I do return I feel I am going backward instead of forward. Memories are bittersweet at best, and the connections you made are always tinged by the awkwardness of time passed, conversations filled with nervous pauses, praying for some words to come into your brain, the default to superficiality. What at the time came so naturally no longer comes naturally at all. It may be why the trip sometimes puts me at odds with Zach, who loves nothing better than visiting places he has been to before. He never goes through such machinations. He connects. I disconnect.

I can't wait to get to Las Vegas. I have never lived there, so there are no relationships to fret over. It is hell, a good kind of hell, a crazy and beautiful hell with neon rainbowed lights like a wave of falling stars, hell as it should be with secrets left behind, and I will need some definite hell at that point in the trip. But with Milwaukee ahead of us and then the trek to Odessa, Vegas seems unreachable. I cannot shake my gloom. I need to talk to somebody. Zach is it.

— It's funny being back in places where you haven't been for a long time. You think about a lot of things. You think about when you were younger. Life seemed so much simpler, more unburdened. I feel old today.

— Yeah.

— Do you ever worry that you're going to die?

— You lived in Milwaukee like I remember when you were thirty-three to thirty-seven you were young.

— My life is behind me.

Zach pauses. He looks through the car window. I wait for something profound like the Peggy Lee song.

— HEY DAD THERE'S THE EMBASSY SUITES!!

Not what I was quite looking for.

II

We grow quiet once we get onto Interstate 94. It is raining and the sound of the drops against the car is comforting in its rhythmic rat-a-tat. It feels like the timing is right.

— Do you ever want to live on your own?

— Maybe.

— Like to have an apartment by yourself?

— Maybe.

— Don't you think you'd be scared of that, be lonely?

— People could come in twenty-four hours to check on me.

— I think you'd be lonely being in an apartment by yourself. I think you'd be happier living with other people.

— Yeah.

— Because you're going to get to that age of what to do once your brother Matt leaves high school and no kids are at home at your mom's.

— Which will be 2011.

— We've got to figure out what to do.

— And by 2011 I will be I will be I will be twenty-seven I will be old so it won't be until 2011.

— I'm worried about you living in an apartment. I would miss you.

— Yeah.

— It feels like somebody's sending you to prison.

— Yeah.

— Do you know what that means?

— What?

— I just feel it would be like putting you away.

— Yeah.

— But maybe you would like it.

— Yeah.

— You seem really happy with your friends and maybe they could live with you.

— Yeah.

— That's when you seem happiest, with Shanna and Andrew and Joe.

— Yeah.

— They make you smile. And you love it when new people come and you all tiptoe on the grass to see who is coming.

Zach removes himself into his silence, not because he is confused but because he is anxious. He pushes his seat back and closes his eyes. He falls asleep somewhere near Kenosha. I remove myself into my own silence. Zach's friends all have impairments of one kind or another. Some have Down syndrome. Some have the same limits of comprehension that he does. Like all disabled people, they are unwanted by society at large regardless of strides that have been made over the past decade, particularly with the expansion of the diagnosis of autism.

Many psychiatrists and parents of classically autistic children feel the definition has become too broad and resulted in an unmerited explosion of cases. Aim has been taken at those said to have Asperger Syndrome — now included in the so-called autism spectrum disorders — because many are high-functioning intellectually, despite difficulties in social interaction. Within the disabled community, an unfortunate schism has developed, a civil war in which we are fighting each other: parents of children who are truly autistic resent parents who they believe are gaming the system by having their children labeled with Asperger's to gain extra support from school districts — in effect free tutoring — and receive unlimited time on the SAT and other tests.

There are always parents gaming the system and there always will be. But the vast majority of cases, autism or Asperger's or whatever else we choose to call it, are real and serious conditions. Regardless the level of function, if you are living outside the social mainstream, you need and deserve help. I know in the case of Zach what a difference intervention made.

As usual, the issue is one of money rather than diagnosis. Schools, looking for ways to cut budgets, want to pay as little as possible for children with disabilities, and make every effort to minimize the condition. So does the federal government, where Zach, for example, is clearly entitled to Social Security because of his disability, but only gets it after his mother makes the annual trek to some office and fights through the bureaucracy. Not to mention that Zach is absurdly given an aptitude test every several years, as if he might transform into a member of Mensa when he cannot drive or cook on a stove or add two-digit numbers.

Zach is just one of millions. It is a despicable situation, since these children should be a priority of our government, instead of the billions spent on futile wars. Many of them, with help, are capable of work and social integration. It is our moral obligation to make them into productive citizens. But without the assistance they deserve, they will always live outside the world or at best on the bare fringes of it. They will remain among the unwanted.

In 1992 we returned to Philadelphia from Milwaukee so I could write a second book. The boys were nine by then, Gerry at a private elementary school and Zach at Vanguard. He had been in self-contained programs all his life, but never in a school where all the students had severe disabilities and special needs.

The school had wonderful teachers and all the services a parent could want. It had small classes. It offered physical therapy and occupational therapy. But it was about twenty miles from our house and drew from a wide radius. Zach had no friends, at least no friends he could see easily. That was always how I justified our decision to stop sending him there: it was just too far away. There was truth to that, but not the whole truth. The rest of the truth was that I felt a shiver every time I pulled into the grassy parking space on the edge of a field and heard the crunch of gravel under my feet as I went to observe. Inside, there were jaunty watercolors and other artworks the students had made with endless coaxing. You could feel the determination in each wobbly stroke.

Zach's classroom teacher was a marvel. There were eight kids in the class, all of them prepubescent boys. She had this ability to see no difference, to treat them as she might treat anyone else. But all I ever saw was difference, these boys scarred and severed from the world at large in their own lock box without a key, eyes receding and eyes darting and eyes befuddled and eyes looking vainly upward for some glimpse of celestial light of explanation. Some of the kids were verbal and some were not. Some could do the simple math and some could not, and some, like Zach, even though he was ten, could do some of it only by counting slowly on his fingers like the endless peeling of an orange. Some had to be constantly told to settle down, and the tiny classroom seemed combustible to me, a place of unknown and captive energy that could explode at any second, the brain being prodded to do what it could never do and these boys just tired of it fucking all, a flick of angry consciousness that nothing made the sense it should and why were they already sealed and shut off like prisoners? And all those boys, those boys, a hothouse of desires that would never be fulfilled because they would never know how to fulfill them.

Whenever I visited, I did my best to be upbeat and was upbeat and treated them with the vanity of normalcy. But I saw them as freaks, sweet lost freaks, a carnival come-on just like the exhibits of premature infants. Whenever I left the school I felt as if the whole world was watching me, had discovered my shameful secret. I walked back past the watercolors with the crooked smiles that broke my heart. I wished the receptionist a cheery goodbye. I waved to teachers I knew. I chatted a little. *Everything's fine, good, yup, Zach is doing great.* He was doing great in the context of what he could do. He liked it there, but I couldn't wait to get the hell out. And I couldn't wait to get Zach the hell out.

The opportunity came when Zach turned high school age; his mother and stepfather and family moved to Haddonfield, a small-town gem in New Jersey about a half-hour from Philadelphia. I had once lived in Haddonfield. It had a smug tranquillity, and I liked the main street lined with stores like something out of a Currier & Ives print. It was safe. It was clean. The biggest crime was teenage drinking, the mice at play with the parents away. It was everything too much of Philadelphia was not for a child like Zach. I knew the time had come for my son to go with them. Most important, it had a public school system that could cater to my son's needs without total isolation from regular students and provide him with a social network.

At the time, we were living on a quintessential Philadelphia block where the houses had been built in the 1920s out of solid stone and stucco and came with sunrooms. But the surrounding neighborhood was balky. Zach liked to walk when he got bored, but I only allowed him to go around the block. I was willing to let go of him because he would be moving to a town that was self-contained and would give him a freedom that even then he was beginning to covet. I also knew in my heart I could not match his mother's ceaseless energy. She would fill his days with her kinetic energy that both awed me and made me ready for a long nap.

I did not miss his daily presence because I no longer knew how to cope with it. I did not miss the nightly regimen of back-and-forth pacing and perseverative behaviors. Most of all I did not miss the abyss that had grown wider and deeper between us, as I watched him in the corner of the red couch silently watching a TV show he could not understand, folding and unfolding the map he always had with him hour after hour until I finally said it was time for him to go to bed. I hated that silence. It meant loneliness to me, his loneliness, his separation from me. My loneliness, my separation from him.

Plus I still had Gerry with me. I still had an unbroken mirror in which I could see many of my parental aspirations. I loved watching him play varsity high school tennis until he firmly told me that I could no longer come to his matches if I continued to bark instructions to him *during* points. I traveled with him to prospective colleges. I watched as he gathered in a girlfriend and amassed a collection of fine and steadfast friends he might keep for life, his band of brothers. They traveled with one another and partied with one another and consoled one another in the endless vagaries of teenage love.

Zach would never have any of that, but he loved Haddonfield, and Haddonfield loved him. He became the de facto mayor since he remembered every face and name and was boundlessly friendly and, like his mother, never shy. His warmth was a balm to the most savage soul. But he was still among the unwanted.

Zach knew virtually every student at Haddonfield High, since all he had to do was hear their names once. He adopted their style of dress, the baggy jeans sweeping the street and the floor-to-ceiling shirts. He adopted their vernacular as best he could. The wrestlers liked him, and the football players liked him, and the cheerleaders liked him, and so did the giddy girls in the skintight jeans with the exclusive butts. They were kind to him, the genuflection of their blond hair as they said hello, offering the airy enthusiasm unique to their genes. He craved their recognition. You could see it in his shy, lowered eyes and the back-and-forth play of his hands.

I watched him once when he didn't know I was there. I heard him say *Hey man* to a football player because that's what he had heard in the hallways of high school. I heard him ask *What's up for the weekend?*, not so he would be included, because he would not be included, but just to feel what it might be like to belong to the common teenage world and its teenage tongue. Then the football player went in one direction and Zach in the other. It was always that way. It would always be that way.

Zach did not seem upset at being left out. All he wanted was the recognition. But I wanted more than recognition. I wanted them to go off together and finagle a six-pack of beer and talk about which giddy girl they wanted to screw. I wanted him to be invited to the hot Saturday night party. Tears formed as I watched my son from the shadows. I wiped them away before he saw me.

I cannot remember any Normals his age interacting with him out of anything more than noblesse oblige. A few of the Normals were kind. They liked him because he was so eminently likable. But as some can smell fear, the Normals smelled his disabilities. Nobody was mean. Nobody was cruel. But the iron curtain had gone up at his birth and no one would tear it down.

All Zach wants, all his friends want, just like everybody wants, is unconditional acceptance. That is what they give each other. Unlike the rest of the world, they see no difference in each other and make no diagnostic distinctions. They demand only proper behavior from each other. They express neither pity nor self-pity; as Zach told his mother when he learned he was going out to dinner one night with a girl who was blind and deaf, "That means I can order what I want from the menu."

As I drive through Wisconsin, I ask myself: Shouldn't Zach *live* with his friends one day? It could be done. Around the country parents had bought houses, found competent and caring twenty-four-hour-a-day in-residence counselors, met all state and federal standards, and then stocked the houses with disabled adults who all knew and liked each other. I found out through a friend a private group-style residence run by a charitable Jewish foundation that sounded perfect for Zach's needs. He gave me the number of the woman who ran it, but I couldn't bring myself to call her.

I still could not overcome the idea that I was sending Zach to prison, although it was becoming less and less clear where the prison was: a supervised home with his friends or living alone with one of his parents. I always circled back to the same aching question: What would happen when his mother and I were no longer here and living with his parents was no longer a choice? There actually was another alternative.

I believed it would be the best option for Zach, or at least the one that would give me the greatest peace of mind. It was also the most difficult choice of all. I would not even be the one to make it.

III

When Gerry was a senior in college, he applied for several teaching internship programs. We spent several days in Connecticut when he was interviewing. One morning, I drove him to the end of a long driveway outside a private school in Greenwich. As he prepared to go inside, I studied him in his coat and tie. I made a quick checklist of the things that were bugging the crap out of me, the shirt that should have been button-down and the black shoes that looked too scuffed. Still the father. I held back. He was nervous. So was I.

I sat in the car after he left, watching him as he walked up that driveway into a building at the top of a hill. I wanted to leap out of the car and call him back, promise to do a better job of parenting, ask for a mulligan. I wanted to apologize for interrupting him during his second serve, to be more communicative, to think less about my career, to tell him the secrets every child should know. But it was too late. At that very moment, I knew that he was leaving me to become his own.

You are filled with so many contradictory emotions when this moment comes. Part of you wants to sob as you recall the days when your child was utterly dependent on you. Part of you wants to cry because you are suddenly overwhelmed by an emptiness you have never encountered before — *Okay, you have done your job as parent, thanks for the memories.* Part of you just wants to sit in the car and beam with pride as you watch your child, who is not a child anymore, leave your confines and begin to build his own. All these feelings were only multiplied by the juxtaposition of Gerry with Zach.

Several weeks later, Gerry was offered an internship at New Canaan Country School. During the summer, on the way back from our vacation on Nantucket, Zach and I exited the bleak black heat of Interstate 95 and made our way to New Canaan so we could see the school-owned apartment that Gerry had been assigned for the coming year. The house, odd-angled and distended and painted lighthouse white, stood on a busy, tree-lined corner. Gerry led the way up a narrow staircase to his apartment on the third floor. He opened the door and there it was, his apartment, spacious, reasonably clean, albeit with a mottled carpet that smelled of the musky interchange of bodies and the ample spillage of beer and God knows what else, the earthy, beefy smell of young males.

Gerry started going through the apartment, figuring out which room would make the optimal bedroom and where to place the hand-me-down couch in the living room. Zachary stayed in the living room with a map of New York and Connecticut, locating the house so he would forever know how to get to it. Gerry and I talked about cable and Internet hookup and credit card rates and different types of mortgages, imagining a future in which he would buy a house. I thought about drawing Zach into our conversation. But he was still inside his map, tracing the routes and highways and streets to where his brother was going without him, and it was better to leave him there. The difference in my twins, always inverted mirrors of one another, never seemed greater than it did that day.

Several months later I visited Gerry again and watched him teach. His interaction with the fourth-grade kids, his confidence, his pat-on-the-head tenderness with the needy ones, and his firmness in squelching the fires of antsy silliness enthralled me. Where had he learned all this? How could he have learned it without me?

The next day, a Saturday, we went to a little diner off the main street of New Canaan for breakfast. We picked it because it was the cheapest place in town, a place where you could still get eggs and home fries and bacon and toast for six bucks instead of the usual one hundred and twenty-five plus tip. The place was crowded and tiny; customers at small square tables ate voraciously and surreptitiously, as if getting such a deal in New Canaan was a felony. Gerry and I could only find seats at the counter. He plowed through his breakfast. I poked around because I was edgy, drinking one cup of coffee after another. What I was about to bring up with Gerry was yet another enormous consequence stemming from 3:30 P.M. on the Saturday when he'd entered the world three minutes ahead of his brother. It had brought him to this place of sole proprietorship. But it also carried with it a responsibility that seemed too awesome.

— How would you really feel if Zach lived with you at some point in your life?

— I don't know.

— I wouldn't think you'd feel so good about it.

— You don't think I would?

I could hear in his voice confusion and hurt. Perhaps he was thinking, wrongly, that I believed he wasn't up to the challenge, lacked the sense of duty and loyalty it required.

— It's a big burden.

— I don't think so. It's a lot of responsibility but at the same time he's my brother.

— You're going to get married and you're going to have kids. It will be hard.

— He'll be part of my family, you know. I'll take care of him.

He was all of twenty-two years old, and yet it was something he had to start thinking about. If Gerry placed Zach in a private group home, however caring and watchful, he could be consumed by ceaseless guilt. If Gerry decided Zach should live with him, the disruption could be intolerable.

"You're a better man than I am," I told him, and I meant it; nothing in my life would ever approach the difficulty of the decision Gerry would one day have to make. He didn't reply.

"You finished?" asked the counterman.

IV

Zach wakes up as if on cue the second we pass the Milwaukee airport. He is on terra firma now.

— I remember this place in Milwaukee it was like Soccer USA I also remember when Gerry was the goalie in soccer I only played soccer in 1991 I think because I had trouble I wasn't good I guess.

— Dad I remember when we were in Milwaukee I remember we first learned about Waldo in Milwaukee.

— YEAH there's the JIMBO'S CAR WASH Dad!

— Remember they had that good hoagie place Cousin's Subs!

— BAKERS SQUARE!! We would eat there and get pies.

We reach Shorewood, the suburb where we used to live. We get out of the car and walk for a little bit through the downtown. Zach recalls instantly what is still there and what has been replaced: the North Shore Bank and the Baskin-Robbins are still around but the Domino's is gone, and the Kohl's has been replaced by the Harry Schwarz bookstore. He immediately wants to drive to his old school. He just wants to sit in the car and stare at it. I tell him we'll do that tomorrow. I don't have the psychic energy right now. I'm just not in the mood for staring.

Chapter 7

Lost in Milwaukee

I

A T THE HOUSE of our friend Lois, on a white sheet of paper,
Zach writes out a list of all the places he wants to look at
today. He hasn't seen many of them for almost two decades,
but that doesn't matter. I haven't seen him this engaged and excited
on the entire trip. He works with his customary diligence. His *a* looks
like an *o* or sometimes a *q* missing its tail. He holds the pen with the
characteristic firmness of a walking stick. He has been thinking about
this list for a long time.

- Bradley Ctr.
- St. marys
- Atwater School
- DUNWOOd School
- COPS ICE cream
- winkies
- olive St.
- JCC

It is a collection of schools and a toy store and several restaurants and the hospital where his half brother Caleb was born and the duplex in which we once lived. He doesn't particularly want to go inside all these places. He just wants to look at their outsides. He wants to see what's still there; he wants to see what if anything has changed.

Shortly before we leave, I finally pull out a clump of pictures from the green duffel bag I've been carting in and out of the minivan each night. When Zach was nine or ten he would pull out scrapbooks from the red drawers in his room and stare at some of these pictures for hours and hours. He sat on his bed with the rainbow-stripe bedspread from Ikea on top of the rug from Ikea, where all men shop after divorce, the silent Ikea secret handshake as we write out with a stubby pencil the list of furniture we must have by this evening because the kids are staying over for the first time and we need to provide a stable atmosphere fast and try not to get too upset when you put something together and there are still very many pieces left.

I mostly left him alone while he studied those scrapbooks in his boy-in-the-bubble mode. I had preoccupations of my own. I was in the thick of work on a new book that was paralyzing me with the fear of failure that always found me. Amid my fear, I wondered how Zach could possibly occupy himself looking at those same pictures hour after hour by himself, sifting through his life like that, turning pages gone flaky and brown like a dying autumn leaf. I wished we could commune together about sports or the weather or even that I could help with homework until I only made the outcome worse as I inevitably did with my other children. But I didn't want to look at old pictures — part of the phobia of going backward — and I had come to the truth that Zach doing something, anything, was better than the tendency of talking to himself and walking on his imaginary back-and-forth gangplank when unoccupied. I thought the study of pictures made him lonely, but I was imposing my own template upon his. The pictures reignited his memory, came alive for him. Still, I felt out of fatherly duty I should at least make some attempt to engage with him. So every half-hour or so, I checked on him.

— Are you okay?

— I'm okay.

— Aren't you bored looking at those pictures? You look at them all the time.

— No I'm not bored.

— Want to come down and watch the baseball game with Gerry and me?

— That's okay.

— You're sure.

— I'm sure.

Zach went back to his scrapbooks, running his fingers over the faded colors of the familiar, reexamining cousins and former babysitters and nurses who had taken care of him when he had been so sick and old friends of mine I had long ago forgotten. It wasn't some idle pursuit to fill in space until bedtime. It was important to him, refueling the hard drive.

Knowing how much Zach had loved looking at pictures throughout his childhood, I thought the pictures in the green duffel bag would help bind us together, give us a common ground. But Zach is surprisingly disinterested in the photos now. Lois and I look at them — my mother and father; Zach and Gerry in red blazers lifted up in each of my arms like barbells at the birthday party I gave them when they were four; Zach at our first house in Milwaukee in 1989 after he had just learned to ride a bike, something I was convinced he would never do but Sarah was convinced he could do and tirelessly worked with him as she did so often.

The pictures bore him. He much prefers to tell Lois about his job at the law firm. He sounds like Sergeant Joe Friday. Just the facts, ma'am.

— I know my way around I start on 51 then go down to 50 deliver mail to the secretaries the home office is on P2 used to be on 49 when I first started working but now I am on P2 so it's interesting down in the basement in P2 you can't get cell service so I am enjoying the job and it's interesting you walk everywhere and I'm downstairs it's interesting if you take the elevator it stops at the lobby then at 38 and then 51 to get to my mailroom you get on this elevator and you have to put your card in and push the button.

Are there any questions?

If not, let's recap so far.

— So me and Buzz we started driving me and my dad you know it's funny he gets me at four fifteen on Sunday and he says like should we leave tonight so we go have dinner with Gerry and we go to Chestnut Hill and my dad finished packing and we got on the road at eight o'clock then we stop in Pennsylvania it's also nice because if we left Chestnut Hill yesterday we would have had to left at five in the morning but we kind of left at eight thirty at night that's not early so we got to Chicago around three thirty instead there was no traffic it was nice we were gonna stop in like Cleveland or Toledo for lunch but we just went to a rest area because we just wanted to get here.

His cadence is beautiful to me, the breathless engagement with which he talks. But abruptly he stops his account and starts the pacing back and forth, the talking to himself. He is depleted. Lois and I finish looking at the pictures. There is nothing we can do to reel him back; he has entered his trance until it is time to take on the list.

II

We drive along Murray Street on the way to the Atwater school, the first school Zach attended in Shorewood in 1989 when he was six. We had just arrived from a year in Odessa, Texas, where I'd been doing research for my first book, *Friday Night Lights*. Until the school district determined proper placement for Zach, there was no choice but to send him to Atwater, the local elementary school, which offered no real additional support for kids with special needs.

— Do you think Dad I did good when I was there?

Before the trip I would have mumbled "fine." Now I will say the truth.

— At Atwater you had a lot of trouble. What do you remember about Atwater?

— I remember my teacher Miss Lauren and I remember she gave me a book to put my baseball cards in.

— You were lost.

— What do you mean I was lost?

— You were having a lot of trouble keeping up.

— I couldn't keep up with things?

— Do you know why?

— I couldn't really figure out what I was doing?

— Do you know why that is?

— Because I wasn't born great that might have been it.

— It was hard for you. It was hard for you to follow. You needed other teachers. You needed help.

We get out of the car to examine Atwater more closely. It is hot. It suddenly feels much hotter, each step leaden, like wading through the thick silt at the bottom of a river. We look at the field adjacent to the school where he and Gerry once played soccer. Zach remembers not being very good at soccer. The other kids were frustrated by him and vocal about it, a chorus of groans when he showed up in his uniform. He played only one season.

We walk a hundred yards to where he attended school, a one-story brown annex. Zach crouches and stares through a grimy window to look for his old classroom. There is a playground nearby with the sounds of families and their kids. I can hear squeals from the swing and the seesaw. But they are faraway echoes that dissolve in the heat. Zach continues to look inside. Then he gets up.

— I remember a couple of times when I fell asleep during class and you had to come get me.

— You've been through a lot in your life; you know that?

— Yeah.

— You know you were really tiny when you were born. You know how big you were?

— How big?

— One pound, eleven ounces.

— Yeah.

— You know how tiny that is?

— No how tiny?

— Like a package of chicken parts.

There is more to say, but not now.

Zach remembers the names of other kids who went to school with him. He calls them his friends, though they never were.

I have my camera bag with me. We walk to the playground. There is a molded dinosaur for kids to play on. I take a picture of Zach sitting on the dinosaur and smiling. It's something to do. He makes a suggestion.

— Dad let's get a picture of me next to the school sign that would be fun.

We head to the main school building. Cars pass like sighs of breath. I take a picture of him on the steps of Atwater. I know why he wants to memorialize this, another concrete point in his space, but I wish he did not. Nothing good happened here.

He was at the school for only a few months before it became clear that he needed to be placed in a self-contained program with extensive one-on-one teaching. But the time it took to place him in that program seemed to last forever, the walk to school every day without any expectation. Other parents congregated after they had dropped their kids off. They knew. I knew they knew. I could hear the whispers I never heard:

That's the father of the poor little boy who is a retard.

"How is he doing?" I would sometimes ask the teacher. I felt like I should say it to show vigilance.

She mentioned his sweetness and effort, a *nice little boy.* But there was also the look that said, *Are you kidding me? How do you think he's doing?*

It was only much later, when I finally gathered up the courage to open the blue box, that I discovered her summation of him:

> Extremely short attention. Needs constant pulling back into lesson. Cannot attend. When sharing usually states the same thing. Little or no communication with teacher and peers. No eye contact. Body acts spastic at times. Fine motor inconsistent, able to cut some days, unable to hold scissors on others. Math readiness is below grade level. Reading readiness — at times aware of upper and lower cases, has some letter correspondence. Very dear, pleasant and agreeable. Cannot follow directions when in kindergarten workbooks without one to one help. Severe attention difficulties.

It was obvious that Atwater was not working. He could never be a part of regular kindergarten. Her assessment was part of the deconstruction of Zach when he was six and everybody was trying to find the proper placement for him in the Shorewood school district with reams of reports and psychological analyses and observations and tests:

Auditory Sequential Memory. Beery Buktenica Visual-Motor Integration. Bender Gestalt. Benton Visual Retention Test. Brigance Inventory of Early Development. Daberon Screening. Detroit Test of Learning Aptitude. Kaufman Assessment Battery for Children. McCarthy Scales of Children's Abilities. Raven Coloured Progressive Matrices. Stanford-Binet. Wechsler Preschool and Primary Scale of Intelligence. Wepman's Auditory.

The results, except for memory recall, gauged by the ability to recite back strings of numbers, were numbing. Visual perception (0 of 10). General knowledge (13 of 30). Gross motor (4 of 12). Unable to write numbers in sequence. Unable to do simple addition. Unable to recognize money. Unable to tell time. Unable to print uppercase letters sequentially. Unable to print lowercase letters sequentially. Unable to print simple sentences.

Was there anything he could do? The final paragraph summation was always the same. Such a nice little boy.

Fuck your summation. Fuck your patronization. This is *my* son. Not a house pet.

As part of determining the proper school placement, he was personally observed by a special-education supervisor one day in the classroom at Atwater. It was time for sharing what had happened over the weekend. All the other children sat on the floor looking at the teacher, rapt and ready, while Zach rocked back and forth. He was desperately trying to keep up. He raised his hand to say that he had ridden his bike. He did not look at the other children when he said it. Suddenly there was a chorus of cries that he was ignoring them, as if he was being haughty and condescending by not sharing in the proper way.

The teacher then put on a record, and the kids sang along. Zach couldn't keep up with the words. After that, the children sat down and were asked about what it meant to eat a good breakfast. Zach was called upon. It struck me as taking a bucket of shit and forcing his head into it. Why would the teacher call on my son when she knew by then that he could not adequately answer? He repeated the question several times before blurting out that he had cereal for breakfast.

The children stood to do a step-movement to a poem. Zach rocked back and forth again and played with his shoe. The teacher called his name to regain his attention. He looked in her direction but continued to play with his shoe.

It was a teacher and thirty kids against one, his incapacities like a thousand open sores for everyone to gape at.

I think of the irritated grumbles toward him when I see the main building. I think of him not looking at the teacher because he was scared and confused and shy and did not know what to say. But then I think of him raising his hand when he was asked what he had done over the weekend. I can see the hand rising up above the murmur of the other kids, a little boy with something to tell even though nobody else thought he had anything to tell.

I rode my bike.

And yes he had, defying all age-appropriate behavior, flying down the street in the brace of the fall wind and the first creep of cold, the master of the world. Then I think about him playing with his shoe in the classroom of Atwater, twiddling the laces with his slender fingers, the silence within him like every voice yelling at him at once with no idea of what to do except not say a word.

We walk back to the minivan and drive to the next place on his list: the house on Olive Street where we used to live. I pull over in front of the house, jerking the shift into park. I am fumbling to find things I cannot find, although I know they are there because I just put them there.

— Goddamn it goddamn it goddamn it!

There is the lone bark of a dog in the cooked sunlight. There is a disembodied voice yelling, "Kenny, come here!" The house, in the center of the block, is a sprawling red brick converted into a duplex. The street is empty. The world is empty. Zach peeks inside windows on the first floor, where we lived, looking for his benchmarks. I peek inside windows with him with no interest in any of it. We left this place long ago, and I can see no reason to ever return.

A woman who lives there sees us lurking and opens the door to find out what we're doing. Zach explains.

— My name is Zach we're driving across the country to places where we used to live.

She lets us inside. Zach makes a beeline for the room that Gerry and he shared, only to find that it has now been converted into an indoor sauna. The woman, recognizing my last name, pulls out a copy of *Friday Night Lights* for me to sign. I sign it. She brings up the television series.

The doorbell rings, and the woman goes to answer it. There is a policeman at the door asking if she's related to the person who parked in front of the house because there is a problem.

— There is no parking on the street.

I tell him that's my car.

— Sorry, that's me.

— Are you okay? Are you tired? Seriously, take a look at your van.

The driver's side door hangs open. My cell phone is on the seat.

— Are you okay? Even your demeanor, a little bit ... Are you tired? You under the influence of anything?

— No, I'm not under the influence of anything. It's just an emotional trip, but I'm not under the influence of anything.

The woman, a former assistant district attorney, comes to my defense.

— He's fine. I can tell you we've just been through the house.

The cop is still unconvinced.

— I wonder if it's okay to let you go at this point?

— My demeanor is fine.

— I know, but your welfare.

The woman promises that I will get a cup of coffee. The cop reluctantly relents.

— I guess I'm not going to arrest you. I'm looking out for your well-being.

The cop drives off, and I thank the woman. Zach and I climb back into the minivan to fulfill the rest of his bucket list. We head toward another school, this one named Dunwood.

I am shaken up by what happened. It's one thing to park on the wrong side of the street. It is another dimension to leave the driver's side door wide open and your cell phone in the passenger seat. The cop was right to question my judgment.

I need to talk about it now.

— The cop thought my demeanor was strange. I think it is. I think I am wearing down here. It seems like a lot is going on, probably emotionally. I am tired, exhausted.

A map of Milwaukee has moved from Zach's hand to his lap. He is peering into it. I look over at it. I see nothing but the crisscrosses of nonsense.

— I need to get a cup of coffee, Zach. How far is the school?

— Not that far. I think it's . . .

He pauses.

— *How far?!!*

— It's just up in Fox Point.

— *Well how far is that?!!*

— Yeah yeah make a left here then we're going to make a right.

— *Where is it?!!*

— It's not far.

— *It is far!!*

— Yeah yeah make a right here it's after Calumet right after make a right here see Dunwood Road go straight.

He has found the Dunwood school after a fifteen-year absence. It was a school that catered to his special needs. It was a good place. We stare at it.

— Yup this is where I went to school.

— Yup, this is where you went to school.

I suggest that maybe we should get out and see if it all still looks the same.

It is a daycare center now, but the layout has been left largely intact. We walk along a linoleum-covered floor trying to find his homeroom. He remembers the number, 107. When we get there, he looks inside for a second or two. That is enough. He is satisfied.

— I remember the name of my homeroom teacher.

It's ridiculous to have driven all the way here and spend all of thirty seconds inside. I force him to look at the rooms that used to be the gym and the library. He looks.

—Yup.

We get back into the minivan. It is a blitzkrieg now so I can just finish the list. An ice-cream store named Licks next to the Fox Bay Theater. The curio store Winkie's, largely filled with ingenious trinkets, like the bottle opener playing the University of Wisconsin fight song. St. Mary's Hospital where Caleb was born in 1991. The little Hayek's grocery store that he walked to with the Carter boys who lived upstairs.

The exhaustion is overwhelming now. I climb into the front seat after the last stop like a battered old man. I don't know where we are. I don't have any sense of my bearings, driving around in a haze. I feel explosive. I am trying to contain myself, although some has already spilled out.

—You *enjoyed* all that?

—Yeah.

—That was *exciting*?

—Yeah.

—What do you think about when you go inside? What do you think about when you go to these places?

—What it looked like and what it was like . . .

—Do you really remember?

—Yeah.

I believe that when he crouched down to look through the grimy window at his classroom at Atwater, he saw all the other children who were there. I believe that when he went to the old house on Olive Street and ran into his room he saw every piece of furniture and every picture and Gerry in the bed across from him. I believe that when he went to Dunwood and walked into room 107, he saw his homeroom teacher and his speech teacher and the alphabet cutouts. I believe that every detail of those places, and a thousand more, remains alive in Zach's brain with uncanny accuracy.

The meticulousness of Zach's memory doesn't reinforce the past. It reinforces his present, a living snapshot that never disappears because in a sense he is still there. No object or face has left him. There is no ab-

stract extrapolation. There is no emotional attachment. Just those images so perfectly remembered they come alive like the loop of a film.

I see how his memory enhances his life, has in many ways become
his life. But memory is different for the rest of us. Memory is as much
emotional recall as it is physical recall. The details in some way become almost irrelevant. Memory can evoke joy or pain or sadness. The
beauty of memory is what it makes us feel, a psychological tool far
more than a literal one. It isn't what we specifically remember. For my
son it is only what he specifically remembers, what he specifically still
sees.

I cannot do what Zach does. Few can, only those equipped with the
"failure to forget." But the vast majority of us do forget as we should.
We remember what we remember because it signifies something, con-
jures up a certain feeling. That's not the case with Zach. He wants to go
to these places to replenish his hard drive.

But I don't want to be here today. I don't want to go back in time.
I can remember barely a single physical element about the Atwater
school or the Dunwood school. But my memories are nevertheless
powerful, the memory of a lost little boy, the memory of facing the
hardest reality of all for any parent that my child would always be different. That is what I remember, not the number of the homeroom.

— Now where are we *going*?

Zach wants to go to some place called Kopp's, or maybe it's Copp's,
for lunch. I don't know how to spell it, much less where it is located.

— How the fuck are we going to go there if we don't know how to
get there?

— We don't have to go there.

— No, that's where you want to go.

— It's all right we can go somewhere else.

— No, if that's where you want to fucking go, then that's where we'll
fucking go.

I call directory assistance to at least figure out the spelling and get
an address. The silence separates. I am increasingly finding the entire
trip pointless, a vain exercise in molding Zach into something he cannot be, fantasizing that the open road would lead to a greater sense of
togetherness and understanding, that in our intimate privacy I would

be able to bore into his soul and pull out a string of sparkles. I want a different son at this moment. I deserve a different son. I glance over at Zach and fill up with familiar self-hatred. I realize the cop was right: I do have an impairment, an emotional impairment, the anger of what happened, the helplessness, the forever haunt of watching my newborn son through a hospital window bloody and breakable.

The restaurant is on Port Washington Road in a town called Glendale. I feel obligated to find it. But I'm just driving in wider and wider circles.

Zach peers into his map and finds Port Washington Road. I try to gather myself together.

— You think I'm in a good mood or a bad mood?

— A good mood as long as I find the place.

He brushes my hand with his.

— It will be all right Dad.

— You're being very supportive of me.

— Yeah.

— I'm out of it.

— Yeah.

Zach spots a sign for Glendale that I missed.

— It's good we're on this road.

We drive a little farther and spot Kopp's on the right, a saucer-shaped building out of the 1950s serving burgers and malts and fries. Zach found it.

He guides me to a parking space in the overflowing lot.

— Yup we got a spot!

We sit on a rounded ledge outside and eat Buffalo chicken sandwiches and thick onion rings. I suck down a malt, and he sips a Diet Coke.

— Dad can I have some money so I can get some ice cream?

It is a question he asked me when he was five. It is a question he will ask me as long as I am here with him.

He gets his ice cream with its ooze of hot fudge creasing over the plastic cup. He eats in the complete wash of his happiness. At this moment, I feel neither pity for him nor self-pity. I feel gratitude. Zach knew how to save me.

Chapter 8

Cardinals and Cookies

I

WE ARE SUPPOSED to spend another night in Milwaukee but our hotel, the squirm-sounding Pfister, built in 1893, is infested with gloom. Our suite appears to have been robbed of most of its furniture. There is a pullout couch in Zach's room, a scarred coffee table once used to play tic-tac-toe with a penknife, a corner armchair that sags like flabby flesh. There is a bed in my room and a scuffed side table without an alarm clock. The bathroom is best approached sideways.

The Pfister is supposed to be Milwaukee's leading hotel, but staying there only casts a pall over the rest of the city. Milwaukee is ninety miles from Chicago and feels the shadow of those bigger-than-ever shoulders, the unshakable reputation of a sickly little brother. It is known for beer, once the largest producer in the world. But the industry has largely subsided. Pabst is gone. So is Schlitz, along with the slogan that became synonymous with the city, "The beer that made Milwaukee famous." The area is also known for wholesome white TV and film characters from a bygone era, benign buffoons who spend an inordinate amount of time bowling — *Happy Days, Laverne and Shirley.* But in the past fifteen years since we lived here, the downtown has remade itself with new condos and restaurants. There are other places to eat now beside Mader's with its leaning towers of sauerbraten and potato pancakes. The Milwaukee Art Museum on the edge of Lake Michigan, whose Quadracci Pavilion was designed by world-renowned architect Santiago Calatrava, makes the museum the most eye-popping in America. Lit up at night, the Calatrava addition shines upon the lake like a thousand white sails.

A sight such as that, the unexpected discovery of a diamond-encrusted necklace, is what makes a cross-country trip cathartic no matter what route you take, even one as hideous as ours. Milwaukee proves that the American city, lost for so many years, can reinvent itself with originality. It still has the feel of a careful place but not a stodgy one. It doesn't take itself with strident seriousness, the best show in all of sports the race around the bases in the seventh-inning stretch at Brewers baseball games where five lucky fans get to dress as sausages — brat, Polish, Italian, hot dog, and chorizo.

But the reconstitution of Milwaukee has not filtered down to my own reconstitution. The events of yesterday have not subsided. My mood. My meltdown. My ambivalence in being with my son. My unexpected resurrection from the pit of frustration because of him. It continues to be a muddle. Zach, despite his limits, has been steady and true, while I have been volatile and inconsistent. I *am* volatile and inconsistent. But I thought I would do better, hold my feelings in check for my son. I also realize all too well what this behavior signifies beyond my intrinsic personality. I am not at peace with my son. I am still not at peace with how he came into the world and what he became because of it. I don't know if I ever will be and I do what I do when in conflict — take it out on someone else, too often someone I love. My sniper attack.

We could order room service for dinner but the Pfister is beyond faith and we want our food before midnight. We could go out to eat but I don't want to suffer through one of those meals where I ask Zach simple who-what-where questions and he gives one-sentence answers until, after about three minutes, I bury myself in smartphone minutiae. We could play tic-tac-toe on the coffee table but neither of us brought a penknife. I feel pent-up, caged, like I did at the very beginning of the trip. I decide suddenly that we need to get the fuck out of there.

— We're done in Milwaukee. Time to move on. Let's just leave now.

— Yeah.

— Hit the road, right, Zach?

— Yeah.

— I've been very depressed. I don't know why.

— The zoo is only nine miles away Dad.

We hurriedly pack and head downstairs to settle with the clerk. It is 8:00 P.M. I acknowledge the oddity of checking out at such an hour. She looks at us like it happens all the time. She avoids asking the standard unctuous question of "How did you enjoy your stay?" because she already knows the answer.

Even Zach is depleted by Milwaukee. He has refreshed all the snapshots of memory he felt were important for his hard drive. He has found closure with the people he has seen while squeezing out new bits of information. He has said goodbye to our friend Nancy, who owned the duplex on Olive Street. He asked after her daughter Lissa, whose name I would not have remembered had I been waterboarded for a year. Nancy gave Zach a picture of her. I watched as he so gently slid it into his wallet like a written verse of Keats, a keepsake of a girl he has not seen forever. He keeps it to stay close to her because she is still there, still in his heart, where all good relationships persist regardless of time or distance, the truest beauty of his failure to forget. He will keep that picture in his wallet forever, and even if he doesn't look at it for another thirty years, he will always recall the exact day and circumstances in which it was given to him.

He has said goodbye to Lois, whom he has known all his life and to whom he feels a special attachment. He has given her a hug, dropping his head into his favored spot, the nape of her neck, and letting it linger as she places her arms around him. *Oh, Zach . . .* We have gone by the streets where we lived one final time, the shade trees in front of the tiny lawns with their bounty of limbs, sentries in the still night. "Goodbye Frederick," he whispers, the street where we first lived when we moved here in 1989. I try to decipher his tone. At first, I think it's wistful. But then I realize it's simply a thank-you to a place and a moment that once was there for him and always will be, an anchor in the moonlight as we roll down the road.

It was in the house on Frederick where I wrote *Friday Night Lights* in 1989 and 1990 in a tiny second-floor study with a computer on one side and a corkboard filled with index cards on the other. No Internet. No smartphone. No Google. No distractions except those inside my own mind. Every day I put on headphones and juiced up the music of Bon Jovi and Tears for Fears and the Alan Parsons Project to stimulate and write with the head-spinning frenzy of Schroeder. It was about the work then, not the commercial prospects and the book tour. It was the most creative joy I ever felt, the only sustained time I woke up not with the dread of writing but with the exhilaration of it. Zach's whisper of farewell is also mine.

Goodbye, Frederick . . .

We both know we will never see it again. But we both carry our memories. The right memories for each of us.

II

The normal route for a cross-country trip would be to continue west, through the lush grain seas of Wisconsin and Minnesota and then onward through South Dakota and Wyoming and Utah and Northern California. That route would show you the Black Hills and the Corn Palace and Wall Drug and Yellowstone and Zion and Bryce and the Grand Canyon and Yosemite. Because I had promised Zach that we would spend time only in places he has been before, our trip assiduously raises its most evocative finger at all of that. Instead, we will now veer south from Milwaukee to Missouri and then west through Oklahoma into Texas. Our next stop is Odessa. We have to go a thousand miles out of our way to get there and still make it to Los Angeles.

Outside of Milwaukee we finally get onto highways I have never driven on before, which does offer relief. For the first time, I feel the *On the Road* abandon of the unknown, humming into a night that will never end, no idea of where we are going to stay because we don't really know where we are going to go, Zach and I just two bad-to-the-bone born-to-be-wild boys in bandannas and biker boots and studded belts pushing pedal to the metal on the minivan so it gets all the way up to sixty-two miles per hour without shaking, flipping the bird at every truck and car and bicycle and kiddie scooter that passes. In reality we are dressed in shorts and T-shirts, gently passing a bag of Cheetos back and forth, each of us taking respectable handfuls without undue piggery. But we still feel the liberation. We feel the badness. We are *bad*.

Our interim stop is Branson, Missouri, tomorrow night. There is some cheating involve, a serious violation of the trip rules. But I have always wanted to go since it represents a distinct hue of America and we need something to break up the monotony of the death march. Branson has its reputation of being a holy-roller Las Vegas, wholesome entertainment without fishnets squeezed into corpulent thighs. I also promised Zach we would go to an amusement park every day. It was a good intention and, so far, a bad delivery. But Branson has a good one, creating yet another incentive, particularly after Zach once again brings up the already very sensitive subject of mode of transportation.

— I have an idea Dad maybe you'll like maybe we should drop off the minivan and fly to Odessa.

— Don't you like being in the car?

— Flying is always faster.

— Yeah, but flying's for pussies.

— Why?

— Because you see things when you drive.

— What things?

— Since we're not going anyplace beautiful, Home Depot.

— I've been to Home Depot.

The amusement park in Branson is called Silver Dollar City. There are thousands, if not millions, of websites that have done very meticulous studies of amusement parks — the wait times, the force of gravity, the pitch and grade and velocity and speed. On all these scales, Silver Dollar City ranks high. It has WildFire, a multilooping roller coaster with speeds up to sixty-six miles per hour. It has PowderKeg, zero to fifty-three miles per hour in 2.8 seconds. It has Fire-in-the-Hole, an indoor roller coaster where a gang called the Baldknobbers sets the town ablaze as you rumble through it. It has American Plunge, where you climb more than five stories into the Ozark sky and splash down in a log flume at speeds of more than thirty-five miles per hour. For all these reasons, it is Zach's definition of heaven. But the distance to Branson turns out to be longer than I thought; we won't get there until tomorrow night, by which time the park will be closed. We will need to make a change in plan and route. I have not told Zach the possibility we won't be going to Silver Dollar City after talking it up endlessly. I cannot bear to keep disappointing him.

We head south on 43 near Lake Geneva. We pick up the Chicago Cubs–St. Louis Cardinals game on WGN, the ultimate *On the Road* romance, the terse beats of the announcers' voices like old-fashioned Western Union telegrams. *Here's the two-two to Ramirez. Ground ball to short. To his right is Eckstein. Gloves. Throws from the edge of the outfield grass and just gets Ramirez for out number one. The 0 and 1. Swing and miss. 0 and 2 to Fontenot. Takes outside for ball one. And the 1-2 to Fontenot. Swing and a miss. And the inning is over.* We hear the I-can't-believe-this-is-happening-again groans of Cubs announcer Ron Santo as the Cards take a 10–1 lead on a three-run homer by Albert Pujols and a grand slam by Chris Duncan. I can't help but feel sorry for Santo, as he gives voice to ninety-eight years of Cubs World Series–less futility. He loves. He loves too much.

Zach has been to his share of baseball games in Philadelphia. He loves the food court set behind the outfield fences at Citizens Bank Park where the Phillies play. The lines are such that he usually misses the first five or six innings, but he does it on purpose. He understands who is winning and who is losing, but if a pitcher was pitching a perfect game with two outs in the ninth and I teasingly suggested that now was a good time to beat the crowd, Zach would be out like a bullet. I doubt he is listening to the agony of Ron Santo. But we at least have progressed from Cheetos to cookies.

— We're having a good time, aren't we?

— Yeah.

— We're eating cookies, right?

— Yeah.

— We're listening to the Cardinals game.

— Yeah.

— What else could be better? It's dark out. The moon is pretty.

— Yeah.

— So what could be better?

— Nothing.

— Name anything that could be better.

— Anything.

III

— Do you ever wish you had a girlfriend, Zach?

— I kind of do . . . like Shanna.

— Is she not your girlfriend?

— Yeah she's just kind of a friend who I just see sometimes.

— But you wish you had a girlfriend?

— Kind of yeah.

— Why?

— 'Cause I just wish I did.

— Somebody you could do things with all the time like Gerry and his girlfriend Alli.

— Yeah Gerry lives with Alli and I don't.

— Would you like to live with Gerry and Alli?

— Gerry and Alli yeah.

— You would?

— I would like to maybe I was gonna say maybe I can stay over like on Tuesday maybe like on a Monday night or even a Wednesday night when I am working in Philly the next day.

As part of his array of activities, Zach goes to dances with other disabled adults. He dances with Shanna when she is there. They work together at the supermarket, and she is a lovely girl with lovely parents. They are faithful companions to one another, going to movies together or having dinner just the two of them at Oriental Pearl on Kings Highway in Haddonfield. He talks to her in a way that he doesn't talk to anyone else, never bombarding her with questions except for "What have you been up to?" and then listening and then telling her what he has been up to and then ending the conversation with "maybe we can hit a movie sometime."

When Shanna isn't there, he dances alone.

— Does that bother you?

— No it's okay.

— You don't mind dancing alone?

— I don't mind.

— Are you sure?

— Yeah I'm sure.

I look over at my son. I can visualize him dancing by himself, earnest and awkward movements to a syncopated beat. The sweet confluence of baseball and Cheetos and cookies gives way to the image of my son in that isolation. As social as he is, even with people he has met for the first time, he spends much of his time that way. He engages at a gathering and then, because of the limits of his comprehension, disengages. He starts talking to himself, while everyone else converses. When I break the trance, because it is a trance, and ask him if he is okay, he always says that he is fine. He never complains or expresses boredom as the world circles around him. In his own way, he is expressing acceptance of who he is and what he will be.

He dances alone.

We clear the border of Illinois, past Roscoe and Rockton and Rockville. We cannot see the landscape in the black night, but we can feel it: farmlands and weary, worn-out machinery still churning out crops of bounty. I have never been in this part of Illinois before and I feel serenity, worth going deeper and deeper into the unknown lands. I can see in the night without having to see at all the humble white-painted house of a farmer with cows lingering outside in lazy obliviousness next to the machinery that has needed fixing for at least a decade. I see lights on at the kitchen table, and I see a husband and wife and kids dishing out mashed potatoes and meat and gravy and beans. The other version of this vision is that too much work and too little money have made the parents so depressed they watch *Dancing with the Stars* without even voting, and the children, no longer addicted to methamphetamine, are making it instead. Which is why it is always good to travel at night.

We stop at McDonald's. We lay out our maps and our meals on a hard wooden table. We ignore the smell of cooking oil and the other customers who look too much like roadkill survivors. Together we make a momentous road trip decision.

— Zach, I think we need to skip Branson.

— Why?

— Because we won't get there until tomorrow night. The amusement park will be closed.

— What about the rides?

— We'll go instead to Six Flags near St. Louis.

— I've been to Great Adventure in Jersey with my friends I like the rides it's nice there except for the bathrooms they really stink.

— St. Louis is a nicer place than Jersey so maybe the bathrooms will be okay.

— Okay.

It is still an ambivalent choice, at least for me. Forget Silver Dollar City. No Yakov Smirnoff's Moscow Circus. No Andy Williams Moon River Theater. No Dolly Parton's Dixie Stampede. Not even Twelve Irish Tenors. Zach pries his cheeseburger from the thin white paper and pulls it apart like Turkish Taffy. I choose the Southwestern Salad, as if it will somehow negate the potato chips and Cheetos and Slim Jims and Snickers and cookies that I carry out of every gas station like a disorganized looter. He looks at the Rand McNally atlas and studies a little bit and traces the route. We will take route 39 and then get on route 74 just for a minute and then go down 55. I don't care to question him. Fuck the GPS.

A child comes in whining for ice cream. An ample woman comes in and orders two hot fudge sundaes. I do not see anyone else with her.

— Are you sure you want to go to Six Flags?

— I want to stay all day.

Back on the road, we pass by LaSalle and Peru near 10:00 P.M. The Cardinals-Cubs game ends. Ron Santo's misery goes silent. Zach falls asleep in the back seat, piled into his bird nest. I am happy to be away now, happy to be with my son, happy we planned the next stop to-gether. I am now comforted by the jagged sounds of his sleep, unlike the beginning of the trip when the sounds seemed so agitated and la-bored. There is a now familiar rhythm in the pump jack rise and fall of his breathing, the oxygen gulped in and out. The miles meld into enduring nostalgia — Gerry and Zach in Odessa in their bright red boots and bandannas; touch football when I was a kid on the wide ex-panse of the sidewalk outside the Guggenheim Museum where white-haired Park Avenue doyennes occasionally got hit on the shoulder and did not react positively; my first kiss, in a cemetery with the white slab of a tombstone staring at my genitals. I never thought Zach and I would reach such a place of unity and contentment. But we have on this night. We are gliding. We are finally what I've dreamed we would be since I first hatched the idea for this trip: a father and son together on the road.

Chapter 9

"It Will Be Okay"

I

W E ARE HEADED for Six Flags today. Zach has forever felt liberation in amusement parks, his primal screams unplugged, his dance upon the moon. The ratchet of the roller-coaster cars to the top before the perpendicular plummet. The loops upon loops upon loops in increasingly perilous circles. Right side up. Upside down. Compressed. Contorted. It is all part of his rush.

I like them as an uprising against middle age. Unlike my son I am not fearless. There is no rush, just the hiccupping heart and the churning stomach straight to the rooftop restaurant of the throat. Some of the rides, named after a natural disaster or a misshapen comic book villain, accompanied by the ennui of teenage operators in striped shirts and scratched-at pimples most likely distracted by trying to come up with new slogans for the front of black T-shirts, offer neither sympathy nor solace.

We haven't slept much, about six hours, but everything about the day seems right. The trip is now truly beginning, Chicago and Milwaukee far more tense and intense than I anticipated. The Carlinville

Best Western is midwestern womb, no bites of bedbugs in blood feast, no faint odor of difficult sex. The room is square-angled like the region itself, bed to the right, blond wood desk to the left, instant coffeemaker of plastic components promising only tepidness. Pets are allowed as long as they don't weigh more than fifty pounds. The microwave costs an extra twenty-five bucks. The trip has been like a board game, one step forward, two steps backward, two steps forward, one step backward. But this day will work. He will not be disappointed. I will not disappoint him.

I knock on the hollow door of Zach's room at seven.

— Are you up?

— I'm up.

I go inside. He tells me he has already been to the computer in the little business center of the Carlinville Best Western. He has Googled the phrase "Six Flags" and carefully studied the rides he wants to go on and in what order — Batman, Sling Shot, Screamin' Eagle, Rush Street Flyer, Mr. Freeze, the Ninja, the Joker, the Boss, the Big Spin.

It all sounds dreadful.

— Are you packed?

— I'm packed.

— Did you brush your teeth?

— I brushed my teeth.

— Did you remember your toilet kit?

— I remembered my kit.

— Give me a second, and then we'll go.

— Okay.

I go back to my room. All my bags are in a little huddle. I hoist them on my shoulder. I put them down.

I taste panic.

The camera bag is missing.

It contains about five thousand dollars' worth of equipment, which can be replaced. But the rest cannot. I have taken hundreds of pictures, but I haven't had a chance to download any of them onto my computer. The tape recorder I used to record Zach and myself is also in that bag. Since Zach's birth, I have taped and taken notes with the possibility of one day writing about him. A book is immaterial now; I cannot replicate hundreds of hours of recordings no matter how great the writerly claim of an audio memory. The panic spreads, the awful feeling of nausea at being unable to undo what has been done. I need a scapegoat. I am good at that.

Zach is to blame for this. Why can't he help me with the fucking driving? Why can't he carry to the room more than his own fucking suitcase? Didn't he notice that when we pulled into the motel last night at one in the morning I was fucking tired after driving three hundred miles? Why do I have to be the one to keep fucking track of everything? Can I please, just for a second, get some fucking help here?

I race into his room.

— Have you seen the camera bag?

— No.

— I can't believe it. I can't believe it. I can't believe it. I can't fucking believe it. We're fucked, Zach. Do you understand that?

— Yeah.

— We're fucked.

— Yeah.

— This is a fucking disaster. A goddamn fucking disaster. What am I going to do?

— I don't know.

— Of course you don't fucking know.

— Can we still go to the amusement park?

— Fuck the amusement park.

He looks at me. He is scared and wounded.

— I'm sorry. I shouldn't have said that.

— It's okay.

I can't handle the stress of the trip anymore. I am falling apart. The last time I lost something invaluable I was with my father. It was an omen of collapse then, and I take it as an omen now.

II

In the summer of 2001, my father, then seventy-five, was diagnosed with leukemia. We took a cab together from the New York apartment to Mount Sinai Hospital, where he was to be admitted. He cried in the cab. It was the second time I had ever seen him cry. The first was forty-four years earlier when his mother had died at the age of fifty-five. He was the kind of man, like so many men of World War II and the "Greatest Generation," who loathed having others do things for him because it meant vulnerability and weakness. But there was no chance for that now.

"I'm scared," he said.

He had never ever said that to me before.

The cry turned into a wail in the dank smell of the cab, heightened by the incense sticks hanging from the rearview mirror. The plastic partition was filled with patterns of greasy fingerprints from impatient passengers pushing crumpled bills through a little tray. My dad was making a confessional inside that crappy shitty cab with the ill-aligned passport-size photo on the faded license and the click of the meter. He hated showing himself like this to me. I held his hand but my grip was weak and limp out of my own fear and confusion. We both knew it. I had to say something.

— It will be all right.

The thing that everybody says in a situation like this. The thing that nobody ever means in a situation like this. We both knew he was going to die. We let go of each other's hands. It was a role reversal of father and son that neither of us could handle. He wiped his eyes, willing the tears back inside him, suck it up, soldier.

— Fuck it.

I helped him get settled in his hospital room. It had the familiar mask of disinfectant to ward off the shit and the piss and pus as death takes its time working through you. I wanted to get out of there as quickly as I could. I hated that fucking smell, the same smell that had permeated the hospital after my twins had been born. I could feel my withdrawal: I had played the role of caretaker with people I loved enough in my life. I didn't want to do it again. I didn't know how to do it again. My father, whom I did so dearly love, was evaporating behind his hard shell like melting candy. So was I in my own wallow of help-lessness, knowing that whatever I did and whatever I said would be superficial and transparent.

It will be all right . . .
Bullshit.
I left the hospital and walked several blocks to the Lexington Avenue subway on 96th Street. I could not escape the guttural siren of his wail inside the cab. It flooded my head. As I approached the subway station, I reached for my wallet to get my Metro Card. The wallet was missing. I once again tasted panic, the stinking coat of bile as your mouth goes dry. I had a bag with me that contained a sandwich. I had put the bag on a ledge of a brownstone window to get the sandwich. I wondered if I had put my wallet there too for some reason. I also wondered why the fuck I had gotten a sandwich. My father was dying, and I was hungry? What the fuck was wrong with me? I knew why. It was a way of further distancing myself . . . *take your dying father to the hospital, then get a roast beef special on rye with extra Russian.*
I went back to the ledge, but no wallet. I ran back to the hospital, but no wallet. I combed the streets and the sidewalks like kicking for quarters in the desert. The wallet was gone, and I knew why. I could not deal with any of this, my hands a juggler's mess and my mind frayed and frazzled like a rope being pulled beyond tautness, a dead son walking to his dying father.
Day after day, I returned to the hospital, feeling lost without my wallet. It was metaphor of course for how lost I felt within myself, not knowing what to say, so saying nothing, preoccupied with my own future instead of with my father and his own lack of future. I acted in ways that were uncharacteristic and despicable, computing inheritance and IRA accounts and how much I would end up with. I am ashamed to this day, and I will always be ashamed. It was a symptom of the continued withdrawal, a way of fixating on something besides the death of a man I worshiped. It was not crass avarice. But my father didn't see it that way. He never said so, but I think he saw me as an ingrate after that, a son-of-a-bitch son. All those years of a beautiful relationship splintered. He said he did not know me very well, when I thought he was the one person in life who did know me well. He was angry and inconsolable at the end. He hated me at the end. He hated everyone at the end. He was terrified at the end.
My detachment was just a front. I so desperately wanted closure. I

just wanted him to say, "You have been a wonderful son, and I am so proud of you," and for me to say, "You have been a wonderful father, and I am so proud of you," but the mutual damage done once he was sick hardened into stubborn scars. He told me he had sat in bed one night unable to sleep, thinking of all the horrible things he had done in his life. He told me that when I was seven, he had umpired a pickup baseball game in which several of my friends were playing. I was frantic to do well. He called me out on strikes even though he knew the impact would crush me. I didn't remember the incident, and I could not come close to understanding why he would do something like that to his own son, his tentative and always fearful son. He apologized for it from his deathbed, but he must have felt some perverse satisfaction at the time.

I moved from Philadelphia to New York to be with him. I was a dutiful son and believed in duty. But there was only sulky silence between us.

If anything held my father and me together, it was the Yankees, who were making their epic playoff run in the aftermath of 9-11. They were magical; the strength of their victories seemed to reflect and enhance the enduring strength of New York. We sat there at night together in the gray glow of the television hooked into the wall. The Yankees brought us solace, and I remembered the time thirty-seven years earlier when he had taken me to the fourth game of the Yankees World Series against the St. Louis Cardinals. When Ken Boyer hit a grand slam to wipe out a 3-0 Yankees lead, he held me as I wept.

I was with him as he lay unconscious at the end. He was stoked up on morphine, the leukemic cells dancing through his veins in one final hoedown. All he could do was gasp as if he was being slowly smothered. I held his hand. But that is bullshit. I did not hold his hand. He did not want to be touched in those final moments anyway. *Just get the goddamn motherfucking thing over with. I am not ready to die but I am dying and fuck all that closure shit. Let you and your sister and your mother fucking sort it out. I got problems of my own.*

I could not bear those gasps. I went to the small waiting room down the hall and bought a bag of chips and watched television. I think it was *Seinfeld*. I came back to his room five minutes later. His gasps had stopped. That's how we left it. Or how we never left it.

He was dead.

III

I run through the corridors looking for the camera bag. I think about the wallet and how I inevitably lose what is vital when I cannot cope. I am convinced now: I forced the trip down Zach's throat, a snake oil salesman selling him on the dazzle of driving across country when the country is a haze to him without the introspection that comes when the horizon floats, with glassy shimmers of heat, and the sun lowers like the loss of a relationship, and the night gently takes over your soul.

How could I have lost this bag with all this information that can never be retrieved or replicated? Because I am a wreck. Because I am boring into my son like a lab rat by asking him intimate questions that make him sad or confused or nervous. I am subjecting him to hours in a car where I can see his squirming boredom no matter how much he fights to ward it off. I see him performing for me, trying to be good for me. It only makes me more selfish. I have responded to so much by getting angry with him when he has done nothing.

I run outside to the car and push the sliding door back, but the bag is not there. I run to the front desk and ask if anybody has left it, a ridiculous question since anyone seeing its contents would steal it, even in the goodhearted Midwest. I give them my cell number and at least they write it down. Then I think that maybe I left it outside the room when I checked in. I ask the cleaning woman if she has seen it. She says no, but she will look. That's what everyone says when they have no intention of looking for anything. Just like saying everything will be *all right*. I sit on the bed in my room, running my fingers through my hair again and again. I have the urge to turn around and go home.

Zach comes in and looks at me. He touches me on the shoulder.

— It will be okay.

I feel the delicacy of his fingers, as if he realizes that touching me too hard would make me cry in pain.

— Thank you, Zach. That means a lot to me.

— Yeah.

We get in the minivan. We forge ahead. We still may turn around and go home, but we will go to the amusement park first. It is the least I can do for my son. I try to make conversation.

— What do you think about me losing the bag?

— I thought it was not good because it is very expensive you bought it like last year June 27 2006.

— It's because I am stupid.

— I'm sorry you lost it.

— I know.

He points to the upper front cover of his knapsack.

— You know like I keep my cell phone in there I always keep it in there.

— You're more careful than I am.

— Yeah.

— Are you going to get another tape recorder you probably need one maybe we should stop somewhere.

— I guess so.

— We can put it somewhere where you won't lose it.

We get onto Interstate 55 South toward Six Flags. I ask him if he is excited about the amusement park. It is a pro forma question. Silence sets in on a day in which there should be excited noise. Zach stares out the window with his tilt. The miles crawl. Drizzle falls across the windshield in streaks. It is 9:00 A.M. and we have traveled 1,384 miles. It is roughly a third of the trip if we make the final two-thirds.

My phone rings. Who the fuck is this? I don't want to talk to anybody I know right now. I answer because I'm unfamiliar with the area code.

— Mr. Bissinger?

— Yes.

— The maid found your bag.

— YOU'RE KIDDING!?

— No, sir.

— I WOULD KISS YOU, BUT I'M UNSHAVEN!!

— No problem.

— Where was it??

— Behind the rear tire of the car that was parked next to you. Must have been there all night. It was a miracle that car hadn't left. The bag would have been crushed.

— I must have put it there when I was taking the bags out of the car last night. It was late. We have a lot of them.

— Yes, sir.

— We're turning around right now to pick it up. And thank you. Thank you so much.

— No problem.

I hang up. I turn to Zach.

— THEY FOUND THE CAMERA BAG AND TOOK CARE OF IT!

— You think they probably took a picture maybe?

That had never occurred to me.

— When did you get the camera where did you get it where did you buy it did they deliver it to you because you bought it online?

— Yes yes yes yes.

— I'm glad you found your camera for once.

— Say funny things, Zach. Make me HAPPY!

— Now it's good that we found the camera that's one good thing but now the next good thing is let's hope we get to the park and the park is open in the rain I'm sure it will be open.

— Maybe it will be just the two of us.

— Yeah.

— Wouldn't that be a dream, just you and me?

— Yeah.

— Thanks for being so kind and patient with me, Zach.

— It's okay.

Chapter 10

I'll Do Anything

I

WE STAND IN a darkened stairway of grated metal. There are patchwork clusters of gum hardened into the tiny holes. There is a wait. Giggling teenage girls, making a beeline from the adjacent water park, line up in still-wet bathing suits. I feel like I'm in a damp cave. I assume that's the point.

Scratchy theme music from the Batman movies builds up in volume. We inch further up the stairs. Small knots of people around us are discussing how to exit without embarrassment. Fears are expressed over what will happen if they remain in line. "I'm taking off my shoes," announces one of the teenage girls. It must mean the ride is so fast that footwear tends to fly off; among all the eventualities I had prepared myself for, losing my shoes was not one of them. Somewhere people a fifth of my age are screaming.

We make it to the top of the stairs and get in one of the cars. I am concerned my glasses will fall off since the shorts I am wearing do not have pockets suitable for holding glasses. Plus for reasons I cannot explain, they are also three sizes too big. I have to hold them up when weighted down with tape recorder and wallet and car keys. I feel like a clown at some low-grade circus where nobody has been paid for months and the only act I can do anyway is the drop-your-pants routine that hasn't gotten a laugh since Rock Island.

Zach is pensive. If he looks worried, then what am I supposed to look like? I already know what I look like. My shorts are continuing to slide. Zach continues to be silent. That makes me more nervous. What does he know about this ride? I'm in no mood for punking.

— What are you thinking, Zach? Tell me exactly what you are thinking.

— About the ride.

— Is it gonna go fast?

— Yeah.

— Are you gonna be scared?

— A little.

— Gonna scream?

— Maybe.

The elevation is ten and a half stories. The length is 2,693 feet, and the speed is fifty miles per hour with maximum G forces of four. The ride features five "head over heels" moments, with the trains traveling on the outside of the track rather the inside in which I have to assume you hang upside down like a bat. As a bonus, the floor drops from beneath the riders' seats. I have no idea why this is a bonus.

The ride makes its first ascent with calculated slowness. There is a cruel pause at the top, then we drop into the first loop. This thing is fast. My stomach is now in my ears. Yet I am screaming in elation.

— ZACH!!!!!!! ZACH!!!!!

Zach's eyes are open. The faster we go around a loop, the greater the G forces sucking our bodies into emaciation, the more he luxuriates in it. The ride ends after two minutes and four more loops. My paraphernalia has remained in my pocket. My shoes did not fly off. Zach is just getting started. I follow like his pet.

— I need to go on the rides all day I can't stop going on the rides.

— Why do you like them so much?

— I just do.

He has the map of Six Flags in his hand. He has figured out the next ride. It is called the Boss. That can't be good. We pass by Miss Kitty's Saloon and a gift shop called Thrill Seekers filled with tacky junk. They have a belt adorned with the Six Flags logo. I put it on so my shorts won't fall down.

—What do you think?

—Good.

Zach as usual is being diplomatic.

I now officially look deranged. Even for an amusement park.

The Boss is said to be one of the top five wooden roller coasters in the country. It reaches a maximum speed of 66.3 miles per hour. It has four drops of 150 feet, 112 feet, 103 feet, and 72 feet. There is a 570-degree spiral helix. I don't know what that is but it can't be good. There are numerous 52-degree high-banked turns. The track length is 5,051 feet and the duration three minutes.

On the ride, I scream Zach's name again. We lift our arms high over our heads to imitate the more experienced riders. We get an eight for enthusiasm, but only a three for style. My arms are a little rubbery at the end.

Next is the Sling Shot, which is true to its name. Zach and I sit side by side in adjoining seats that remind me of dental chairs except that we're strapped in. I think a lot about dental chairs. The Sling Shot catapults us up, then heads back down again. It does this for far too long in my increasing squeamishness. Zach is impressed.

—The Sling Shot is my favorite so far.

—The Sling Shot? The one where we went up high and then went upside down? That was your favorite?

—Yeah.

—You're insane. That was one I hated.

Zach is not focused on my feelings.

We go on the Screamin' Eagle and the Rush Street Flyer and the Ninja and the Joker and the Tidal Wave and Mr. Freeze and the Log Flume and the River King Mine Train and Tony Hawk's Big Spin. We eye the Superman Tower of Power, the amusement park equivalent of scaling K2. It is a relatively new ride, manufactured in Switzerland. It is twenty-three stories tall, or 230 feet. Then the contraption you are in drops sixteen feet per second and has a free-fall speed of approximately sixty-two miles per hour. Zach eyes it with longing, but it is closed. A year earlier, a young woman on the same ride at another park in Louisville had both her legs amputated at the ankle when a cable snapped in mid-flight.

The day winnows down, the thick humidity muted into slick vapor. The park has emptied out, all those thrill rides now forlorn without anyone to thrill, the sadness of empty roller-coaster cars still in forced climb. I sit on a bench and watch Zach as he rides the Teacups; he's the only one aboard. It is a kids' ride, far too demeaning for crusty souls of the Boss and Mr. Freeze. They would never be caught dead there, too much to live down. But Zach doesn't care. I can hear the gentle whir as the red and yellow teacup cars undulate up and down. A few screams scatter in the distance like a faraway car alarm. Zach's arms are spread out behind him. His eyes are closed, his head bent back slightly. The warm air encircles him.

II

We sit across from each other at a blue Formica table. He eats French fries and I eat a foot-long hot dog with a crumbling bun that leaves bits of soaky mustard on my shirt. It is only a matter of time before I become the official Six Flags mascot, unshaven, barely belted, flecked with mustard like some rare skin disorder. We are done for the day after seven hours. We need to head to Oklahoma so we can make Texas by tomorrow.

We walk to the exit. I see a ride I haven't noticed before. It is called Dragon's Wing. You are hoisted 153 feet high to the top of a crane. Then you pull a ripcord and basically bungee jump in a horrific free fall. I make a terrible error in judgment.

— You want to try it?

— Yeah.

Wrong answer.

— It's dangerous, Zach.

— Yeah.

— We could get killed.

— Yeah.

— I don't think your mother would like you to go on this.

— Yeah.

— It's really dangerous. Are you sure you want to try it?

— I'm sure.

I am screwed.

The line moves far faster than I thought. I see other people do the ride. I ask them what it's like as they get off.

— Just don't pull the ripcord.

I once again gauge Zach's willingness to go on this thing.

— Hey, Zach, do you want to pull the ripcord?

— No.

— I don't think this is a good idea. I really don't.

— Yeah.

— Do you want to get hurt?

— I don't want to get hurt.

— Are you sure you really want to do this?

— I'm sure.

— All right, fine. We'll fucking do it.

— Okay.

— But it's stupid.

— Okay.

— We went on every other ride today. What's the point of doing this one?

— I don't know I just want to do it.

— What does that mean?

— I just want to do it.

I can handle the roller coasters and the like. I have been on them many times before and have learned to brace myself for the worst. I have never been hoisted up by a crane and then dropped. Why would I? Why would anyone?

We put on our bondage outfits, which resemble wetsuits with Velcro straps and strategically placed hooks. We are yoked together tightly so that we face each other, nose to nose. A cord is attached to the hooks and we are slowly hoisted to the top of the crane. At the top, two workers stand on a little perch. It's hard to hear them, but I think they're talking about hair, or nails. Through their headsets, they get clearance from down below. They count down for us.

— Three . . . two . . . one . . . Go.

Fuck it . . .

I pull the ripcord . . .

We free-fall, our bodies initially parallel to the ground that rushes toward us. My arms are wrapped around Zach. His arms are wrapped around me. His eyes are closed. Mine are open. We fall faster than I thought possible. My mouth is dry. The churn of nausea in my stomach travels upward with far too much speed. We miss the roof of the entrance by what seems like inches. I can feel Zach holding me tightly. Then we swing high, flinging out into the sky. I feel an exhilaration I have never felt before. I am screaming at the top of my lungs. When we swing low, I can feel Zach holding me more tightly. Then we swing high again over the amusement park.

Zach and I merge into one, arm around arm, shoulder against shoulder, the press of his body against mine. I never had that when he was an infant in the hospital. I wore a gown and mask much of the time. He was almost always attached to the tube of that ventilator, the in-and-out hiss of the breathing he could not do himself. I held him in my arms and clutched his matchstick fingers, saw his infinitesimal toes emerge from beneath the blanket, ran my hand over the little cap he wore. I saw those brown eyes the size of a faraway star you can barely see. He was so strong. He was so hopeless. Was I holding a baby or was I holding a medical specimen, a miracle, yes, to be alive but a miracle of what? But now he is my lifeline, and I am his. If we let go of each other, both of us will surely shatter.

We swing low again, until a worker on the ground pulls on a rope attached to the cord and reins us in. We are lowered to the ground and disentangled. I stride and strut in my wetsuit back to the entrance, offering expertise to the terrified virgins.

— Don't pull the ripcord.

Most images fade in life, no matter how hard you try to keep them. They become hazy and blurred. At best you use your memory to inflate them back up. But this memory will always stay as it was. Just like my son's memories, it will always be set in concrete, no need to gussy it up or dress it in new clothing. This moment is momentary. I know that. But maybe for the first time in my life I feel that Zach and I share the same mental ground, think the same way, seize the world on equal terms.

— It was quite beautiful when we were arm in arm.

— Yeah.

— I will never ever forget today. I will never ever forget being with you.

— Yeah.

— Will you ever forget it?

— I won't forget it.

— You promise?

— I promise.

— Do you love me?

— I love you.

— Are you sure you love me?

— I am sure I love you.

— And I love you.

— I know.

— How do you know?

— Because you're my dad you have to love me.

Chapter 11

Scene of the Crime

I

WE LEAVE SIX FLAGS and head to a nearby Waffle House. Zach chooses it because there is a Waffle House in Carlisle, Pennsylvania, where Gerry went to college at Dickinson. If nothing else thus far, he has learned that the country is bound together by certain institutions wherever you are—Embassy Suites, Waffle Houses, Best Westerns, Holiday Inn Expresses. It is almost as if Zach, because of the way his brain organizes, planned the country himself with reliable monuments that always orient you. Zach has also invoked the Waffle House in Carlisle because he misses Gerry. He's proud of what he has just done and he wants to share the joy of it with his brother. Zach makes a call.

—Hi Ger I can't wait to see you Thursday we went to the amusement park it's like Great Adventure in Jersey but it's Six Flags near St. Louis Dad and I bungee jumped Dad pulled the cord we went on all the roller coasters and we went on this one the Boss and I went on the Teacups myself and we went on Mr. Freeze and Batman we went on

Ninja we went on the Log Flume we went on another ride where it got
very wet the Tidal Wave!

Zach hangs up. We quickly finish eating since we have several hours
of driving ahead.

— C'mon, Zach. Time to make tracks.
— Where are we going?
— We need to hit Tulsa.
— Tulsa's in Oklahoma will I get my own room again?
— You like that, don't you?
— Yeah.
— Because it makes you feel grown-up?
— Yeah and oh Dad.
— What?
— Let's not leave the camera.

We get onto I-44 West and drive for several miles, until I can no longer
ignore that there is something dragging beneath the car and scraping
the asphalt. I bang on the dashboard, which is the only way I know
how to fix a car. It has no effect. I then naturally assume the worst, the
high of the bungee jump replaced by the doom of disaster:

*The underbelly of the minivan is hanging out like entrails. It is very
broken. We are stranded in Oklahoma. We shall be stranded for several
days with nothing to eat but a few old Cheetos that lodged in the front
seat cushions.*

We pull onto an exit ramp and find a place to stop. I get out and look
under the car. I see a long piece of hard plastic that has wedged itself. I
pull, and it comes loose with such ease there must be some punch line.
Fixing the car couldn't possibly be *this* easy, because nothing is ever
this easy: my "repair" must have somehow punctured something, the
muffler or the gas tank or the transmission wherever it is and whatever
it does. I open the hood of the car and peer in, an exercise in meaning-
lessness since I don't know where to start to look and wouldn't know
what to do even if I did know where to start to look. But back inside
the van I find that the radio still works, so everything must be fine.

As far as I can tell, Zach has paid no attention. He has remained in
the passenger seat, and it looked like he was talking to himself most of

the time. But he has been watching with that unique style of his that is so deceptive, never letting on that he is the least bit interested. He offers summary judgment based on an ad for Staples:

— That was easy.

Around 10:00 P.M., we find a Best Western off a strip of overdeveloped highway near Tulsa. It is called the Trade Winds Central Inn. I like the name because it represents the eternal optimism of America, evoking beauty where there is none, trade winds where there are none, *something* where there is none: the name reminds me of housing developments called Piney Woods where there aren't any pines or woods in sight. A club and restaurant called the Elephant Run are attached to the motel. No elephants; the name makes perfect sense. Black letters on a white sign offer AARP and corporate rates, none of which seem to attract much business. There is a gray refrigeration truck in the parking lot with a ladder hooked to the roof, catty-corner to a Ford Explorer. Behind the parking lot is a Shell station. Behind the Shell station is a restaurant called Johnnie's. Behind Johnnie's is a Circle J Mini Mart. Near the Circle J are two three-way lights for the highway.

America.

II

As we leave our rooms the next morning, we run through the mandatory checklist.

— We have everything, Zach?

— Yeah.

— Have your wallet?

— Yeah.

— Have your keys?

— Yeah and my phone.

— Good.

— You didn't forget your camera did you Dad?

— You think I'm stupid, don't you.

— Yeah.

He senses that he may have hurt my feelings. His fingers slide gently over my arm.

— I love you Dad.
— Who else do you love?
— I love everybody.
— What about the dog?
— I sometimes love the dog.
— You don't even like the dog.
— Maybe.

We are hoping to make Odessa in West Texas by nightfall. It is the most brutal segment of the trip, six hundred miles of mostly sand and scrabble and dust bisected by two-lane tarmac like a strip of runway blackness. It is Zach's idea to go to Odessa, a homecoming for him after nearly twenty years. He is aware that I wrote the book *Friday Night Lights* but unaware that I was threatened with bodily harm when it came out in 1990 because of unflattering depictions of racism and misplaced academic priorities where students leaned back and learned little, subsumed by high school football gone mad with crowds of twenty thousand and teenage kids subjected to unconscionable pressure in the name of winning a state championship. The animosity toward me finally lowered once Tim McGraw and Billy Bob Thornton came to town to shoot the film of the same name in 2003, and thousands of residents were invited to appear as extras. I became an afterthought. The Hollywood lights are always blinding, and Odessa officials had received assurance that the controversial themes of the book would be largely sidestepped. There is still a hard core who considers me vermin — a Yankee Jew who should have been denied a Texas visa. I don't quite share the homecoming feeling.

Zach is desperate to see a family called the Chavezes, with whom we bonded when we lived in Odessa in 1988 and 1989. We've kept in touch with the family, but Zach hasn't seen the patriarch, Tony, in nearly ten years.

— Remember eating dinner at the Striped Bass in Philly with Tony on November 16 1995 that Thursday?
— Zach, we've been through this. I don't remember yesterday.

—I do.

We're also going to see Boobie Miles in Odessa, the Great Black Hope running back I wrote about whose high school career ended with an injury before the season even started. He was the book's essential character, a figure of tragedy because of his shattered dreams, scorned by the town of Odessa with epithets of "nigger" after he got hurt and no longer mattered on the football field. Because of the book, he achieved a fame so at odds with the desperations in his own life and only intensified by the 2004 film where celebrity re-occurred. I have been close with Boobie ever since the publication of the book, a relationship going on two decades. I have become a surrogate father and he has become a surrogate son. I have received hundreds of calls from him and in almost all of them I have heard the genuine pain in his voice — unable to hold a job, unable to pay the rent and the electric bill, in and out of jail for petty offenses for which he can't afford minimal bail, hit in court with overdue support payments. There is love between us. But there is also the subtext that what he really wants from me is money, and I am only enabling his self-destruction.

III

As we drive through the sand and scrabble and dust, Zach's memories of Odessa fill the minivan like the sudden appearance of ghosts.

He remembers going to Palo Duro Canyon in Amarillo when we first got there.

He remembers that our neighbors Billy and Bonnie had a dog named Rascal.

He remembers that they used to have us over to watch the Dallas Cowboys.

He remembers that he once helped Billy plant a tree.

He remembers that he had his first taste of Dr Pepper.

He remembers that Gerry and he took Spanish once a week with a woman named Virginia.

He remembers the Raindance Car Wash.

He remembers that the Chavezes had a dog named Lucky.

He remembers their house had a pool and a slide.

He remembers that my first book agent stayed at the Lexington Suites and bought black cowboy boots.

He remembers eating Frito pie.

He remembers Brian and Sandra.

He remembers visiting a nursing home called Seabury Center and visiting Mary and Olivia.

He remembers Ed Shugert and his wife, Mary, and going bowling.

He remembers Gerry and him taking swim lessons at the YMCA with a teacher named Gilbert.

He remembers going to the Carlsbad Caverns.

He remembers Gerry and him walking with their raincoats and boots on during a rainstorm.

He remembers all these things from when he was five.

I realize I have been wrong in thinking that Zach's memory does not richly enhance his life. The rest of us, when we ask how so-and-so is doing, don't listen to the response. Our eyes furtively dart toward the hors d'oeuvre table as we hope that the hosts are not vegan zealots. It is ingrained social behavior to not listen. But Zach always listens, and because he remembers what he hears, his relationships are always fresh and current to him, able to pick up exactly where he left off even if it was twenty years ago. The passage of time is irrelevant, as if there has been no passage at all. The ability forges new hope that there will be something else in his life besides bagging groceries and stocking supplies. But the hope is still tempered, always the bittersweet.

— Hey, if you could be anything in life, what would you be?

— Like anything in life?

— What would you do?

— What would I do?

— Yes.

— I don't know how to think of it.

He stares at the map of Texas he has bought.

— What about a reporter? You love gathering information.

— And Dad you should go to the law firm Christmas party with me.

He has abruptly changed the subject again, another reaction born of his own sorrow. He knows he will not be a reporter, just as he also knows that he would love to be one. He told me that once, but as he has gotten older he has let the possibility go, an indication of his maturation and his increasing grounding in reality. Like all of us, aspirations do die.

The Quiet sets in. I refuse to default to extended brooding over what my son will be, won't be, should be, should not be, would be, will never be. The exhilaration of the bungee jump is still within me. I cannot forget his arms clutching me, needing me. Needing each other. Nor can I forget the liberation I felt, which occurred only because of his resilience in making me do something I never would have done without him. He stood firm even when I confronted him with the possibility that we would die. I did not mean it. At least partially.

— You're fearless. Like a child in that way. Completely fearless. There was one ride we didn't do because it was broken, the Superman ride. That would have been crazy.

— I would have been scared?

— Yeah, but you would have done it. We would have done it. We did the bungee jump together. I'll never forget how beautiful that was. We were arm in arm. You wouldn't let go of my arm, do you know that?

— If I let go I would have fell off?

— You would have flown.

IV

We pass by exits for Sapulpa, Oklahoma, home of the rockabilly duo the Collins Kids who played on Tex Ritter's TV show in the 1950s, and a baseball player named Don Wallace who had one season with the Los Angeles Angels and hit .000 in six at-bats. We pass by the exit for Sand Springs, a Tulsa suburb that was occupied in 1826 by the Cherokee Indians during their forced march from their original southern homelands on the Trail of Tears.

It becomes noon and we have been driving for about three hours. We need to stop somewhere and break up the monotony of the day, not an easy thing in Oklahoma. I decide we should see the memorial to the 168 victims of the bombing of the federal building in Oklahoma

City in 1995. I think it is important for Zach that he bear witness to at least one site of historic and social significance during the trip. When I ask him about the bombing, he knows nothing about it.

There are two walls of black granite, referred to as the Gates of Time, that stand at opposite ends of the memorial. The space in between runs the length of a football field. There is the Field of Empty Chairs symbolizing those who died. In the middle is a reflecting pool. The memorial has the feel of a modern outdoor church, the solemn power enhanced by its very understatement. It does what a memorial should do — push you to fill in the images of that beyond-tragic day, the falling building and the trapped children and the noble efforts of salt-of-the-earth volunteers who worked for hour upon hour to rescue survivors trapped in chunks of rubble.

We stand at the black granite of the first Gate of Time, which commemorates the exact moment of 9:01 when the bombing began. We move to the inside of the memorial to the Field of Empty Chairs, made of granite from the destroyed building. There is a short inscription, which I ask Zach to read aloud:

> The field of empty chairs is to the 168 Americans who were killed April 19, 1995, on a Wednesday.

What Zach said is wrong. The inscription actually reads:

> The field of empty chairs is to the 168 Americans who were killed April 19, 1995.

He has inserted "on a Wednesday" automatically.
— How do you know it was a Wednesday?
— I just figured it out in my head.
— Are you sure?
— Yeah it was I'm sure.
I later check.
It was a Wednesday.
Next, we pass the reflecting pool so still you could walk upon it without a dapple. I am taking pictures, embarrassed by the constant clicks, an affront to the sanctity of those who died. In the distance, I hear someone with a thick southern accent ask a park ranger, "How

are those boys that tried the first attack on the World Trade Center being treated?" I keep taking pictures, the chairs to the fallen, the reflecting pool, the gate at the opposite end of the memorial commemorating the moment at 9:03 when the building fell. Zach musters every fiber to understand, but I can tell he doesn't understand. Then his eye catches something.

— See the baby ducks Dad take pictures of the baby ducks!

A mother lies still in the grass with three offspring behind her in a zigzag. It is the lone moment of life in a place dedicated to the dead. Zach finds it.

We get back on the interstate. One of the highlights of Zach's day is deciding what to have for lunch. He has settled on Mexican. We find a Taco Tico in Elgin. He squeals "yay!" when he sees it, then he points out the crucial differences between Taco Tico and Taco John's.

— They have those places in Wisconsin Taco John's my teacher Dave goes to Taco John's but actually they make the tacos they put them on hamburger buns so they call them at Taco John's Taco burgers.

I must remember that.

— How do you think this Taco Tico is?

— I bet it's good trust me.

— Trust you?

— Yeah believe me.

Not a chance.

— I don't think it's open.

— No it's open it says it.

— Then why is it so empty?

— I don't know.

— It looks scary. We're not gonna get killed in here, are we?

The interior is trimmed in green and beige, and the windows have been painted so you can't see out. On one wall, a mural shows a red pepper shooting at something. A worker dressed in black with a headset leans over the counter as if she might fall dead from a working life immersed in fast-food tacos. The only other diners are a couple. The man has steely white hair flattened out like the Dead Sea. He shoots me a glance that says blue-state foreigners are not welcome. He looks like he could skin me from head to toe while eating his second Taco Tico. Zach has the chicken quesadillas and eats with gusto. I have the beef salad and probe for shrapnel.

V

We make the Texas line at 2:54 P.M. at Burkburnett County. The weather has turned, splotches of blue losing out to the encroaching clouds. Near the border, on our right, sits the hollowed-out socket of a wooden shack. Hard not to wonder what it once was used for — a bunkhouse for cowboys herding cattle, the world's first 7-Eleven, a one-woman whorehouse. There are wheat fields on the left with gigantic rolled-up spindles and a clump of trees chattering in the breeze like shy schoolgirls and the rusted bones of an abandoned car. We have about 325 more miles of this before we reach Odessa, about seven hours.

— What do you think of Texas?
— Pretty good.
— Pretty good? Pretty ugly.
— Why?
— What is there? What do you see?
— Nothing.
— That's Texas. Telephone poles and a lot of mesquite.
— And grass.
— A little grass.
— Was it like this when we lived in Odessa?
— Even worse.

Zach falls asleep. The miles melt into one another on Texas 277, a dried-up gulch. Zach doesn't sleep for very long. He is having terrible trouble sitting still, repositioning himself almost every second. He talks to himself until I look over and ask him what's going on, and he stops with embarrassment. The two hundred proof of his purity and ability to find good even in wrenching tragedy has no outlet here: there are no baby ducks. But he keeps trying because he wants to please me and also show he is engaged.

— We're passing a lot of interesting places.

— Like what?

— Seymour.

— Ever been there?

— Nooooo.

— What's interesting about it?

— Um I think they are I think what's interesting about these um places um 'cause I think um I think um what's exciting about them is um because um they are in um they are um interesting um they have interesting names.

— Should we go see it?

— Never.

We stop at one of those gas stations that appear every hundred miles. The white of the clapboard has turned gray with remorseless windblown grit. An attendant comes out. He regards us with blank eyes, a surrender to the relentless terrain and so little to do in the bottomless canyons of time. Zach says he is reminded of Yellowstone.

— Why does this remind you of Yellowstone?

— 'Cause you know like in Yellowstone there's nothing there just that hotel and nothing to do there really and also we didn't have anyone to see on that trip.

— You hate trips where you don't have people to see.

— Yeah.

— That's why we are taking the most unscenic route in America.

We go through the main street of Seymour, Mike's Pit Barbecue and Sonic and Maverick's Café and the Movie Gallery and a discount food store that closed down. A Ford pickup carrying cattle slogs in the opposite direction. A little bit out of town, we pass a Chevy Trailblazer, then a Chevy pickup with six-packs of beer and soda in the back covered in plastic. Then nothing but the dry gulch of the tarmac.

— You want to drive cross-country again?

— Noooo. . . .

— Why not?

— Because I'll be tired after this one.

— You'll never want to do it again?

— NO.

For all my dismissiveness, there is something mesmerizing about these lands. Just as so much of America is being submerged by the homogenization of new waves of overdevelopment, there is also the vast America that remains untouched. It reinforces the promise of America, a country capable of greatness because it is physically still great, still new frontiers.

VI

We reach the outskirts of Odessa at 7:15 P.M. We stop at the Flying J Travel Plaza where Zach buys a map of Midland-Odessa. There are several to choose from, and he carefully studies them all before making his selection. The Flying J sells personalized mini license plates. I remember when we bought Gerry and Zach ones for their bikes when we lived here. I remember the outfits they wore in this newfound land, blue jeans and those red cowboy boots and flannel shirts and black cowboy hats. I was following the legendary high school football team the Permian Panthers for the 1988 season, then the winningest team in Texas state history. I remember when Sarah took the twins to the last game of the regular season in their pajamas.

I remember the freedom I felt in Odessa, away from the newsroom hothouse of the competitive *Philadelphia Inquirer* where we all sat starving for attention. I knew nothing about writing a book. But I knew I was onto the best story of my life almost from the minute I arrived in Odessa in July of 1988. The Permian coaches and I took off to Houston for the Texas North-South all-star game. The trip was long, about 430 miles, so we spent the night in a motel where the head coach got a single room with two double beds. There was a traveling party of seven, and I am not sure but I think I slept in the double bed that contained only three of us, although one of them was large. Very large. And he snored. Loudly. Very loudly.

I stayed in a motel off the interstate when we got to Houston. It cost $129 for the week and truckers were all over it. I understood why when I turned on the television and several channels showed deeply serious porn, making it a nice place to unwind after watching the monotony of practice. During the all-star game itself, an official left the field complaining of a stomach ailment, then came back on and dropped dead. It understandably took more than a few minutes to remove his body from the field. There was the requisite shock, but after a while one of the coaches began to mutter under his breath, "Let's get on with it here."

They did.

I knew it was going to be a story unlike any I had ever encountered.

It only built from there — the injury to Boobie in which he tore his anterior cruciate ligament and you knew his life had changed in the freak millisecond of his cleats getting caught in the turf in the twilight. Added to the book were the ingredients of the open racism, the surreal travel of the football team to away games on chartered jets, more money spent on athletic tape than on new books for the English department.

Friday Night Lights went on to sell close to two million copies. It became the film, then ultimately a long-running TV show. It was the story I was destined to write like every writer has a story he or she is destined to write, the one you have inside you because you only really have one inside you. I knew when it was published I would never top it no matter how hard I tried, and after almost twenty years, I still have not topped it. It all happened when I was thirty-five. The success opened all sorts of avenues, but it also hung over me. It was a wonderful thing to be known for something that had lasted for so long. It was a terrible thing to be known for something that had happened so long ago. It sounds like self-pity, but it wasn't self-pity. It was the fear of being tapped out and topped out, the rest of my life a vain search.

As we drive into the outskirts of Odessa, we go by places that once thrilled me because of their rawness but now only haunt me. The back lots selling rigs and horse-head pumps and water trucks and jangles of pipe and compressors; the shabby mud-colored motels where men with dirty fingernails and thick boots pay seventy-five dollars a week while they work the oil fields, the downtown where you could still see the faded embers of the J. C. Penney's sign and the one for Odessa Pawn pockmarked with bullet holes. I had never seen anything like

Odessa, stitched together without any planning but in rise and fall to the oil bust or the oil boom. It had the dazzle of discovery for me, a third-world country. But that was then.

Zach senses this without my saying a word to him.

— Do you think we'll ever go again to Odessa after this?

— I don't think we will.

— Why?

— I just don't think we will. You'll get older. I'll get older. It will be harder to get to.

— Do you like being in Odessa?

— Sure I do.

He knows I am lying. It is why he asked me the question.

The deeper we drive into town, the more his enthusiasm unleashes. He squeals when he sees the Raindance Car Wash. He does the same with the Dairy Queen over on 7th. And the pond in front of the YMCA where he and Gerry fed the ducks. And the nursing home where he visited Olivia and Mary, calmly noting they aren't around anymore because they are dead. And the house we lived in on Richmond, which of course he finds without a map. I try to feign enjoyment, but too many memories are jamming me. I hope this will not be a replay of Milwaukee. I must also come to terms with the most difficult relationship I have ever experienced outside of my own family.

Chapter 12

Boobie

I

BOOBIE MILES LIVES in Midland now with Evelyn, his girlfriend of the moment. She is steady and of even temperament, a low-burning flame on the stove. I believe that, at this point, Boobie has four children with three different women. It may be more. It's been hard to keep track over the years. I don't know how many will be living with him when we see him. It may just be his newest child, Evan. His beautiful twins, James and Jasmine, a flurry of keyed-up energy with the call of "Daddy" like seagulls, could be there as well. He loves his children. He has tried to be a good father despite his nomadic existence, from Odessa to Midland to Monahans to Dallas and then back again.

Zach is curious about Boobie. He is determined to understand. It is confusing to him why I give money to someone who is not a part of our family.

—What does he need money for?

—Because he doesn't have a very good job. Life is hard for him sometimes.

— What do you mean life is hard for him sometimes what's hard for his life sometimes?

— It's just hard. He has a lot of kids to support. And he gets down on his luck and he doesn't have a very good job.

— Yeah.

— He's kind of like a fourth son to me.

— Yeah.

— I worry about him.

— Yeah.

I hope a special bond kindles between the two of them. I hope that Zach will understand the role that Boobie has played in my life and embrace him, drawing on the gifts of intuition I never fully appreciated until this trip.

— You know when people like you and when they don't?

— Yeah.

— You do have a sixth sense about the sincerity of others. As Tony Chavez says, "The thing with Zach is that you always know he is telling the truth."

— Oh.

— Do you know what sincerity means?

— No what does it mean?

— It means that you know in people who is honest and will never hurt you.

— Oh.

I wonder how Boobie will be, whether he will ever make the remotest peace with what happened to him years ago. I know the answer. We all face it, that moment of clarity in which you realize you will never be what you imagined. He faced it at eighteen as a senior in high school when he ruined his knee as a running back. He had dreams of playing college football and then pro. He had a right to those dreams as much as any athlete does, although they are false dreams 99.9 percent of the time. But, God, was he good. Most kids in high school, however impressive their statistics, are still gangly when they run. They rely on speed. Boobie had speed (he ran the hundred-yard dash in 10.3 seconds). And he ran his two-hundred-pound body like a man. Whatever the reality, the dreams of what could have been still consume him.

When the movie *Friday Night Lights* was being made, there was a measure of redemption for Boobie if you could call it that. He was cast in a small role. When he went to Ratliff Stadium in Odessa for the filming of a scene, hundreds of locals in the stands as extras gave him a standing ovation. They did it to prove that they were not the racists who called him a "big dumb ole nigger" when he was in high school and joked about how, like a horse that had pulled up lame at the track, he might as well put a bullet in his brain. Boobie succumbed to the measure of celebrity he gained that night. You could see the glow and beatific smile of someone who was something again. He said it felt like he had been given the senior season that had been stolen from him. He did interviews. He met all the actors. They acted like they liked him. They're actors.

Before long, Hollywood packed up its gear and left. Billy Bob Thornton went back to his band. Tim McGraw went back to Faith Hill. Boobie's character in the movie, played by Derek Luke, was its linchpin, and the film couldn't depict Boobie without acquiring his "life rights." I had helped obtain the life rights of the key kids in the book in the early 1990s for one hundred dollars up front and a thousand in total if the film was made. I acted as the conduit after it was made clear the film would never go forward without my obtaining them. I was young and desperately wanted the film to be made. I felt enormous pressure not to come back empty-handed; I was told this was the only offer, and either the kids took it or the movie disappeared. It was the first of my experiences with Hollywood, and I had yet to learn that when it comes to so-called non-talent — everyone but the actors themselves — everything was a degree of conceit and manipulation.

I met with the kids at a Mexican restaurant and extolled the virtues of signing the agreement, how exciting it would be to have your life up there on the silver screen. I knew I was acting as instructed by the producers. I still felt filthy and loathsome, but that didn't stop me.

Mike Winchell, who was the quarterback in the book, listened without a word and did not sign. He rejected the emphatic pitch because he wasn't sure he wanted his life depicted. He waited until the film was about to be made and got a much better deal: I was a decade wiser at that point and told him to ignore the studio's lies that they could make the film without his rights. I told him to hold out. At least he got in the low five figures. But he also got what he really wanted — a new set of golf clubs.

Boobie didn't originally sign either. He wanted to be in the film if it was ever made, but he also knew he was the essential character and deserved more than a hundred bucks on signing. I frantically made a side deal with him for three thousand up front and ten thousand in total out of my pocket if the movie was given the green light. He still should have gotten more. I thought that the tragedy of his plight would ignite the humanity of at least one of the battalion of producers, and promises were made to supplement what Boobie had already received, which as far as they knew was a lousy thousand dollars anyway since they had no awareness of the side deal. Those promises were forgotten as soon as they were made. I gave him the ten grand for the film to honor my commitment. I had given him thousands already in response to his calls for help. He used the movie money to enter into a strange financial arrangement with his girlfriend at the time to buy a daycare center in the empty, echoing town of Kermit, near Odessa. The daycare center went bust, and the money disappeared.

He was broke again. But his celebrity post-movie still had some mileage left in it. He was recognized at the local Holiday Inn. People came up to ask if they could have their picture taken with him. It was the same at the Permian Mall where he was stopped for autographs. It was like being in a glass-bottom boat. Boobie may not have seen it but everyone else did, the sand and muck of the bottom.

Still, in the wake of the film, a few people in Odessa were affected by his story. They wanted to help and offered him jobs. The jobs were menial, but they meant a steady wage and benefits. They called me, and I vouched for him. He had a beautiful smile and a deep-throated laugh and he could be a "gentle giant" as Tony Chavez called him. At first he had to walk to work, about five miles. Then he said he needed a bike so I bought him a bike. He said he had a bead on a car that cost only a couple of grand, so I gave him a couple of grand for a car. He stopped showing up for work. They had no choice but to fire him. He became basically penniless. He still had child support payments in every corner of Texas. He still got stopped for autographs in the mall. He still got hit with a spate of paternity suits by women he hadn't heard from in fifteen years because they presumed the combination of the movie and book had made him rich. What came to him over the years came from my own pocket. Sixty thousand. Seventy thousand. Maybe a little bit more.

For as long as I knew him, I don't think he ever had a driver's license or car insurance. He was repeatedly arrested for his failure to carry such documents. He'd call from jail and say, "Hey!" like a long-lost cousin. He'd say, "What's going on!" and I knew exactly what was going on: he needed bail. After one release, he said he had finally zeroed in on something that he knew he could do and would last. He wanted to become an air-conditioning and refrigeration technician. He reasoned that most people in the summer would always need air conditioning. He seemed sincere. It meant going to a place called the Career Training Institute in Huntsville, Alabama. "They'll even pay my airline ticket!" he gushed. They fucking should have: the tuition for roughly one month of training was $11,900.

He had to take out a loan but he needed someone to cosign. I did not research it. I did not think about it. The money requested was ridiculous without the guarantee of a job. Yet I kept hoping that this would be the thing that would stick. I should have said no. I couldn't say no. I didn't say no.

He flew to Huntsville and e-mailed me the results of a rudimentary test on which he had scored a 100. He circled it with an exclamation point. He was trying to prove he was serious, and I think in his own way he was serious. After the course ended, he disappeared. The institute called me and said they had referrals for him for possible jobs but didn't know how to get in touch with him. I told them I didn't know where he was either. Like the Fugitive he was always on the run, not because of outstanding warrants (although he had a few of those) but because he never had a place to stay for longer than a few months. He used the kindness of friends and girlfriends and cousins and grandmothers. Sometimes he got a place for himself, but inevitably the bills piled up, and there were only so many times I could pay the rent and utility bills. He ended up at least once at a homeless shelter. The phone numbers he gave me lasted at best for a few months, some for a few weeks or even days. Over the years I had collected three dozen numbers for Boobie.

The bills from the Career Training Institute tracked me closely, the loan ballooning to $12,317 at an interest rate of 10.5 percent. On the days when I wished I was not a writer, and the older I got there were too many of those days, I wished I had opened a career training institute charging 10.5 percent on tuition loans. I finally paid the debt off. I didn't tell Lisa until the whole thing was over. She wasn't livid but incredulous at how naive I was. She said I had no one to blame but myself. I told her that Boobie needed help, and guiding him toward a career was constructive. She agreed, but she told me that paying over twelve thousand dollars for something I had never even bothered to research wasn't helping anybody. It was wasted money for both Boobie and my family. She said if we really wanted to help Boobie, he should move in with us in Philadelphia. She was right.

So when Zach turns to me now with puzzlement and asks me why I give Boobie money, the answers I give him are truthiness at best. I tell him that Boobie needs it because of that hard life. I say that I am doing it for Boobie, but I wonder if I am really doing it for myself — expiating the guilt I amassed from witnessing his treatment in high school like a football animal. But all writers silently soak up despair for our own advantage; like dogs rolling in the guts of dead animals, the stink of others makes us giddy. We deny it but we lie in denying it. Without Boobie Miles, *Friday Night Lights* would have disappeared. I know that. So maybe I was paying him off.

II

Zach and I stop first on the main street in Odessa before heading to Midland to see Boobie. When I was contemplating doing the book, the street is one of the sights that hooked me. I have never tired of the time warp of it. It has not changed an inch, as far as I can tell. There is the closed-down movie theater with the name "Ector" in vertical letters of white on red like a streak of tears. The honky-tonk pawnshops like a roaming carnival sideshow selling guns and microwaves and rows of wedding rings like pulled molars. The red stoplight swinging to no one in the wind. I leave the car to take some pictures. Zach stays inside. By accident, I have left my tape recorder in the record mode in the car, and I listen later that night.

I hear him breathe a husky breath. I hear a whisper rise to a rasp. I hear him say, "Stay! Stay!" I hear him folding and unfolding his map in a steady rustle. I hear him humming. I hear a sigh. I hear a singsong voice saying, "Just Dave a question!" I hear a staccato hum. I hear him say, "He's doing a story on Dave!" I hear him take a gulping inhale. I hear furious chatter. I hear a low murmur. I hear a desperate inhale. I hear high-pitched laughter. I hear enough. For all that I have seen of my son that is so uplifting, disabilities remain and in some aspects are only getting worse, particularly these raging debates with himself. They scare me, and yet he has shown remarkable discipline in restraining himself in my presence during the trip. His war of words is a compulsion. I have compulsions as well. I try to control them but often cannot. He does a much better job than I do.

III

We find Boobie's apartment over on Wadley in Midland. The day is gray and threatens rain, the few slants of blue shuttering early. He shares the apartment with Evelyn, the mother of his newest child, Evan. Boobie loves Evan, picks him up like a football and beams at him as Evan rolls with giggles. Boobie's love is abundant in general, when he doesn't dwell on his life.

It is impossible for me not to think of Boobie as the perfectly sculpted teenager he was when I first met him in 1988. As a junior he once gained 332 yards on eight carries in one half. But I never got the chance to see him play at full throttle; I only saw him on film. He came back in the middle of his senior season with a knee brace after the injury. He wasn't ready. His breakaway speed was gone. He seemed scared. He was slaughtered on the field, the defense aware he wasn't the Boobie he once had been. He played in one game and then quit.

His big arms still show the vestiges of strength. But he has put on considerable weight now; he will later tell me he has diabetes and weighs close to three hundred pounds. His face is round, no hard-lined jaw. He is almost forty now.

— I'm tired, you know what I mean. I need a different surrounding. People always want something from me, man.

— Well, they think you're a star. They're stopping you for autographs.

— All the time. I go in the mall, we be in the mall, and kids come up and say, "Are you Boobie Miles?"

He has trouble keeping jobs because he gets frustrated over some-thing. He has no impulse control. He goes off on me in certain mo-ments. He hates me in those moments. He feels used by me in those moments. He hates the book in those moments. Just as I sometimes do.

When I was away on vacation with my family in Maine shortly be-fore the trip, he called me once then twice then three times then four times. In the space of half an hour. Maybe because he was in jail for not paying a speeding ticket or a domestic abuse problem or not making a court-ordered support payment. Maybe because he was flat broke. He was furious when I didn't call him back. He left a series of messages.

— The least you can do is call me back, man.

— Will you please call me back?

— You don't call me back. Fuck you.

— I made your fucking book and you don't do shit for me so fuck you, you're like fucking everybody else.

Eventually, I called him back, just so the messages would stop. I yelled back at him.

— I'm the only one who fucking helps you. I give you more fucking money than I do my fucking kids.

We started yelling simultaneously. The only distinguishable words were *fuck* and *fuck you*. I hung up. He hung up. I calmed down. He calmed down. He *was* my son. He knew he was killing his only lifeline.

He called me back about ten minutes later with a whole different tone. I asked him how he could say such things to me given I helped him out repeatedly. He apologized, said he just didn't know where else to turn. He promised this would be the last time he called me, which of course it would not be. He gave a convoluted story that he was coaching a peewee football team and they traveled to San Angelo for a game and he used a credit card for food and lodging that he was given permission to use and the card was no good and the charges were rejected and now they were coming after him and he needed a thousand bucks to stay out of jail.

I knew it was a mistake to give him the money. But I also know that helping him is not a mistake. He is at the dark bottom of a well. No matter what steps he takes to climb out, he isn't even close. He will always be wrapped in what could have been.

Could have been. The three most overused and worthless words in the lexicon of athletes.

He has a job now at Target, unloading trucks at night. It is lousy work. He is convinced he got it because of the notoriety of the film. If true, it is all he substantially got from the film.

— It's easy money. Just something to jump on.

— You have to work, Boobie.

— Yeah.

— You need to work. I'm still surprised you can't find something in the oil field. It's booming again.

There is work about forty miles to the west in Monahans. He has lived there before but it is "too little" for him. And it is little, a pop-top of a town like so many in West Texas where the wind blows dust and dirt in the winter and the sun beats down like heated foil in the summer. Boobie tells me there is no movie theater in Monahans. Boobie tells me that kids who live there have nothing to do but drink in front of the local supermarket. Boobie tells me that he has to go to Midland or Odessa if he wants entertainment.

I have been to Monahans when Boobie lived there. We went to a playground with James and Jasmine. They were four, maybe five. They loved and adored their father, and he adored them. Jasmine went down the slide a hundred times, her legs long and graceful and her coordination inherited from her father. "Watch me, Daddy, watch me!" she yelled. Boobie watched Jasmine as he pushed James in a swing. The sky had no limits, and a little breeze went through. We were the only ones there. There was no sound except for Jasmine saying over and over, "Watch me, Daddy! Watch me!"

There was such weariness in Boobie's face. I looked for the vestiges of youth and could not find any. In the metal glint of the swing I studied my own face. I was nearing fifty and terrified by it. I too looked for the vestiges of the person I had once been when I wrote *Friday Night Lights*. I couldn't find it either. How had both of us gotten here? What had happened? Dreams found. Dreams lost.

The park was a perfect green rectangle in the desert sea, a thumbtack on a corkboard. It had been built by the city, or maybe it was the county, with bloodless bureaucratic precision. I heard the whine of the swing as it went back and forth. The wind became a hollow squawk.

In the playground's joylessness, I watched Jasmine and James in their joy. I felt selfish. I loved Boobie at that moment and knew that I would always love him. I also never felt lonelier in my life, the hollow of that wind like walking through an abandoned house and finding a toy, a teapot, coated in ageless dust.

Zach wanders around the apartment. He explores the rooms to center Boobie in his mind by focusing on objects, a picture, a desk, a bed. As an extension of that, he wants to see precisely where Boobie works.

— Can we go to the Target?

— Huh?

— Can we see your Target?

— Yeah, we can go by Target.

— What street is your Target on out here?

— Midland Drive, I think.

— How long will it take to get there from here?

— Here. Take you roughly ten minutes. Eight to ten minutes. About five.

Zach looks at the map of Midland he has with him.

— Yeah so you're on North Midland Drive is where your Target is right?

— Yes, sir.

— Where's it off of?

— It's off of Midland Drive. There's no other street there.

— Remember when you played football in high school?

— Yeah, and I was pretty damn good, wasn't I?

He lowers to a whisper, a distant voice from far away.

— Pretty damn good.

The flat-screen television is on in the afternoon. ESPN offers numbing chatter about who will win the Heisman Trophy. Boobie switches channels to a Dallas station with live coverage of police chasing a stolen car on the highway. Zach could care less about the car chase. But the physical presence of the television interests him, another way of making a link to his own life.

— I guess that's a flat screen right that's what we have at home built into the wall my brother's getting one soon for his birthday.

Boobie watches the car chase.

— Boobie do you have central air in this apartment?

— Yeah, built in.

— Yeah.

Everything slows down, like being trapped in a tiny room without windows. Zach on the couch blurting out questions. Boobie still trying to piece back together the broken puzzle parts of his life. Two disconnected wires that I thought would merge.

We mindlessly watch the car chase in Dallas. It feels interminably dull despite the best effort of the anchor to make it dramatic. It looks like a board game with little cars chasing one another. I find myself focusing on the religious artwork hanging on the white walls. I grope for things to say but can dredge up nothing. The car chase gives us something to do and allows us to be silent.

I have told Boobie that we will go to Wal-Mart and do some shopping for Evan. I have done that with Boobie before for James and Jasmine. We walked through the aisles, indiscriminately grabbing from the racks paper-thin garments with movie and television logos and throwing them into a metal shopping cart. James, sitting in the cart, wanted everything he could touch.

I don't want to go to Wal-Mart. I don't want to empty out the filled-to-the-gills shopping cart in front of a cash register clerk more glum than the clothing itself, stuffing the crap into an overabundance of plastic bags. I give Boobie the money instead, a thick roll of twenties that comes out to five hundred dollars. I tell him it's for clothing for the kids. He nods. As we move toward the door, we tell Boobie there's going to be a cookout tonight at the Chavezes'. He seems delighted to have been invited. He says he'll come over before the midnight shift.

IV

On the way back to Odessa we hit the 2,500-mile mark on our journey. In two days we will arrive in Los Angeles. Gerry is meeting us there, but the on-the-road portion will end. I have never felt more tied to Zach than I do now. I have grown used to having him next to me. I love his peculiar yet trenchant insights, blurted out with a quirky on-the-nose brilliance. And he is happy to be with me.

— The trip's almost over. Are you sad?

— A little.

We can feel the wind across the flanks of the minivan as we enter Odessa. We stop at a 7-Eleven to get a drink. There is a car wash next to the 7-Eleven. Zach wants to get one. The car is filthy, splattered with smashed bugs. But it's a rental car, so there is an obligation to return it filthy.

— Why do you want to get a car wash?

— It's just something to do.

We place the left front wheel of the minivan onto the track. Zach is the pilot.

— Yes here we go.

I realize that this is like an amusement park ride for him, a sense of liberation and freedom in the cacophony of bells and the sound of the drizzle of the presoak and the thunder of the high-pressure wash.

We go to the cookout at the home of Brian Chavez, the tight end and brilliant student I wrote about in *Friday Night Lights*. Chavez went on to Harvard and has taken over his father's law firm in Odessa. Even though Zach has barely seen the Chavez family over the past decade, he has aimed his fixation at them. A great part of it has to do with the comfort with which they embrace him, treating him as a member of the family no different from anyone else. Zach senses that Brian is a guy's guy, always with a new girlfriend and fond of trips to Vegas, and he likes hanging with him. He also likes confiding in Brian's father, Tony; he's impressed by the cushy luxury of Tony's 700 Series BMW. He tells Tony that he wishes we were driving his car across the country instead of the minivan. He really does hate that fucking minivan.

There are two women at the cookout the same age as Zach, one Brian's girlfriend of the moment and the other the girlfriend of his brother Adrian. Zach repeats their names in a mantra, *Melissa and Prissy Melissa and Prissy.* He is infatuated with them, taken in by their kindness and pretty, perky faces. He particularly likes Prissy's blond hair that feels of summer blossoms only made in Texas. *Melissa and Prissy Melissa and Prissy.* Say it fast enough and they merge into one. *Melissa Prissy. Melissa Prissy.* They are sweet and gentle to him. They instantly take Zach for what he is, a kind and endearing person with some obvious quirks. They make no pause of reluctance or discomfort. It is the same with the Chavez family. And it strikes me as far more than ironic that it is here in Odessa, where so many people hated me and I hated certain aspects of the town with equal ferocity, that every single person we encounter treats Zach the way he should always be treated, which is just like everyone else.

About twenty people are at the barbecue. Zach is shy with *Melissa Prissy* so he hovers around Brian. He asks Brian where he plays cards in Las Vegas. He tells him about Gerry. He tells him Gerry is going to Penn. He tells him he is going to see Gerry in three days in Los Angeles. He tells him the plane is scheduled to arrive at eight forty-five at night. He tells Brian he is excited to see Gerry. He tells Brian he has felt kind of bored without Gerry.

Brian seems satisfied that he has all the information he needs on Gerry.

— Hey, Zach, you want a beer?

Brian thrusts one out to him.

For the first time in his life, Zach takes a beer.

I watch him as he laughs and is cheered and gets hearty slaps on the back, just a regular Odessa shitkicker. He takes tiny little sips, each one with a grimace because he finds the taste strange. He holds on to that bottle. His hand tightly grips the dripping base of it as if he will never let go. He is at the center of the circle. He is out with the boys. He is exactly where he wants to be.

Chapter 13

Mom and Dad

I

WE LEAVE ODESSA early in the morning, heading west toward El Paso on Interstate 20. Odessa has been the most powerful part of the trip, incredible given how portions of the town will always believe me guilty of writerly homicide. Odessa is also developing into a favored vacation spot; Zach, based on his love of the Chavez family, now wants to go there every opportunity possible. Once again Zach and I have set a road trip first: nobody in the history of the world, ever, has chosen Odessa for a vacation.

In an increasing series of revelations, none has been more gratifying than Zach's interaction with the Chavezes. The cookout reoccurs as I drive: seeing my son at the center of the circle with a sweaty bottle of beer in hand, the only accouterments missing a cowboy hat and concealed weapon, actually unconcealed and more than one, to make him a true West Texan.

The day before the cookout, Zach asserted his independence and individuality even more. He wanted to spend the night with the Chavezes; their house was Grand Central Station, the constant in and out of children and grandchildren and associated friends, including *Melissa Prissy*.

He was reluctant to ask me. He did not want to hurt my feelings by utterly dumping me on my butt at the Elegante Hotel. But that was a minor part of his reticence. He wasn't sure if I would say yes. So he went to the matriarch, Irma Chavez, to ask me if it would be all right, a sharp strategic move of negotiating through an intermediary. If Zach had approached me directly, I would have said no because I felt it would be an intrusion. The house was already full because it was always full, the West Texas version of *Cheaper by the Dozen*, patriarch Tony relegated to the bathroom to watch *Desperate Housewives* on a black-and-white television with rabbit ears because the six other TVs in the house were being used by others.

Irma did not mind one more body. She had been a school principal in Odessa for many years and her tenderness with children, everyone actually, was limitless. We went to the hotel so he could pack for the night. It was remarkable to me that Zach, who had not seen the Chavez family for twelve years, would want to stay there no matter how high his level of comfort and their bottomless graciousness. I thought he would be fearful given how tethered he was to routine.

— Why do you want to stay over there?

— Because I have never done this before I think the guests Melissa and Prissy and you know because I think you know Melissa and Prissy they're my age you know.

It seems incomprehensible to me. No matter how great his fondness for them and their fondness for him, they exist on a different plateau. I assumed they were years apart because of the vast differences in communication.

— They are?

— They're in their twenties very close to my age.

That distinction is increasingly crucial to him. I still view him as a man-child, but Zach, although aware of his limitations, never sees himself that way. In his own mind, he is a peer to others his age and it is only natural that he be with them. It is the pull of human instinct.

— It's more fun than being in a hotel room with me, isn't it?

— Yeah because I kind of get bored.

I'll remember that.

I began to pack his belongings in a plastic bag. I told him he didn't need to bring his shaving cream and razor. He was insistent because he wanted to look his best. We drove to the Chavez house on Opal.

— All right, give me a hug and kiss.

— Okay.

— You have a great time.

— Goodbye.

He walked toward the house.

— YOU GOT EVERYTHING??

— Yeah.

The door opened. "Hi Tony!" he said in his lilt of love. He disappeared from me. For a moment I felt just like I did with Gerry when he disappeared at the top of the hill in Greenwich for the school interview; I knew Gerry would never return as he once was. And now Zach was building his own wings, step by careful step, an intricate model with all sorts of tiny pieces that are difficult to fit, but still building. It was inspiring to witness, even if I went to bed at eight because I had been stiffed. As I think about it in the early stages of a 550-mile day trying to make Phoenix, I am still inspired.

Until the cell phone rings. It's Evelyn calling about Boobie. She says he never came home. I ask if he went down to the Southside of Odessa where the drugs are. She thinks the answer is yes (although Boobie later says the answer is no). Zach hangs on every word of the brief conversation. The potential of chaos in others always perks him up. He is the child of two reporters.

— He got lost last night?

— I don't know. I don't know what happened. I just don't know what happened. I should never give him money. It makes the problem worse instead of better.

— He didn't go to work probably lost his job?

I respond not with derisive bitterness but sad frustration and discouragement. Another job most likely has been lost.

— Probably.

— Why didn't he want to go to work?

— I gave him money to help his family and he didn't. It's very sad. He's a wreck. It's hopeless.

— How will he get money?

— Not from me. I can't give it to him anymore.

— You think his parents could give him money?

— His mom is alive, but his dad is dead. And his uncle who took care of him is dead.

— Yeah.

— You're lucky because you're well taken care of by your mother and your dad and Lisa and Paul.

— But Boobie's not well taken care of?

— He's kind of alone and very lost.

— What does that mean that he's very lost?

— He just doesn't know what to do with his life, and he's not getting any younger.

— Well it's not like you're Boobie's dad or anything.

— You're right. I'm not his dad. I'm your dad and Gerry's dad and Caleb's dad. And I have to remember that.

— How come you sort of would like to be his dad in some ways?

This question is more than just astute; it shows an *abstract* thought process of trying to figure out my motivations for being a father to someone I am not related to. He doesn't understand and he wants to understand.

— Well, because I've known him for a long time, and when he couldn't play football anymore he sort of lost purpose in his life. He wanted to be a pro football player, and once that dream was gone he became a wreck. He just floated from job to job. I gave him money, and I think he's going to use it for his family, but now I'm not sure he does. It's really stupid of me, and I feel really bad about it.

— Boobie I guess is a very nice guy?

— He's a wonderful guy. He's got a big heart. But he's not responsible. Do you know what it means to be responsible?

— No what does it mean?

— What do you think it means?

— You have to be responsible about your things like not losing your bags.

Punked yet again.

We drive in silence for about forty-five minutes and pass Monahans. Zach's hard drive suddenly goes code red. He knows that Boobie once lived in Monahans because he must have heard me talk about it. He is also fascinated that Boobie has been to jail. It is a subject Debra and I had broached with Zach several years earlier after he had used the school e-mail system to tell his teacher that he wanted to "kill" him. It was the first time, and the last, I ever heard him express any thoughts of violence. He explained that the teacher had told him he couldn't do something he wanted to do. I was upset, but there was undeniable gratification in Zach's willingness to express his individuality, that he had grown tired in his life of only following commands and never being trusted, although using the school e-mail system was not the best way to conceal a threat. This was also the post-9-11 era and he probably would have been arrested had he been a regular student. The school let it go because it was Zach. I did not, although I knew he did not mean what he said. It was also an opportunity to explain some realities that most children at the age of ten would understand.

— You're lucky you didn't go to jail, Zach. What you did was terrible. You threatened a teacher. Most kids go to jail for that.

— What's jail?

— It's a place where people go when they have done something wrong.

— What do they do to you in jail?

— They lock you up and bad things can happen. You don't want to go there.

— I don't want to go there.

— Do you understand?

— I understand.

— What happens in jail?

— Bad things happen in jail.

I believe he did get the ramifications. But an unintended byproduct is that Zach now becomes animated any time he hears the word *jail*. It excites him because it is taboo, and he does like taboo.

— Where was Boobie in jail out here or somewhere?

— In Odessa.

— Oh in the city how many months was he in for like?

— Just a couple of days.

— Like a couple of days or a couple of months how many days?

— Four or five.

— Was he okay what did he do in jail?

— He sat around. He was fine. It's not a good place to be. You don't want to go to jail. I've told you that already.

— It wasn't a lot of fun there probably?

— No, jail's not a lot of fun.

— But then he got out?

— Then he got out.

— Annie your sister got put there for something.

— Drunk driving. It was a bullshit charge.

— Annie your sister's birthday is next Monday August 6 do you think you'll ever get over feeling sorry for Boobie?

— I don't know. I'm very disappointed with him. But I do feel sorry for him.

— I think Boobie should go to like some psychiatrist like I did.

— Well, maybe.

— Well what about you do this do you still see Doctor Hole I saw Doctor Hole one time does Doctor Hole talk to people on the phone?

— I don't think that would help.

— Well you could probably think of some ways to talk to Doctor Hole about trying to fix his life.

The random threads of his hard drive have come together into a cogent and intriguing suggestion. The only word that comes to my mind is *wow*, although I am positive Doctor Hole does not make house calls. If he did, it would have been easier for him just to move in with me.

II

The itinerary is Phoenix tonight. Then Las Vegas tomorrow, where Zach and I will have our dream date. The best hotel on the strip. Fancy restaurant. Hot-ticket show. Gambling.

After nearly three thousand miles, we still are still dragging bottom on the scenic scale. We have felt the epic vastness of the country, even from Milwaukee to Odessa. But with the exception of the Calatrava addition to the Milwaukee Art Museum and the Oklahoma City bombing memorial and a statue of a giant jackrabbit in Odessa to commemorate all the real ones that live there, we have seen nothing beyond the vastness. I am not sure the jackrabbit qualifies.

I ask Zach if maybe we should go to the Grand Canyon on the way to Las Vegas. I tell him it is the only place in the world where you never feel any sense of disappointment or diminishment, a fissure so big it touches heaven and bores into hell. His feelings are still scarred by Yellowstone and the idea of having to walk in search of what he is convinced will be nothing. Plus he doubts he will know anyone there. I tell him all we have to do is park the car, take a look, and then leave. He says he'll think about it.

We get onto 10 West at the Jeff Davis County line in Texas. We are about twenty miles from Van Horn. A freight train crawls along a track to the side, dozens upon dozens of unmarked double-decker cars of green and red and blue. It is the only spot of color in the thirsty gray landscape. There isn't a single structure in any direction except for a few shacks of pockmarked wood about to cave in with the next gust of wind. A handful of cattle graze, lowering their heads with slow rote to scoop what few odd-lot strands of grass still exist. A Southwestern Motor Transport truck moves west. Allied Van and Warner Enterprises trucks move east. The speed limit out here is eighty miles an hour. You can get to where you want to go as quickly as you want. But I want to linger in the lost, beyond the groping chitchat of yawning babble. Out here, no telemarketers who butcher your last name.

No friends who never feel like friends, going through some preprogrammed list of banalities before they ask you for something. No mul-
tiplex with sticky, popcorn-infested floor. No dry cleaners. No bank
branch. No Starbucks. No competitor to Starbucks. Just a land that
refuses to concede. The empty. The beautiful empty.

— I could do this forever with you.

— Yeah.

— Should we just do it forever?

— Yeah.

— Just drive forever?

— Yeah.

— Stop at places where we know people.

— Maybe.

— But you would have to be in the car a lot.

— It's kind of uncomfortable.

Thoughts mainline into my veins. Boobie. *Friday Night Lights*. The
bungee jump. My future. My son's future. My parents.

My father has been traveling with me the entire trip, telling me I'm
going too fast, telling me I'm going too slow, asking me if I remember the trip to Dartmouth, wondering if after all that happened I still
thought he had been a good father. But in the lost land of West Texas,
my mother taps me on the shoulder as well. I am a little surprised; I
always favored my father over her. But it makes sense to think of her
now, given how she and my father were so inextricably intertwined at
the end. Of all the things that have happened in my life, none will ever
come close to what I went through with my parents at the end. Except
for what happened when my twin sons were born.

I ask Zach if he thinks about them very much. He remembers when
my father, whom he called "Goggie," went to a section of Nantucket
called Monomoy. My parents had owned a house in Nantucket since
1960, and my father moored his little sailboat about a hundred yards
out in the bay. He trudged out to get it, invariably getting his pants wet,
as the water was always higher than he thought and ran halfway up his
chest. It was always at this point he also realized he had left his wallet
in his pants pocket, followed by a "son of a bitch!" so loud it carried all
the way downtown to the Unitarian church.

As we near El Paso Zach offers several solutions to Goggie's predicament.

— Next time maybe he should have gone into the water without his wallet because maybe that would have been better.

— Anything else?

— He should maybe have worn a bathing suit.

— Do you miss him?

— I miss him so much.

— What about your grandmother Ellie?

— I miss her too although sometimes she got mad at me.

III

My father carefully pondered purchasing a house in Nantucket. So did my mother. Despite occasional agreements, they were an odd couple, mismatched in many ways. My mother generally liked being cheerful. My father, when he wasn't the most charming man in the world, liked being sullen. For their honeymoon in 1950 they went to Bermuda. They were supposed to be there for two weeks but came back after one because they had nothing to say to each other. In the wooing stages my father claimed that he loved to play board games, which my mother adored. She figured that's what they would do if all else failed, until he announced that he hated games. Yet they became inseparable. They also ended up working together with my mother's brother and her mother at the investment banking house Lebenthal & Co. It was a family business that had been started by my grandmother and grandfather in the 1930s. As in just about every family business, the shouts and screams at the board meetings could be heard across the Hudson into New Jersey.

My father was the president of the firm, and after a previous career in advertising where even the hat he wore looked beaten to death when he came home from work, this was a dream job. But he really lived by obsessions that started in passionate love and ended in blunt rejection. On impulse, after playing pool one night at a bar, he replaced the dining room table in our New York apartment with an antique pool table. He took hundreds of hours of lessons from an expert teaching pro named Joe Stone, an intense and demanding little man ripped from the pages of *The Hustler,* who generally told my father he was hopeless. My father kept a little pamphlet Stone had written called *The Correct Angle,* containing diagrams looking like Rube Goldberg drawings. My father gave it up without warning after two years, but the pool table stayed.

When my sister and I, now adults, visited the apartment, we ate Chinese takeout on TV tables in my parents' bedroom since there was no other place to eat. Worried perhaps that we weren't getting enough variation, my father ordered from half a dozen *different* Chinese restaurants, proudly producing their menus in a special folder he kept. He was also proud that he never had to give his last name: they instantly knew from the sound of his voice. In the Chinese takeout capital of the world, New York, I think he finished first in the rankings every year.

My father and mother thought the house in Nantucket was a reasonable deal at twenty thousand dollars as long as the sellers threw the furniture in. Things were different. The island had not yet gone through onepercentification. Over the years they put the house back together room by room. They wallpapered. They sanded and buffed the floors. My father was an impatient imperfect perfectionist. He did everything twice, condemning the first attempt as a "piece of shit." He had a tendency to run out of things; I think it was just an excuse to go to the hardware store and make sure nothing new had come in given his pathological love of tools, most of which he never touched again after buying them because he didn't know how to use them. They wallpapered three walls of the room off the kitchen in one style, then the fourth in a completely different style after they ran out of the original. "Fuck it," he said, "no one will notice anyway." Everyone did.

My mother and father fought every step of the way as they remade the house. You see things when you are growing up. You surmise things more right than wrong because your feelings are still raw and unclogged. I never thought they were in love for much of their marriage. My father seemed to resent my mother's charm. Underneath his life-of-the-party pomp and circumstance were insecurity and brutal self-denigration. I don't think he ever felt particularly needed by her.

She was fiercely independent, having gone to work in the 1950s when no wife worked. She never revealed her interior, to the point of being unknowable. I realized at an early age that my sister and I truly existed solely to prove our worth as her worth. When we disappointed, I did anything to avoid her airstrikes of humiliation. It worked, and it did not work. Sometimes I could feel my balls ache. But she had shine and such style and marvelous observational wit. She had high cheekbones and wore a brown fedora that made her look like Gloria Vanderbilt. She hugged people and called them "dear boy" and "dear girl." She could solve the *New York Times* Sunday crossword in two hours. She gave to every charity imaginable, until my father enforced a ceiling of fifty dollars per year. But she exceeded it anyway, since she paid the bills. She was one of those mothers who became more and more golden over time. My fear of her lessened and her love of me found a home.

But medical problems started in her forties when a tumor developed on her pituitary gland that affected her eyesight. She was treated with massive radiation and recovered but was never quite the same to me. After her retirement at sixty-two, she spent most of her time in bed. My father discovered a definable place with my mother as she became ever more fragile and delicate. He worried about her and took her to an endless series of doctors and rushed to her aid when she began to have a series of fainting spells. She also became increasingly disoriented and it was clear that her mind, which truly was a beautiful mind, was rapidly going dark.

In the early summer of 2001 she fell off a curb on Fifth Avenue and into the street after blacking out. She was hospitalized at Lenox Hill. My father kept vigil fourteen hours a day. His only respite was an occasional meal at J. G. Melon's with friends where the waiters sometimes decided you merited serving. He sat in the corner of her room, talking to her or reading the paper or watching television. He pushed her in her wheelchair along the corridors just to give her a different setting. They finally were together.

Until the pain in his back became intolerable and he reluctantly knew he had to do something. He hated doctors. He also went by the theory that what you don't know is the best thing to know. But he saw his physician and was diagnosed with acute myeloid leukemia. I remember the call. I was standing in the kitchen. He called me at least once a week. He always said, "It's your old man, just checking in." I figured this was the usual weekly check-in.

— I've got fucking leukemia.

— Do you know what kind it is?

— I don't know what fucking kind. I didn't fucking ask.

— What hospital are you going to?

— I don't fucking know yet. I think Mount Sinai. They're calling me fucking back.

He didn't want any more questions. We hung up.

My father was admitted to Mount Sinai several days later. Just before he left for the hospital, I could tell he wanted something he had never expressed before. He was desperate for a kiss from his wife, a stroke of the head, a promise to visit as soon as he got settled. He wanted reassurance but she lay in bed with her head to the side, her left hand flapping up and down in agitation, unable to cope with his illness and his hospitalization and likely not understanding any of it. He threw a few things into a bag, a razor, shaving cream, toothpaste, and toothbrush. He looked at her with pain and hatred, fifty years of marriage filed down to this.

"Bye, El," he said. "See you later."

She said nothing. She was terrified without him.

My mother only became worse. Two days later she fainted trying to get out of her wheelchair. My father had just been hospitalized, and now my mother was hospitalized. She was released without any precise diagnosis. Her days of walking even a few steps without assistance ended. She spent all her time in two places, the wheelchair and the bed. She became incontinent, and I had to change her diapers once.

I don't recommend it.

My mother was not aware that my father had leukemia. She asked repeatedly where he was, why he was gone, when he was coming back. She went to the hospital to visit him once or maybe twice. My sister and I walked her across Central Park one day in her wheelchair, stopping at the cart by the Great Lawn for the hot dogs slathered with mustard she loved so much, her appetite never at a loss. The park, once the epicenter of my life, seemed closed off to all but a handful of people. They made no eye contact with us, as if they knew. We circled the Metropolitan Museum and passed the Guggenheim, fixtures of my New York life that no longer held meaning. We arrived at the entrance of Mount Sinai on Madison Avenue, crammed and crazy in the shuffle of people who had no idea where to go because nothing was clearly marked.

We went up the elevator and awkwardly jammed the wheelchair into his room. She recognized him but was puzzled and gave him no encouragement or sympathy. My father became increasingly angry. He had his laptop computer in front of him and was trying to get a program to work and complained that the "fucking thing is broken." He wanted all of us to leave. We became a Diane Arbus photograph at that moment, a freakish fractured family that would never heal.

He came back from the hospital about three weeks later. The chemotherapy seemed to work for a while. His white cell count went down. He joked when he saw the oncologist for the weekly blood check. He never felt self-pity. Instead he felt defiance and said he never thought about the disease. He got tired of the endless restrictions — no booze, no high-calorie food, no this, no that.

He and I were out together one day, when we went into a Starbucks on the West Side so I could get a cup of coffee. He peered into the pastry case at all those cakes lacquered with frosting. "Fuck it," he said. He bought a piece. We sat at a table, and he ate with rapaciousness. He never looked at me, and we never spoke. His eyes darted back and forth, yearning and terrified instead of satisfied, like a terminally ill little boy knowing it was only a matter of time.

IV

My mother still lived in their apartment after he died. She still sometimes called to him. She sometimes said she had just seen him in the living room.

Her diagnosis had still not been pinned down — aspects of Parkinsonism, aspects of Alzheimer's, aspects of low blood pressure that caused her fainting, the suspicion of depression. She was on twenty different pills. My sister and I took her to a neurologist at Columbia Presbyterian in November of 2001, a month after my father's death. He believed she might have hydrocephalus, an abnormal buildup of fluid in the brain. A shunt was inserted to relieve the pressure.

In early March of 2002 she was rehospitalized after fainting and having difficulty regaining consciousness. She was placed in a single room with a view of the Hudson River. She loved New York. At her peak she had sopped up all of it — plays, musicals, ballet, museum openings, the opera where she occasionally had to wake my father because his snoring was disturbing the other patrons. I believe the view brought her a certain serenity, that the connection to New York would always be there with the Hudson in front of her. She watched the little cities of the ships move up the river. She could see the George Washington Bridge. The on-call neurologist came in one day to test her aptitude. "What is your name?" he asked her.

She paused. She stared out the window into the brittle light of early March when winter is no longer winter and spring isn't yet spring. It was somewhere around her seventy-fifth birthday.

"Eleanor Lebenthal Bissinger."

She said it like a five-year-old standing up in class for the first time, trumpeting to the world that she had arrived. It was the last thing I remember her saying. The shunt had become infected. In trying to get rid of the infection, her kidneys started to fail.

Four months and ten days after my father died so did my mother, quietly and without complaint. I felt relieved. I felt lucky. I no longer had to bear witness to a mind that had vanished. That was the good part, I suppose. The bad part is that you never get over your parents dying back to back, critically sick at the very same time. You feel exhausted, cheated, angry, pulled in every direction because of their simultaneous needs but never knowing quite where to go. Parents die, but they should never die like this, the father livid at the world, the mother permanently sealed in her own world. You also know your children, no matter how much they loved their grandparents, will never fully overcome the scars. I worried particularly about Zach. He had lost great-grandparents, but he never shed a tear, his only curiosity to see what they looked like in an open coffin. This was different. I did not know how he would react. If he'd react at all.

Zach held special territory in my father's heart. The place where they worshiped each other the most was Nantucket. In one of the first steppingstones of self-assertion, Zach visited alone one summer when he was fifteen or sixteen. Since Zach was not easy to entertain, my father was apprehensive. But he compensated for it. Zach could gladly eat salmon every day of his life so my father wrote up a menu for the entire week and came up with four different ways to prepare salmon — grilled, poached, sautéed, stuffed with crabmeat. He put in vegetables to act like he was doing the right thing. Dessert was always crammed with chocolate.

Every morning at eight, they got in the car together and drove side by side to the Downyflake. My father, after much inner debate over calories and cholesterol, ordered scrambled eggs and bacon and hash browns and toast and then complained about it the rest of the day. Zach had a muffin. Then they went to the car wash only a few hundred yards away and got my father's car washed. Afterward they went to the entrance and watched other cars get washed until Zach said he'd seen enough. Ten minutes. Maybe fifteen. It was their version of fishing in the pond.

My mother's relationship with Zach was well-meaning but taut and tense. She could never quite accept his condition. She took him to see *The King and I* on Broadway when he was nine or ten. Zach constantly shook his box of candy because he couldn't sit still. She became livid and she slapped him. When I asked her about it, she was convinced he had done it on purpose. A pattern developed. Zach saw an opening for attention, positive or negative, much like he did with Gerry when they were younger. He'd pull on the brown fedora she wore. "Goddamn it!" she'd say, her pursed lips like the slit of a knife. He'd take her pocket-book. She'd chase after him. I found him in the yard of the Nantucket house once, terrified and breathing heavily. I took Zach's side and lectured her on the fact that he was different and she had to accept it. But she wasn't buying.

Yet it was Zach who gave the most touching eulogy at her funeral. He insisted on speaking. He wrote the words out himself. His voice was clear and his words direct. Everyone there was familiar with his condition and probably did not think he was capable of speaking in front of an audience with any poise. I didn't think he could either. But he did, in unfiltered words straight from the heart.

"I love you, Ellie," he said at the end. "I shall miss you very much."

V

At 2:19 P.M. we pass the Continental Divide. We have driven 2,942 miles. At 2:56 P.M. we cross the border into Arizona. We have driven 2,991 miles. We have decided not to go to the Grand Canyon. I feel ambivalence but Zach feels none. He looks quite relieved.

Dark clouds hover over the mountains like vultures, turning them black. Then straws of white light poke through the clouds like secret stairways. Sections of the mountains heat with an amber glow, then turn black again as the cloud vultures return.

The car drives itself as if speeding toward one of those straws of light, lifted up by it, my son and I soaring. Then the clouds turn dark again and press as if they might crush us.

Chapter 14

Hollywood Blue

I

WE END UP DRIVING over six hundred miles today. I am snappish. Zach as usual remains steady in the face of my flash thunderstorms. He has never talked back to me; I used to think it was always out of fear, and sometimes it is when I am purposely trying to scare him out of those behaviors that could become destructive. But his even temper is more than that; confrontation is simply not part of his nature, except when he threatens to kill his teacher. The right hemisphere of the brain, in addition to gripping onto concrete facts and experiences with crampons of steel, also seems to create imperviousness to others' wig-outs. He doesn't get rattled, life too short to waste his energy on such angst. I still have no real idea of what he sees of the world when he looks out the window, but it is never ugliness or cynicism or degradation. I like to think it is salmon.

Zach and I barely glimpse downtown Phoenix, which is fine because I have seen it before, tall buildings plunked and packed into a moonscape. We stick to our route through the labyrinthine interstates, as close to a futuristic version of the Jetsons as you can get where all human impulse is missing and commercial impulse overloads the most materialistic soul. Billboards skirt Interstate 10 for Whataburger, Bowdry RV Center, Gila River Casino. We pass a mall whose name I can't read. It doesn't matter. The same repeat offenders — Home Depot, Bed Bath & Beyond, PetSmart, Sam's Club, Verizon Wireless, Ross, Best Buy.

I am also cranky because it has been the longest day of driving of the trip. Plus Zach must be famished.

— Are you hungry?

— Not yet.

— Okay.

— Let's eat in Phoenix.

He wants to eat in the downtown of Phoenix rather than somewhere out here along its version of the Outback. Not going to happen.

— There is no Phoenix.

— Well I think Phoenix is a city right?

— It's not a city. It sprawls all over the fucking place. I've just driven six hundred miles, and I'm not driving twenty more to get into Phoenix.

— Maybe just eat at the hotel it will be nice to get out of the car won't it you'll be happy for me?

— I'll be happy for me.

I need directions to the hotel, and I'm trying to read the AAA guide while driving. The print is small; the pages are thin. I turn too many at a time. I can't read without taking off my glasses. When I take off my glasses the road becomes blurry. Phoenix, we have a problem.

I hand the book to Zach and tell him where to look. He seems confused. It is taking forever.

— Are you looking at the right page?

— I am looking at the right page.

— No, you're not. We're going to miss the fucking exit.

— It says 139 1-10 51st Avenue see we're right.

We check into the hotel. We eat dinner. Zach takes out his map and studies it and announces the best route to Las Vegas, up Interstate 10 and then over to 95. He hungers for Gerry again and calls him in the middle of dinner.

— Now wait did you have tennis tonight how are you going to get to the airport you just gonna take one plane so Thursday you have to work right so what time do you usually start school every day how do you get to school where do you take the subway from?

He hands the phone to me.

— Hey, Dad. How has Zach been?

— He's been great. How's it going?

— There's a lot of work. Plus student teaching.

— You sound tired.

— I am tired.

— I'll let you go sleep.

— I'll see you in two days.

Zach eats voraciously, as usual. I have to tell him, as usual, to slow down between bites and use his knife and fork and cut the meat into small pieces. The cutting is hard for him, despite the endless physical therapy he had when he was young and had to learn and relearn the simplest actions, build a tower of ten blocks, cut a three-inch circle, maintain balance on a green ball to improve equilibrium, do five sit-ups.

— Sorry Dad.

— It's not going away.

— I'm sorry.

— You don't have to be sorry. Just relax.

After each bite he takes the napkin from his lap and wipes his face. He glances at me to make sure he is performing correctly, as if he is peeking nervously from behind a curtain. I avert my eyes from him. I am sorry. I change the subject to another snippet of *Zach, This Is Your Life! With your special guest host, your father.*

— Do you know why I let you go to Haddonfield when you were thirteen?

— Why?

— Your mom loved you. I thought it would be a really nice town for you, which it has been.

I cannot bear to finish. All I think about are the possessions that I took from his room after he was gone, so little that all of it could fit inside a single cardboard box — a wooden plane we once painted together in wobbly colors of red and green and yellow with his initials, *ZB*, on it, a snowball of Batman sent by a film director looking to dump unsold promotional items, an old-fashioned toy featuring baseball players in white uniforms with curlicue mustaches, the stack of photo albums he left behind because he was moving on and never was burdened by sentimentality. Was it all that he needed while he lived with me? Or was it all that I thought he needed? I had tried to engage him in other activities . . . did I really?

The only sound as we eat is the dull scrape of cheap silverware on cheaper plates. We drove too far today. We are tired and we are hot. We were in the car for fourteen hours. We go upstairs to our rooms. Zach says he wants to use the pool. I ask if he wants me to go too. I say it out of love. I want to be with him.

— No if that's okay it's good for me to do things myself.

After he leaves, I go downstairs and spy on him through a glass window. The pool is empty. The light from the overhead bulbs is in mourning. A few plastic lounge chairs are sprinkled about like forgotten mannequins. I watch Zach in the Jacuzzi with his arms stretched back against the plastic sides, the soft, pale bloom of his belly. I can tell he is talking to himself. He seems so alone in that fraying light. I also know after three thousand miles that he feels no isolation as long as the water bubbles up and swirls through him in the elixir of his own definition of freedom. He has himself, and as I have discovered time and time again, he relies on himself. There are only so many prescribed facts of what is your birthday and where do you work and where do you live and how do you get to work that can fit into a lifetime.

I go back to my room. I insert the plastic room key and hear the little click. I think of him propped like a pillow against the back of the Jacuzzi with those outstretched hands, conducting his own verbal symphony in total contentment. I don't know whether to laugh or cry, be sad or proud. I am all those things.

II

— Where are we going today?
— Vegas.

— So tell me why you need to shave?

— So I look good?

— You don't want to look scraggly. They won't like us as much there. I'm gonna shave too.

I make sure the water is hot in the sink. I tell him to take off his watch, which he wears religiously with the stringy Velcro strap since knowing the exact time is almost as important as knowing somebody's birthday. He dips his hands to cup the water so he can splash it on his face and soften the beard. It is an uneasy physical action. I take his fingers and gently iron out the stiffness. I help him pat off the excess water and apply the shaving cream. He lays it on in mountains, and I take his hand and help him make a circling motion to rub it in. I know he is twenty-four, and part of me says *Why am I doing this?* But the intimacy I feel with him is like the spontaneous kiss of a little boy, because he is forever my little boy.

I take the razor and apply short but firm strokes because of the recalcitrance of his beard. I do his neck. He laughs because it tickles, another vestige of eternal boydom. I refill the sink with water so he can get rid of the excess shaving cream. It is once again difficult for him, his hands unwieldy. I take a towel and gently remove the remaining shaving cream from his sideburns and the groove under his nose. I help him apply a thick and even layer of after-shave unlike the globs he usually applies. I admire my barberesque handiwork. I admire him.

— Dad's shaving you because it's party time!

— Yeah.

We get on the road. I focus on Las Vegas as much as I can, but I feel Los Angeles looming. It was the scene of my greatest personal and professional failure. While the gloom and doom have since receded, I still ponder what happened. I avoided dwelling on it during the trip, but now we are only a few hundred miles away.

I moved there in 2000 as a co-producer for the ABC television show *NYPD Blue.* I had written only one script in my life when the call came from legendary producer Steven Bochco. He had read it, liked it, and nearly two years later contacted me like a scene out of that old television show *The Millionaire.* I was beyond flattered. Bochco had in-

vented the modern television drama with *Hill Street Blues.* He continued with *LA Law* and *NYPD Blue.* He had more impact on television
as we know it than anyone else in the modern history of the industry.
He thought I could make the transition from journalist and nonfiction
author to television writer. So did I.

After I wrote a shitty script in my first assignment, I knew Bochco
had given up on me, a lark that had become a loser. He was quite nice
about it: he took me and another writer who had equally bombed to
lunch at the commissary on the Fox lot. The food was wretched, the
hamburgers so stuffed with extraneous accouterments that it was a
game of hide-and-seek just to find the overly seasoned meat. Bochco
assured us we'd get the hang of it. He just had a heart and was letting
us down gently into the forgotten.

Roiling through me in the minivan is how I had left my children behind in Philadelphia. I cried on the flight to LA, knowing I had made
a terrible mistake but still forging ahead. I told the woman next to me
that I was going to Hollywood without them. I looked for solace from
her but she rightly gave me none. She was literally the only one who
disapproved of my decision; everyone else, whether family or friend
or foe, applauded the careerism of my move because of the perceived
glamour and the money I would be making. Hollywood is still always
Hollywood.

I came back to Philadelphia for a week every month, at least at the
beginning. Zach seemed fine with it, safely ensconced in the flurry
of activities his mother had planned for him. Caleb, nine at the time,
always had a little bit of Hollywood pixie dust in his eyes and thought
the whole thing was cool; he too was well taken care of by his mother.

But Gerry, a junior in high school, was livid with me. We had been
inseparable. Now he was being transplanted to his mother's house with
the wretched angst of college looming. The change could not have
come at a more pivotal moment in his life. He never told me at the
time — he was too loyal a son.

I *was* devoted to my three boys. Despite the two divorces, one of
them was always with me, although I was never quite sure who it would
be because the advance planning needed a slide rule and abacus. But
I was buoyed by the universal encouragement of going to work for

NYPD Blue. Because my whole life pivoted on success, how could I resist another dose of it? In my mind of constant misinterpretation, I assumed the only reason people liked me was because of my success; I had to keep it up. Whatever somebody said, however it was said, the only thing I ever heard was *What have you done for me lately?*

I remember a Sunday when Lisa was making waffles and bacon for the family. Earthy and sugary smells filled the kitchen. A liquid stream of gold sunlight poured through the window. It was a perfect morning when the house is a womb. Zach was there and for the first time in his life a friend had slept over. Yet I ignored all of it. I had pathetically stopped reading the *New York Times Book Review* five years earlier because of my raging jealousy of other writers getting rave reviews. Without hyperbole, the nonfiction bestseller list sent me into hours of depression and bitterness so I could not look at it either. I did take a peek at the cover that morning and without reading the review railed at the writer. Lisa pointed out the success of *Friday Night Lights* as an antidote to my insecurity.

— I wrote that fucking thing close to twenty years ago. All I do now is write shit. I am shit.

It went on some more. Lisa tried to be patient. But she had heard too much of it during our marriage to be patient. The refrain of my marital history. Zach was there with a *friend.* And I was going off in front of them.

"We have no fun," she said. "That's what really bothers me. You suck the joy out of everything, and then you die, and what's the point?"

I forced myself to be cheerful. I still seethed.

III

I worked for *NYPD Blue* for eleven months before I returned to Philadelphia in April of 2001. Shortly afterward, I was given an assignment by *Vanity Fair* that took me to Daytona Beach. I stayed in one of those hotels built with high ambition but gone shabby, eaten away by salt and sea. I was on a high floor with a view of the ocean, tired waves barely making the shore. The Atlantic looked so impotent.

I couldn't get out of bed the first day because of my twin feelings of Hollywood failure and father failure. I had left like the bon voyage of a brand-new ship and now I was returning in a life raft. Nor was I even sure of what I was returning to. Would I be the same father I once was, just pick up where I left off? I finally got up naked and tried to get dressed but lay curled up on the floor with my nose pressed against the algae-colored carpet. The sodden smell of mildew filtered through my nostrils. I felt it was what I deserved, a naked man on the floor with his knees pulled up to his chest. My heart pounded with fear, the moment when a professional writer realizes that he has been caught, his fraud discovered, success always accidental, failure always inevitable. Whatever words I had within me, and we all have a finite amount, had run out. A writer has no chance of survival if he has no confidence. I had no confidence anymore. *NYPD Blue* had killed it. I lay naked on that algae-colored carpet for an hour. I wanted to stay there forever. I finally got dressed. I did the reporting I had to do to get the story done. It turned out well enough to make me think that perhaps I was not professionally dead.

Gerry settled back in with me in Philadelphia. There was quiet between us, friendly-fire quiet: he finally shot out that he'd hated what I had done, felt abandoned. He was a junior in high school; the prospect of finding the right college *was* terrifying to him. Where the hell was I? Three thousand miles away prospecting for gold.

Why had I done it? I thought I would make millions. I thought I would create shows and then write seven-figure screenplays. What would I have done if I had succeeded? I would have stayed, which may have made me rich but consigned me to hell. So failing was fortuitous. I rediscovered what was vital, fatherhood, the best part of me.

I talk about much of this to Zach in Arizona as we pass Sun City, the epicenter of retirees with excellent natural tans. On a paved path next to the road, a little man drives a little golf cart, fast and furious. Bocce ball beckons.

— I get nervous when I think of getting to California.

— Why?

—I just do. I have bad memories of it. Working at *NYPD Blue* was very hard.

—Why?

—I didn't do very well. They didn't like me. I failed.

—Oh you did.

—Yeah, I did. They didn't like the work that I did. It was very humiliating.

—Yeah.

—I realized they didn't give a fuck about me. I was just a piece of meat. You know what that means?

—What?

—It means that people just don't care about you. It means that you're disposable. If they don't like the work that you do, they just fire you.

—After like you live in a place do you care to like remember your way around?

—Not really. I've always had a hard time there. And it's been only harder after *NYPD Blue.*

—Did you miss me when you went to work in LA?

—Yeah, I didn't see you very much then. I shouldn't have gone. I missed you guys terribly.

—But what you had to?

—I thought I had to but I really didn't. I was selfish I guess. I thought I was gonna have a new career but I didn't.

—Oh.

—And I was selfish and I forgot what was important.

—Yeah.

—Being with my boys was much more important and I regret what I did.

—But I remember you lived there from like Memorial Day you got there on Memorial Day of 2000 and you got back on April 30 of '01 I remember Dad when you had first got to LA on Memorial Day you lived in a hotel I guess for a little while.

—The Residence Inn. It was pretty awful.

—What wasn't good about it?

— It just wasn't homey and it was just awful.

— It didn't look very nice?

— No.

— And I remember Dad you got Goldfish 'cause you thought of me and you got Goldfish I guess the crackers that I liked 'cause you got Goldfish to think of me that day.

Zach loved Goldfish. I would buy a big box of them and lie on the flower-patterned bedspread of the hotel. I would cram Goldfish in my mouth, not to savor them but to savor my son.

IV

We are closing in on Lake Mead with Las Vegas roughly an hour away. A wedge of lightning blazes across the sky. A shield of mountains in the background provides cover.

— We're almost there. Excited?

— Yeah.

— I hope we get a break in the weather.

— But the pool's outdoors at the hotel?

— Look how pretty the scenery is, Zach. Look at this.

— But the pool's outdoors right?

— Look at this, isn't this beautiful?

— Is the pool outdoors?

— This is so beautiful.

— I can swim all I want?

Waiting for Godot . . .

Several minutes later we get to Hoover Dam and wait in a traffic jam to pass through the tunnel that burrows through the dam. I am awed in the presence of the greatest engineering project in history.

— What do you think?

— It reminds me of the Lincoln Tunnel.

He says this because of the waiting traffic and in a certain sense he is more right than wrong. Although I also believe he is the first person ever to compare Hoover Dam to the Lincoln Tunnel.

We pass Boulder City, about half an hour away from Vegas. Zach is fidgety. He is out of focus. He is folding the map in his hand at magician speed.

— I know you're getting antsy because you're gonna fold and unfold that map so much it's going to rip into two.

— Dad Railroad Pass Hotel Casino.

— Should be less than half an hour.

— Railroad Pass Hotel Casino.

— That's right.

— It's called Railroad Pass Hotel Casino.

He's fishing for a wordplay game with the added ingredient of a pinch of pestering. He is bored. He wants to get there. I am bored. I want to get there. I won't fall for the bait.

We first glimpse Vegas over the crest of a hill. Xanadu in the desert. A city spawned from a secret meeting of frustrated architects required to take LSD. We arrive in the city about 4:00 P.M., its garish, giddy, goofy Sodom-and-Gomorrah glory going strong despite uncharacteristic gray skies and the threat of rain. Zach sees the restaurants Morton's and Roy's and gets excited because they also have outlets in Philadelphia. Just like his excitement over the Embassy Suites, this concrete connection with home putting more cement in his mental mixer. He sees the Westin and reminds me that we stayed at a Westin in Chicago. He sees the Luxor Hotel, or the Luxari as he calls it, and says that is where Brian Chavez stays when he gambles. He points out Harrah's, or Hurrah's as he calls it. I point out the Bellagio. Zach goes to movies, even though he understands so little of them, so I ask him if he has seen *Ocean's Eleven*. He has not. I point out Treasure Island. Zach doesn't respond. We see where we are staying, the Wynn, a gleaming black curve rising forty-five stories.

— I want to give you the night of your life tonight. We're going to go out for dinner. We're going to a show. Then we'll hit the casino.

— When?

— Tonight.

— Oh tonight.

— Yeah, we'll stay out late. You're gonna have a beer.

— In Las Vegas you stay out late?

— Oh, yeah. Like 'til midnight or 'til one o'clock.

— Oh.

— Would you like to do that, have a real nice night out?

— Yeah.

Chapter 15

Viva Las Vegas!

I

OUR SUITE AT the Wynn is exactly what I hoped it would be, a two-bedroom spread of classy design, with just the right dollop of sinful *beurre blanc* to remind you that you are in the home of the rococo.

The entryway is covered in creamy white marble that extends into the living room, in whose center lies a red patterned carpet of muted hue. A pair of white couches face one another, each flanked by two lamps with glass bases and red shades on side tables. There is a flat-screen television perfectly centered between the picture windows. The TV is one of four, including another one in the living room, which only plays music. There is a bar behind the white couches with two high-backed chairs color-coordinated with the lamps and carpet. Opposite the bar is a white L-shaped couch with a table for dining. Elegant framed prints hang on the walls. The ceiling has a mirror with recessed lights. There is a master bedroom and a smaller one. There is a massage room, an opulent surprise even for Vegas, nothing like having your muscles kneaded after you've lost your life savings and what you further embezzled. The bathroom is bigger than any New York studio with a shower bigger than any New York studio to the right and a tub bigger than any New York studio to the left. On each of two sinks are four brown-ambered bottles of the finest shampoos and shower gels.

Back in the living room, Zach is gazing out the expansive picture window, which displays many of the city's glitziest casinos. He surely must be impressed.

— What do you see out there?

— The highway.

He wants to go swimming at one of the outdoor pools. I ask him twice if he'll be able to find his way back to the room, given the Wynn's size and maze of tunneled hallways. Zach has simply become dismissive of such questions: he's already memorized the floor plan. He puts on his baggy bathing suit hanging below the knees, obviously a new line of sportswear from the Amish. Off he goes.

I go into the living room and turn on the flat screen dedicated to music. A song comes on, Nat King Cole's rendition of "The Very Thought of You."

I stare out the window toward Treasure Island and the unfinished skeleton of the Trump casino. The trip is winding down, and I already miss Zach terribly. My friend was exactly right: when I stopped looking for epiphanies, I found something far better. Just as the song says, *it is the very thought of you*. Like the moment of the indoor pool at the Holiday Inn in Phoenix, I want to be near him. He doesn't want me to intrude, and I have learned to honor that. I go downstairs just to watch him.

The pools cascade into one another, nine of them in all, a seamless surface of aqua. Zach is on a white lounge chair. No one is near him. There is the tall glass of an empty nonalcoholic drink on the table next to him. He is reclining in his bathing suit. A towel covers his legs. A server comes by and asks if he would like another drink. He says he would. Per usual, he gives the room number. He could stay there forever, charging drinks to the room, maybe escalating up to a sandwich, then a 100 percent cotton Villa towel for $159. Who knows, maybe even another belt. I leave knowing he is king of the world. At 5:00 P.M., the exact minute I told him to return, I hear him insert the key. Time to prepare for our dream date.

II

We walk through the Wynn casino toward Corsa Cucina, an Italian restaurant known for re-creating the "heart and art of the Mediter-ranean." Its setting tries to re-create a homey Italian trattoria, but it's more Wild West brothel. Overdone chandeliers speckle the ceiling and the carpet is meat-eater rare. While dress is casual the price is not, but at least nobody is wearing shorts. Zach has on khaki pants and a yellow polo shirt, having carefully dressed for the occasion; it is his most flattering look and he is adorable. We find the restaurant along the periphery of the casino floor. He is holding a dining guide to Odessa — Texas Burger, Watts Burger, Whataburger, Wingstop, What-ever. I ask him why he is holding a dining guide to Odessa when we're in Las Vegas. He says he doesn't know.

Our table offers a view of a nearby blackjack table with high-backed chairs of red and green and blue. The color scheme is meant to add vitality, but there rarely is much vitality in the blackjack gulag of a casino floor. Gamblers lift their cards and glance at them without ex-pression, fold or place bets with assembly-line repetition. Glumness rules, winning chips slid back into color-coordinated stacks and los-ing chips swept away with nothing more than a shake of the head. At a high-stakes table, where the minimum bet is a hundred dollars, there is only one man. He is playing two hands at once at five hundred a hand. His arm is propped on his elbow on the table and he's leaning on his hand as if listening to a convention seminar on the newest trends in vacuum suction. He absently sifts the remaining chips in his hands, a mini accordion. He looks like he is about to drift off. He places his five-hundred-dollar bet anyway, knowing he is going to lose.

A syncopated salsa beat plays over and over. Slot machine bells go off incessantly, like the high-pitched honking of false car alarms. In what seems like four or five miles away because of the casino's size, there is the occasional collective yell at a craps table where the shooter has hit his number. At a roulette table in what must be a different time zone, a cry goes up when the ball clicks into a number that somebody has sprinkled his chips on. A gambler at a blackjack table that has gone cold pockets his chips with arthritic slowness. He seems totally defeated. He finds another table and gives the dealer a thousand dollars for another round of chips. The dealer spreads out the ten one-hundred-dollar bills like a bank robber tallying an easy score. This is not going to end well.

It becomes quite depressing, but nothing will get in the way of Zach and me tonight. We have come too far in miles and emotions. We sit at a corner table, a perfect setting for my dream date vision. I go over the menu with him, point out what he might like—spaghetti maybe, or veal Parmesan, or calamari for an appetizer.

We order drinks. I have a white wine. I ask Zach if he wants a beer, but he says no. He just wants water. The drinks come, and we clink our glasses together.

—Cheers to Las Vegas. Cheers to us. I love you. What do you say back?

—Cheers.

—What else do you say back?

—Cheers to Las Vegas.

—Do you love me or not?

—I love you.

—Are you sure?

—Yeah.

Zach's arms jerk back and forth. It is a minor tic. But it is also a possible sign of being lost in Las Vegas.

—Do you find this overwhelming?

—No.

—You're very ticcy.

—DAD I don't find this overwhelming.

—Are you all right? I hope you're not having an attack. Do you find this fun?

—Yeah I find this very fun.

—It's different. Remember what Gerry said before we left?

— That it's something new to learn.

— Something new to do. That's what life's about.

We order our dinners. He is glassy-eyed at this point. I hand him a hundred dollars to gamble with, hoping it will perk him up. The money is meaningless to him.

— Do you know what roulette is?

— What?

— You spin the wheel and you pick a number.

— Yeah.

— You know what blackjack is?

— I don't know what it is.

— You try to get to twenty-one.

It is an intentionally empty response. If I tried to explain the game to him for the entire night, he still would not understand. And he seems so far away now, in the Space.

— Are you okay, Zach?

— I'm good.

— Are you sad?

— No.

— You seem a little sad. Are you tired of me?

— No I'm good.

I should have tried to explain to him the basic concept of twenty-one. So I try. He knows what a face card is but cannot grasp that it equals ten. Or that an ace can equal one or eleven.

The entrées come. Zach plays with the straw in his drink. A woman with a baby in a stroller passes by. The din of the casino is beginning to sound like a collective murmur in which no words can be made out. Zach and I just can't stare at each other all night, so I start a new conversation.

— Have you ever fallen in love with anybody?

— No.

— Have you ever had a girlfriend really?

— I think I like Shanna.

— Do you know what sex is?

— I've heard about it before.

—What is it?

—When you sleep together.

—Have you ever slept with anybody?

—No.

—Do you want to?

—No.

—Have you ever kissed anybody?

—No.

Somebody yells "Happy Birthday." The television screens show a catastrophic bridge collapse in Minneapolis. Nobody stops to watch.

—Do you hate it when I ask questions like that?

—A little.

—Why?

—'Cause I just do.

—Questions about what?

—The reason I don't like when you ask the questions is that sometimes I don't know how to really answer them.

—I'm sorry.

—Yeah.

—It's hard.

—Yeah it is hard it's very hard to answer them.

—I am sorry.

—It's okay.

—I'm your father. I thought I should ask those questions.

—I know you're my father.

I continue to look around the casino floor because there is nothing else to do. Zach is emotionally gone. I don't try to reach him and I don't feel like it anyway because of my own disappointment that the dream date is crumbling. There is a white neon sign for three-card poker. Men in blue shirts and black shirts walk past, some aimlessly as if lost and some with purpose as if escaping. A man in a red shirt drinks a beer and actually laughs at his losses. A knot of Hasidic Jews crowds a slot machine with their urgent whispers and disagreements. A man in a white cowboy hat and brown boots smokes a cigarette.

Zach gulps his food down in his typically large bites. My voice rises with the same reproach I made the night before. When will teaching him to eat ever stop? When will my scolding stop?

— PUT THE FORK DOWN. TAKE A REST. NOBODY IS GOING TO TAKE IT FROM YOU.

We finish dinner without a word. Why should he say anything? I raised my voice at him not because of the way he eats, but because he doesn't understand blackjack or anything else in the casino. I am more than upset. I am pissed. It is unfair to Zach — he can only do what he can do — but fuck unfair. Don't I ever have the right to be unfair with a child like Zach? My hopes are in the zone of the irrational, but fuck irrational. I want this night to work; I want the dream date to come true.

III

— I feel like gambling, Zach, and losing a lot of money. You think that's a great idea?

— Yeah I think it's a great idea.

— Want to lose a lot of fucking money?

— Yeah.

— It's bad, losing money.

— Yeah.

— I'm feeling very self-abusive. I want to lose a lot of fucking money.

— Yeah I think it's a great idea Dad.

— What should I lose money on?

— How about craps what Brian Chavez plays.

— Yeah, I'm gonna lose a lot of money on craps. I'm gonna lose. Everything. Fucking everything! That's what I feel like tonight. Come on, let's go. Let's lose some money.

We find a craps table. I watch the shooters in a semicircle peering into the green felt. Cigarettes are Super-Glued to their lips so you can see a tiny indentation. Half-full drinks sit next to them with condensation dripping down the glasses in slow streaks. The fatal dice roll of seven bounces onto the green felt time after time. The stick man sweeps up piles of chips like a stadium worker sweeping up peanut shells. The table is cold. I am cold. I lose five hundred dollars in five minutes before I quit.

We get lost in the ridiculous maze of the Wynn trying to find our way out. We end up at the golf and pro shop.

— How the fuck do you get out of this place?

— I think you can go down this way.

Zach is right, of course. We finally make it outside. The neon lights bounce and dance to their private disco beat. I point out the Frontier. Then the Venetian, where Lisa and I stayed when we got married here in 2004, just the two of us. Zach's interest finally perks up at the mention of the Venetian because it enables the concrete to solidify for him. He wants to know what room we stayed in and which floor. He wants to know if we ate at a restaurant there. I tell him I don't remember.

— Oh.

We get to Treasure Island early for the show and play slots poker. I remember Zach as a child playing Go Fish with my second wife, so I think the basic concept of poker is something he can grasp. But Zach doesn't understand the game, what buttons to press to hold certain cards in your hand, such as a pair. I end up pushing the buttons for him.

We go to the main auditorium and take our seats in row DD, numbers one and two on the end. We are seeing *Mystère,* the Cirque du Soleil extravaganza. Much of the show's voice-over is spiritual non sequiturs flowing one into the other in indecipherable nonsense.

> Only when the questions become more important than the answers will the solutions emerge.
>
> The Ancient Bird hops down the Songlines that furrow the brow of the desert. She taps her beak along the path that only she can see clearly. Every click of the crooked bone raises a puff of dust, a few notes, a few memories. A shiver ruffles her sun-worn feathers. The joy of remembrance fills her with surprise, as always. The mystery of memory.
>
> *Mystère de la Mémoire.*

Oh, my God . . .

The narrative line is only an excuse anyway for exquisite feats of acrobatics in costumes that look as if they were designed by Liberace in particularly manic inspiration — aerial high bars, one-hand balancing on wooden squares no bigger than the size of a palm, trampolines, Korean planks in which performers jump on a seesaw device to form a four-person tower, Chinese poles on which performers maintain balance only with their feet. A puffed-out clown in a baby costume with a bottle around his neck bounces a huge orange rubber ball and throws popcorn at the audience between acts.

Zach's arms and legs twitch back and forth and he closes his eyes and quietly talks to himself. I put my hand on his thigh and ask him if he wants to leave, but he says no, he's okay. He only says this because he knows it is important to me.

There is a moment in the show when one male performer grasps the hand of another performer with a single hand and stretches his body out in a perpendicular line four feet off the ground. The strength and grace required to achieve this feat are unimaginable. I turn to Zach who is expending every ounce of his willpower not to fidget. It is torture for him. The whole show is a blur. Tears fill my eyes, as I face the fact that, all night long, I have done nothing but push my son beyond all limits of what is reasonable and right. The tears trickle down my cheeks, and I turn my head so Zach will not see them. I want to hold his hand. I want to entwine my fingers with his. But he is in his twenties and no longer wants to hold hands with his father in public.

The show ends, and we head back to our suite at the Wynn. We should have gone back there hours ago. The neon lights of the hotels and casinos are played-out, pitiless.

We arrive at the suite. Zach changes into the T-shirt and underwear that he uses as his pajamas and slips into bed. We play the don't-say-the-word game.

— When I leave here I don't want you to say *Mystère*.
— Okay good night.
— Good night.
— Good night.

— Good night.

— Good night.

— Just don't say *Mystère,* that's all. Good night.

— Good night.

— Good night.

I leave the bedroom and walk about fifteen feet.

— MYSTÈRE!!

I march back into his room.

— What did I tell you not to say?

— *Mystère?*

— So why did you say it?

— *Mystère.*

— This is your fault.

— Dad Dad Dad Dad.

It is what he wanted all along, a vigorous round of cuddies. He runs around the bed. I chase after him. He squeals with delight. I throw a pillow at him to catch him off-guard, then leap across the bed and grab his legs. He's toast now. I pin him down and tickle him furiously. He giggles furiously. He squirms loose. I grab him again, tickle him again until we are both out of breath.

I kiss him good night.

I go to bed but I cannot sleep. Why did I do what I did tonight? I should have known our dream date wouldn't work. Everything I have learned from and about him on the trip cannot eradicate that so much will always be overwhelming and incomprehensible to him. I just felt there was a chance because of his flowering. He has blossomed. We have blossomed. It gave me false hope, even though I instinctively knew when I saw him lying on the white lounge chair by one of the outdoor pools that this is where he wanted to be, ordering tall nonalcoholic drinks and charging them to the room, happy into the night before a blanket of blue.

Chapter 16

Coming into Los Angeles

I

L AS VEGAS IS TIRED in the morning, a sequined hooker waking with mascara streaks of black tears and dagger slits in the stretched holes of her fishnets. Like vampires, gamblers see the rising sun and scurry inside the closest coffee shop to avoid daylight. They sip black coffee and stare ahead, steeping in the sourness of a spurious last-chance run. In the shock of sun, the Eiffel Tower at the Paris looks like a keepsake key chain. The vertical Bally's sign looks as worn as *The Last Picture Show*. The Mirage and Treasure Island and the Venetian and Caesar's Palace crowd together like subway riders elbowing for space.

We need to leave to wash away the disaster of last night. Surprisingly, I don't whip myself anymore for what happened. I placed Zach in a role he could not play, like all parents sometimes do with children. Yet as bad a dream date as it turned out to be, Zach did take another step forward: for the first time ever, he defended himself. He told me to stop asking the probing questions. He said he didn't understand them, but my intuition tells me there were some he did. Instead he was building a wall around feelings that he considered to be personal and proprietary to him.

When you have a child like Zach, you do feel as if you own his life, that he is obligated to reveal whatever he thinks and feels on demand. This belief is understandable because you do literally own him as a result of the court-ordered process of guardianship, in which your child answers questions from the judge with a quiet "yes" and doesn't fully grasp that he's giving up every right he has, usually to his parents. Some of those rights must be given up, financial decisions and health decisions and decisions of where to live to make sure he is in the best environment. But it should not equate to the entire loss of his individuality. It was only a moment at a restaurant last night overstocked with banal noise, but Zach cordoned off a part of himself with yellow police tape. The issue of sex was something he *did* understand, at least on the surface. But the issue also bewildered him and made him nervous and perhaps most of all embarrassed him. By asking me to stop bringing it up, he was telling me not to embarrass him anymore. In his quiet and nonconfrontational way he was asserting himself as a young man, not a man-child to be picked at and forever probed, not to be deprived of trying to make himself whole.

We make our escape on Las Vegas Boulevard and almost immediately get stuck behind a rental camper with a tableau of a mountain range on the back. It becomes our view, a fake string of snowcapped mountains painted on a camper stuck in traffic in an imaginary land that has lost all illusion in the glare of day.

— What did you think of the gambling?
— It went well I thought.
— Went well? You lost twenty bucks.
— Yeah I lost.
— Didn't that bother you?
— I liked it.

We escape the city and get onto Interstate 15 South toward Los Angeles. It's a five-hour trip, and we should be there in the afternoon. We have now traveled 3,206 miles. The journey from coast to coast will officially end today. Gerry is coming to meet us. If Zach has been my heart, Gerry has always been my soul. I look forward to having my heart and soul both with me, but right now there is instantaneous nostalgia.

— This is the last day that we have to drive anywhere. Doesn't that upset you?

— A little.

— It does?

— Yeah.

— I thought you hated the car.

— Well I didn't like it that much.

— It makes me sad.

— Yeah 'cause the driving's gonna end after today.

— I like driving with you. I like having you next to me. I just like having you next to me. I even like it when you're asleep.

— Yeah.

— 'Cause I love you so much. I just enjoy your company.

— Yeah.

— You're a good traveler.

— Yeah.

— I think you did a lot of things just because I wanted you to do them. And I appreciate that.

— Yeah.

The closer we get to Los Angeles, the more excited he gets. Zach spent summers and school vacations there with his mother and stepfather as a little boy. So he of course remembers the sprawling sprawl the way he remembers everything, in perfect bite-size pieces. The closer I get, the less excited I get. I will never quite shake my Hollywood blues. Zach is buoyant. I am brooding.

II

We are about fifty miles away from Los Angeles. Zach clutches the Rand McNally atlas and per prior arrangement guides me through the freeways. We get on Interstate 210 West then Interstate 605 South then the Santa Monica Freeway.

The nearer our destination of the Beverly Hills Hilton, the more Zach recalls. He remembers that I was in Los Angeles from October 25 to November 6 of 1996 — about eleven years ago — to interview infamous detective Mark Fuhrman for a piece I wrote for *Vanity Fair*.

— Do you know who he is?

— No.

— He was a detective on the O. J. Simpson murder case.

— Was he nice?

I couldn't possibly answer a question like that.

We exit the freeway at La Cienega and onto Wilshire in easy striking distance of where we are staying. It is perilously near to the Fox lot where *NYPD Blue* was located.

— I think this is how I used to get to work.

— Yeah.

— Just being near here, my stomach is really tight.

— What does it mean it's tight?

— It's nervous.

Zach's breathing is like an overwound metronome because of his excitement. Suddenly it slows and he becomes reverential.

— *The La Cienega Hand Wash* . . .

Suddenly he is yelling.

— RODEO DRIVE I REMEMBER I REMEMBER THIS RESTAURANT CRUSTACEAN!

I am seething.

— Everything takes fucking forever in Los Angeles. The traffic's been shitty for the last two hours.

— THERE'S THE BEVERLY HILLS HOTEL!

— About goddamn time.

— I LIKE BEING IN LA!

— I wish we were back in Odessa or even weird Tulsa.

III

We check into the hotel. Zach and Gerry will be in one room; I'll be next door. We drop off our bags and go to the home of my cousin Pete

Berg, the film director who made *Very Bad Things, The Rundown, Friday Night Lights,* and *The Kingdom* and is currently shooting *Hancock* in Los Angeles, starring Will Smith. He is also the creator of the widely acclaimed television show *Friday Night Lights.* In his prior life, he was an actor with a recurring role in *Chicago Hope* and a slew of movies, including *The Last Seduction* with Linda Fiorentino.

When he was growing up, he was often in the psychic doghouse whether he deserved it or not. Our extended family all figured him for an early death or at the very least the nomadic life of one failed job after another. Since I had spent my life trying to impress my extended family and be the Good One, his impending doom did bring me a certain amount of satisfaction. I still wore the crown of King of Accomplishment. But he double-crossed me.

He had great talent if he could find the right home for it. Hollywood became that home, probably the only home that would take him given his mix of visual genius and attention deficit disorder and fine appreciation of mayhem. Like getting into fights with drunken Marines. Like taking Caleb aside as a teenager and showing smartphone pictures that beautiful naked women had sent with the hope of convincing him in person they were perfect for a role in one of his films. Or buying Zach for his sixteenth birthday a Playboy key chain in the shape of a woman's bent-over butt. Like visiting Zach and me in Philly and telling the limo driver at twelve thirty in the morning to suddenly stop so we could run up the famous *Rocky* steps of the Philadelphia Art Museum and then turn to face the city with our fists held high. "If he wasn't working in Hollywood, he'd probably be in jail," Kyle Chandler, who plays Coach Taylor in the *Friday Night Lights* TV series, told me. But behind the naughty-boy reputation is a pure heart. Honest. Kind. Warm. Thoughtful when he remembers. Or at least when his assistant Lindsay reminds him to remember.

It is impossible for Pete not to love Zach. It is impossible for Zach not to love Pete. It's like a sixties love-in, with me in charge of finding the munchies but otherwise outside the bong circle. It does strike me that two of my children, Caleb and Zach, would be perfectly content to live with Pete in Hollywood and leave me behind in Philadelphia. (What goes around always does come around.)

— Peter how old are you Peter?

— Me, I'm forty-five.

— When will you turn forty-six?

— March 11.

— It will be a Tuesday.

— How do you know that?

— In my head.

— Remember Peter we spent Thanksgiving on Nantucket.

— I remember.

— Ninety-three November 25 remember we took a walk remember.

— You know why I remember?

— Why?

— Because you have a crazy memory.

— Peter I think I saw you remember at the movies remember in Manayunk.

— What date was that?

— It was September 30 2004 for *Friday Night Lights* you came to Philly.

— You remember that? What theater was it?

— It was called Main Street remember you met my dog.

— Your dog was there?

— In the parking lot you met her her name is Maddy.

Peter is disoriented at this point. Too many memories and moments and Zach hasn't even warmed up yet.

— You know what, Zach?

— What?

— Nobody can lie to you.

IV

Pete is taking us to a party in Malibu for those from NBC who have been nominated for Emmys. Pete is among them for the pilot of *Friday Night Lights,* which he wrote and directed. I'm dreading it, a walking scowl, a nobody there only because of his cousin. Zach loves parties, any party — birthday, holiday, bowling, pre-funeral, post-funeral.

He goes into them without any of the habit-formed anxiety, anger, jealousy, and competition that I go into them with, *this person is an asshole, stay away from that person, this person by some miracle made a hit, how is it possible for him to have a career better than mine?* He goes because he likes food. He goes because he wants to see people he knows or to figure out some tangential connection with somebody he doesn't know, listening carefully for a single word that suggests a link to his hard drive. He has no qualms talking to strangers, nor is he put off by strained interaction. If this moment at this party doesn't work out, then on to the next moment and the next party.

Pete takes Zach under his wing.

— I'm going to introduce you to everyone I know. You stay with me, okay? You and me together. We'll get through this together. If there are any cute girls, you introduce me.

— Will they have good food?

— I think they will.

— Like caterers they'll walk around with trays.

— Yup.

Zach disappears into the sea of chatter. I suddenly feel more self-conscious than ever. I talk about the television show a little bit, as if I have something to do with it, when I don't other than selling the rights to my book. Or else I ask people I vaguely recognize questions I could care less about, trying to keep up conversation until I figure out my exit strategy. I am acutely aware of my male pattern baldness. I feel bloated, a helium balloon being filled with air. Everyone else is thin and works out six times a day. Showoff assholes . . .

Around me, the chitchat has descended into profound inanity. I actually hear someone say, "Women and wine was something I just couldn't feel passionate about anymore."

I find Zach on the outdoor deck overlooking the Pacific folding and unfolding a map. I ask him if he has talked with anyone. He says a woman. I ask him if he knows who she is. He says he has no idea. It turns out to be the wife of Brian Grazer (since divorced), the hugely successful film producer who runs the company Imagine Entertainment with Ron Howard. I ask him what they talked about. He said he asked her if she had a house on Nantucket. I guess he asked her that because based on his observation she had the glamorous polish of a woman who looked like she was from Nantucket. She said no, and the conversation ended. He is much more concerned with the food servers.

— They're coming with something good.

Zach plucks a strange little object from a tray and wolfs it down. So do I. I have no idea what it is, but it *is* good. Zach disappears. I find him hovering over the raw bar. There are crab claws and oysters and shrimp so big they must have been on steroids. Zach takes an oyster before making a beeline for the table where a chef is carving up tenderloin. On the way, he plucks a lobster salad appetizer. The food is so good that Zach decides he'd like to learn how to cater a party. He asks me what the job would be like. I tell him he'd have to work quickly and not be allowed to talk to anybody.

— Maybe then it would be better maybe if I just eat.

Pete doesn't feel like staying at the party very long, Zach is gastronomically satiated after the tenderloin run, and I never wanted to be there. We leave and drive back to Pete's house. Pete asks Zach about Gerry, who is on the plane now. Here comes the flood.

— When he was in college you know up by Harrisburg I didn't see him as much and actually it was his junior year he lived in Australia from February to June I didn't see him for months he was living last year up in New Canaan Connecticut because he was teaching at a school up in Connecticut so I missed him a lot and his girlfriend actually his girlfriend's family is in Chicago but it was funny Peter his girlfriend last year well she was up in Middlebury Vermont at a college up there and she couldn't speak she couldn't speak we couldn't talk to her because she had to speak a different language Spanish now that Gerry is in Philly Peter I'll see him a lot more because he's only twenty minutes from me.

Peter gets that disoriented look on his face again. I think he may have regretted asking the question.

Zach isn't finished.

— Peter do you like horses?

— I'm allergic to them.

— You don't like them?

— I love them but I sneeze. Do you like them?

— Yeah I like them.

— What else do you like?

— I like e-mail.

— Do you have a BlackBerry?

— I don't have a BlackBerry but I have e-mail and Peter I'm also working at a grocery store and a law firm have you ever had to worn ties when you've had to be an actor?

— Yeah, a bunch of times. Do you like to wear ties?

— I love to wear ties.

— I'm shooting in downtown LA. We'll walk off the set when you see me and go to Brooks Brothers.

— How many ties can I get?

— Two.

— Remember the last gift you gave me?

— No.

— It was the Playboy key chain showing a woman's butt.

— This is gonna be ties, Zach. No Playboy nothing. We're going classy now.

Pete checks his e-mail. But Zach's memory fascinates him. He probes it from a different direction, testing Zach's knowledge of historical events.

— When was George Washington elected?

— I wasn't alive then.

We arrive at Pete's house. We pick up the minivan and drive back to the hotel. Zach is still in the clouds. Like an alcoholic still feeling the booze, he goes on a memory bender — the parties he has been to that have been catered, with dates and name of the caterer, a shirt and tie we bought at Tommy Hilfiger's store in Los Angeles so Zach could look sharp for a friend's surprise birthday, the time we went to the La Brea Tar Pits.

— You've been so happy since we left Vegas, Zach.

— Yeah.

— Why?

— Because Gerry's almost here.

V

I am awoken by the giddy squeal of Zach at midnight.

Gerry has arrived. I go into their room.

Gerry and I hug. The pull is strong. I have forgotten how much I miss him, his laugh, his earnest presence, the possibility of extended conversation. He is tired, exhausted, a full day of graduate classes before flying here. He listens as Zach gushes about the trip but his eyes are slits. He slides into sleep in the queen-size bed in the room. Zach, in a cot next to the bed so he can be as close to Gerry as possible, ratchets down.

I go back and, just like Gerry, slide into a queen-size bed. I am exhausted as well, but for a brief moment before drifting off I think of the room next to me. I think of my twins, so night and day, the gap too great to ever be closed, and yet wishing, in a way I have not wished for in years, that I will wake up tomorrow and there will be no space between them, the imagined no longer imaginary.

Chapter 17

Picture Perfect

I

ZACH EMBARKS ON HIS usual morning inspection of the hotel pool. Then to the restaurant for a hearty breakfast he "put on the room bill." Gerry and I are left alone upstairs. Zach, before he left, told Gerry what resonated with him the most on the trip. It turns out to be Odessa, where he spent the night with the Chavez family. Gerry says he mentioned it four times.

— In other words the best part of the trip was when he wasn't with me.

— He was just really proud of doing something on his own.

— I know. I missed him. I went to bed at eight.

— What was the best part for you?

I relish retelling every detail:

— He saw the bungee jump at Six Flags. I said, "Zach, do you want to do it?" He said, "Yeah, I want to do it." Then I knew I was in deep shit and then I got mad at him on purpose to try to talk him out of it — "Zach, this is really dangerous, someone's gonna get hurt, you have no idea what you're doing, you could get sick. I don't think this is a good idea. It's REALLY STUPID." He looked at me and said, "No, I would really like to do it." So I looked at the guy working the thing and gave him the money, and I was scared shitless, and they put us in these rubber body suits with all these straps sticking out of you. It's like a bondage costume. You're in the prone position and they lift you 153 feet off the ground. And then who's going to pull the ripcord? Well, he's not gonna pull it because he's too scared. If he had to pull it, we'd still be up there. So I have to pull the ripcord. As I'm getting on, a woman is getting off and she says, "Boy, the one thing I would never do again is pull the ripcord. It's much better when someone else pulls it." So you get hoisted up and hoisted up and pretty far off the ground. You pull the ripcord, you know you're descending to your death. But we were totally bonded we were just arm in arm and he held my arm and you're swinging back and forth through the air, and it's one of those memories that I'll have forever, that you want to last forever.

Gerry gives that laugh of his I love. It is a laugh from the deepest part of the belly, without fake or fraud, as unconsciously honest as his brother is unconsciously honest.

Gerry looks like me. He has inherited my short stature, although he's a smidgen taller. He has my sturdy cheekbones and trim-lined nose. And he shares my moods, the something-stinks scowl passed from generation to generation of Bissingers. He has the same reaction to adversity that I do, a house-of-cards collapse where it's over, *just fucking over, and leave me the fuck alone,* and then an equally determined rebuilding. He also has within him his mother, her open-door, midwestern accessibility.

I know that Gerry and I are going to talk now about Zach. It is still the refrain of the trip, to talk to my children seriously and broach taboo topics whatever the repercussions. I was hoping the setting would be more cinematic, an empty church on a weekday maybe, outdoor steps at dusk, the kitchen table after dinner where we are the only ones left, and we pass a bottle of wine back and forth. A small room at the Beverly Hills Hilton is not what I had in mind. Gerry is also fiddling away at his laptop, checking e-mail while he talks, and I kind of wish he would fucking stop, but it's become habitual for anyone born after 1920.

Gerry is so affable anyway that I can't be mad at him. We've been in alignment all our lives except for that one year when I was working in Los Angeles. Because he spent much of his youth living with me, I made a major contribution to his growing up. I am proud of that. And yet for all his feet-to-the-floor mentality, every time I see him I can't quite believe he is here the way he is here.

In all the focus on Zach, I have often felt that the miracle of Gerry, perhaps a greater miracle than his brother in terms of survival and subsequent thriving, was never given the proper coming-out party. Because Zach weighed so little, Gerry's birth size of one pound and fourteen ounces made him seem like a behemoth. He too had severe complications at birth. His breathing was more advanced than his brother's, but he still needed supplemental oxygen and endured bouts on the ventilator. Yet he was so chubby when he came home that in a moment of acute parental paranoia, I fretted that maybe he was too chubby and would grow up to be chubby. I was afraid to ask the question, so my wife wearily asked it for me, knowing how pathetic it was. The doctors mercifully responded with dignity, spiked with a touch of their own weariness: "No, he's not too fat."

Gerry's learning curve was not always smooth. But he did reasonably well in elementary school and proved himself to be a very good athlete at youth soccer and Little League and tennis. I cheered him on with loud pride and burdened him with car-ride-home admonishment that left both of us sulky. I did feel better when he played on a travel soccer team and the Irish coach, a man of generally sweet temperament, morphed into such a monster that he simply left the team one game during halftime so disgusted by the play of twelve-year-olds. We parents coached the team ourselves, and I think it was the only fun all of us had the entire season.

Gerry's athletic skill created a false sense that he had overcome his birth trauma with no residual effects. Another universal ritual of fatherhood. There was no neglect in tracking his learning: he was tested on a regular basis. We did discover that he was one of those children who could grasp concepts as long as he had extra one-on-one, and not just the whirl of the classroom. But every time he scored a goal in soccer, or hit a home run, or made a spectacular catch in right field in the Little League all-star game, I was convinced that it would all be fine. I was frantic that it would be fine: if Gerry carried the fear of becoming his brother in even the slightest way, I carried the same fear. I needed a child who had inherited my traits of work and ambition and drive. I needed that certification as a parent. Children are our voyeuristic porno, the stuff of our parental fantasies. Instead of applauding all that Gerry had done, I only put pressure on him to do more.

When he was thirteen, he didn't do his math homework for two weeks. I only found out because of a note from the teacher. He was drowning at the private school he attended in Philadelphia. He had problems of processing that could no longer be buried in the backyard.

The hardest conversation I ever had with Gerry took place when I told him that I thought he might need to go to a specialized high school for slow learners. My opinion was sacred to Gerry. He always trusted me to protect his best interests. I did have his best interests. I gently gave him all the arguments. I told him it would not be fair to place him in a situation where he was set up for failure. The new school would give him time to process the vagaries of math and science and the grammatical strictures of writing. I told him kids there went on to college. I told him not to take it as a sign of weakness. I told him nobody was giving in or giving up.

But I was giving up to a degree. It was surrender, an admission that he too was a product of being thirteen weeks premature and weighing less than two pounds. He had gained three extra minutes, but he hadn't gained enough.

We got an application. We started filling it out at home on the dining room table. We called and made plans to visit. He then spoke up quietly, but with urgency. And it wasn't just urgency. There was anguish in his voice, that *whether you know this or not, Dad, you are going to destroy every image I have of myself and need for myself.*

— It isn't the right place for me.

— I think it is, sweetheart.

— I don't want to go. I don't want to change schools.

— I think you have to.

— I don't. I can do this.

— I am worried you will be set up for failure.

— Please let me do this.

— You will need tutors.

— I don't care.

We joined the ranks of three billion other parents and put him on Ritalin. I have no idea what good it did. Maybe it was just a placebo. Maybe it was penny candy, like the multicolored dots I had licked off white paper as a kid that tasted like sweetened chalk.

Gerry's determination changed him. He began to work harder. He conquered math. He went on to take calculus in college. I had never taken calculus. It sounded like a foot disease. It was a foot disease.

Some drug didn't motivate Gerry. It was his resolve to prove that I was wrong and that parents don't know everything about their children. He later told me he never felt as much pain in his life as he did when I suggested the special school, except perhaps for when I abandoned him to go to Los Angeles. He said he didn't want to disappoint me by having to change schools. He said he did not want to disappoint himself. What he did not say, but I knew, is that he didn't want to be remotely like his brother no matter how much he loved him.

II

Gerry and I talk some more in the cramped hotel room where it feels like tiptoeing around land mines, clothing and towels and bedspreads everywhere. He has stopped using the laptop. He is interested in what I learned on the trip not because it is my perspective, but because it adds another layer to his own perspective on his complicated brother. I go first.

— Zach needs his own life. I really realized that in Las Vegas that being in the right type of environment and private group home is the right thing to do.

— Kind of confirmed that? Or you weren't sure before?

— I wasn't sure but he needs to be with friends. They may not be the kind of friends you have.

— Probably not.

— But I think he needs to be with other people.

— But I also think he needs to be with people who, whatever you want to call it, are normal. He loves hanging around with people who aren't on his IQ level. I don't think he gets as much satisfaction with maybe some of those kids he went to school with.

— He loves the dances and the outings.

— Do you really think you could put him in a home?

— I don't know.

— I think you do know.

Gerry is speaking to me with authority; he is reversing the roles of father and son. I welcome the switch because he is such a crucial cog in it all. I also welcome it because I need more help making the decision than Debra alone can give. It will not come tomorrow. It may not come for ten years. But it will come.

All I thought I had sorted out on the trip about Zach's future hasn't been sorted out at all. I thought I had figured it out in those moments of pitch-perfect quiet, maybe in Texas, maybe in New Mexico, maybe on that empty two-lane bisecting the mountains of Arizona with the clouds offering up darkness and light. A private group home with his friends seemed so right. But nothing is ever right with a child like Zach. Damned if you do. Damned if you don't.

— Vegas and the casinos were kind of overwhelming to him. I wanted it to be perfect but it wasn't. The show *Mystère*. He tried really hard to take it all in, and I look over at him, and I kind of get teary because he's trying really hard, and I think of all that he misses in life.

— But you can't look at it like that. I looked at it like that for a long time.

— You did?

— And then you start to feel guilty.

— What? That you were the first one out?

— I struggle with that a lot sometimes. I guess when I look at it from the perspective of all the things that I get to do, and he doesn't, I think I just feel guilty.

— It was pretty arbitrary, those three minutes.

— It sure was.

Gerry *has* inherited from his mother and me his dogged work ethic. He *has* laid out the tracks of his life with the same precision I laid mine out — getting his master's, becoming a full-time elementary school teacher for several years, then getting a PhD in administration to become a principal. Like me he often mumbles. But now he is making a confession I always sensed he wanted to make but never could.

— It's always "You're a twin. Oh, what does your brother do? He works at a law firm. Oh, is he a lawyer?" Then I explain he stocks supplies, then a lot of people feel badly and I say, "Oh, you don't have to feel bad." And then going through that exchange a lot of times you start to feel, "Why wasn't it me?" When I was younger, I guess I felt a lot like it should have been me. Then I went through this embarrassment of him a lot.

— Do you ever feel embarrassed about him now?

— No. I think sometimes I try to control him. So maybe subconsciously I do feel embarrassed by him. But not really. Just let him be him. Now I think he's really happy, which is the best thing. It's not that he doesn't get to drive a car or didn't go to college.

— I guess it boils down to how you define a life.

— You define life by happiness. That's what life is about. For everyone that's a different thing. I look at some of the kids I work with student teaching and they may not have the same limitations as him but they have nothing, no support. No parents. Nothing. So he has been lucky to have all of that.

— I guess I'm the one who still feels guilty. I feel guilty that he misses out on so much. I just wish I knew him better. I know him, but I wish I could break through. I learned so much about him on the trip. He gave me so many surprises. I still wish I could have the same conversations with him that I have with you so we can interpret and talk and analyze.

— But he can't do that, and you can't expect him to do that. It's unfair to you and it's really unfair to him.

— But every parent has aspirations for their child.

— The basis of my relationship with Zach has always been different than my relationship with anyone else, and a lot of that means communication in a different way or doing things — taking him out to eat, telling if you've seen someone he knows and what they are wearing and where they work and what floor they work on. Just doing things together has been the connection.

I finally realize I've had it backwards. All my life I have had it backwards. Whatever happens with Zach, I know I can no longer think in terms of what is in my best interests, even if I think they are also in his best interests. Zach will be where he will be. Because he needs to be. Because he wants to be. Because as Oliver Sacks said, all children, whatever the impairment, are still propelled by the need to make themselves whole. They may not get there, but they forever try on their own terms.

III

Zach returns to the room. As the three of us discuss our plans for the day ahead, I see something I hadn't noticed before. It is a picture of my parents propped up against the TV with an inscription to the side: "Good Times Were Had by All." I am guessing it was taken three or four years before they died. They are shoulder by shoulder with the Nantucket house behind them. My father smiles broadly. His chest is slightly thrust out as if he were back in the Marines. He swells with pride. My mother is diminutive, a whisper. But she is leaning ever so slightly into my father, and part of the beam of his smile is that he will always take care of her for as long as he can.

In the aftermath of my parents' deaths, I had placed the picture in the bookcase in the family room in Philadelphia. I had passed it every day for almost five years, most of the time sweeping by it in the earnest haste of the mundane, but sometimes lingering in front of it to see what I wanted to see — the urgency of their mutual need, the infinity of companionship, their love of Nantucket, survivors of marital warfare who finally realized it is just easier to put down the arms and declare permanent truce.

I am shocked to see the picture in a guest room at the Beverly Hills

Hilton. It doesn't take long to figure out the source. Just before we left Philadelphia, Zach quietly placed it in his magic knapsack and waited to take it out until we arrived here.

— What made you bring it?

— I just wanted to I thought it was nice we all stayed together here remember?

— It is nice. It's beautiful. Thank you, Zach.

— Oh you're welcome.

It was in Los Angeles at this hotel on Thanksgiving of 2000 that we as a family last came together — my parents, my three boys, my sister and her husband, Mark, and daughter, Sarah. There is no coincidence in our repeat visit: I wanted to return to the hotel to see what feelings, if any, would be evoked in both myself and the twins by staying here again.

Lisa and I were already living in Los Angeles in 2000. The rest of the family came in from their respective departure points — Philadelphia, New York, Nantucket. Lisa and I wanted the trip to be special, the highlight of a time we knew would be short-lived because of the daily bloodletting that was *NYPD Blue*. We spent Wednesday night on the road at the famed Madonna Inn in San Luis Obispo, where each room was modeled after a certain bizarre theme — the Jungle Rock room with rocks everywhere like a mountain slide, the Golfer's Room with a carpet in the shape of a narrow and winding fairway leading to the bathroom, the Caveman room that really did resemble a cave, and on and on and on. The place was strange and creepy, no real fun getting up in the middle of the night to pee and smashing into a boulder. My father was ebullient, endlessly energetic, staying up until the wee hours with my sister at the hotel bar, getting so drunk they might as well have been speaking in tongues. We had dinner Thanksgiving day in the enchanting town of Cambria and spent the night there. Then we went to San Simeon and the Hearst Castle.

My father was a joyous man at this point in his life since he was no longer working. But there was extra joy that holiday, and I could tell it was for my benefit. He knew I was struggling, and he was worried. He would never say it directly to me, but he wanted to stop my bleeding.

My mother's mind was already very hazy then. You could see it loosening. But she was determined with great nobility to keep up.

The Hearst Castle was a maze of narrow stairways. The physical exertion was becoming difficult for my mother. There was an elevator, but she refused to take it, just as she refused her usual impulse to stay in her hotel room and take to her bed. She wore her Gloria Vanderbilt hat. She spent hours applying makeup. In watching her navigate those narrow steps with both hands on the lifelines of the guardrails, you could see the fight still within her.

On the trip back to Los Angeles from San Simeon, she rode in a car with Lisa and my sister and niece. She regaled them with her wit and trenchant observations of others and word games and songs from Broadway musicals. All the best of her was on display in that car.

The day before my parents left, we went to Universal Studios. We insisted to my mother that she stay behind to get some rest. She refused again. As we were about to get on the Back to the Future ride, she announced that she wanted to join us. She was adamant. She said it looked like fun. We believed her because we so wanted to believe her.

Midway through the ride, she began to panic. "Get me the hell out of here!" she grimaced. There was nothing we could do. My sister held her hand and coaxed her the rest of the way. My father asked her how it had been. "Awful," she spat out. It became clear that she had no idea why she was on the ride, and where exactly she was.

The next day, trying to catch an early-morning flight back to New York, she fainted in the hotel bathroom. As in other fainting incidents, there was no discernible cause. But in this instance I knew — the exertion of the trip had pushed her too far. She wanted to be part of the family, not some invalid. It was her last hurrah. It was the last hurrah for all of us. There would be no more group trips to Los Angeles or anywhere else. Eighteen months later we would no longer be a family unless you included attendance at my parents' funerals.

For the first time since their deaths, I feel a sense of closure. Or at least a reckoning. The inability to say goodbye to both of them, the emptiness that accompanied their equally convulsive deaths, has loosened.

The bitterness gives way to this pinpoint of memory nearly a decade ago here in this very hotel, where love and laughter flowed so freely.

If Zach hadn't brought the picture along, I would not have reached closure. Intermittent memories would have popped up, but because of the photo, and seeing my parents side by side in love and peace, they were now with me in my own love and peace of who they always were. Zach knew that would be the result. Otherwise why would he have brought the picture? I could have but it was Zach who did, placing it against the television as a symbol of their eternal presence.

Good times were had by all.

Zach made sure that would never be forgotten.

Chapter 18

Zach and Gerry

COUSIN PETE INVITES US to the set of *Hancock* on location in downtown Los Angeles where a huge conflagration of bullets and fire and blood is to explode between the police and a gang of bank robbers. At the moment, filming is between takes. We shelter underneath a cabana-style awning that you see in fancy resorts where corpulent men with wormy curls of upper chest hair read the *Financial Times* next to women too young to read.

Pete watches the scenes as they are being filmed on two monitors feeding into the cameras. A row of producers — Michael Mann and Akiva Goldsman and Scott Stuber — sit behind him in a row in high-backed chairs with the grim seriousness of Stalin, Roosevelt, and Churchill at Yalta. The fate of the world is not at stake, but a 150-million-dollar-budget film is, which in the minds of these men is equally important. Behind them is another row of flunkies whispering into their wrists. I think they may be finding out when the break in filming is and what's for lunch. Equally serious business.

The lead, Will Smith, isn't in the current scene. He is dressed in a black neoprene suit playing a dissolute superhero tired of his job. Zach is in the cabana beside Pete, and his man crush once again has him seriously stoked. Pete gives Zach the megaphone and tells him that he can yell "action" for the next scene. He yells too early, and chaos prematurely erupts.

— Zach! Zach! Zach! You need to wait.

— Oh sorry.

Then he giggles.

Gerry hangs to the side, not wanting to step on his brother's star turn. These moments of lucidity in Zach are riveting, and Gerry refuses to trample upon them. He instead laughs appreciatively at his brother's quirks, Zach's hard drive suddenly equipped with a new Intel processor. Gerry is dying to meet Will Smith but is too shy to introduce himself. Zach recognizes Will Smith from his music. He is not too shy to introduce himself.

— HEY WILL SING "MEN IN BLACK" FOR ME!

He looks at Zach and laughs as if it is some off-key practical joke. Zach looks intently at Will Smith, waiting for him to sing. Will Smith declines. Zach stops paying any attention to him. Why should he if Will won't sing? It's a song he wants. He's not interested in idolizing a man whose birthday he doesn't even know.

We leave the set and walk the downtown promenade of Santa Monica. We duck into a Barnes & Noble at the far end. Gerry pokes and picks, still tired out from his cross-country flight. Zach speed-walks to the map section. He buys one of those combination movie star/crime scene maps. It is a curious purchase for Zach given what it highlights. He must have chosen it by process of elimination because he already has half a dozen maps of Los Angeles. He also chose it to further concretize Los Angeles with physical symbols. He was drawn to it in particular because the map showed actual locations and addresses of people.

Unfortunately those people were movie stars, whom he has no interest in at all, their celebrity status irrelevant. The same is true of crime, where his eternal innocence and optimism shield him from the ghoulish desire to see the sites of horrible murders and fatal drug overdoses

222 • FATHER'S DAY

whose killers and victims he has never heard of anyway. Why someone with trace brain damage has his priorities in far better shape than the rest of us, who thrive on such idiocy, is a question for psychologists and philosophers.

Like Gerry and me. We ask Zach if we can see the map because we *do* thoroughly enjoy both movie stars and crime scenes. It is surprisingly comprehensive, particularly on the crime side. The location of the alleged O. J. Simpson murders is shown, of course, as well as the Charles Manson murders. But there are some other incidents that might otherwise go forgotten. Like David Spade being attacked by his personal assistant with a taser. Or the death of George Reeves, who played Superman on television. Or Oliver Stone's arrest for driving under the influence and felony hash possession. Or the somewhat symmetrical discovery of the body of producer Don Simpson on the toilet *with a copy* of Oliver Stone's biography in his hands and twenty-eight different chemical substances inside his body including Valium, Vicodin, and Ativan. The map also comprehensively pinpoints the homes of movie stars, although there are some on-the-bubble stretches — Monte Hall, Nick Lachey, Jaclyn Smith, Peri Gilpin.

I hand the map back to Zach because it is his.

— Oh you and Gerry can keep it.

— Then why did you buy it in the first place?

— I don't know I just did I liked it shows where people live.

— You barely looked at it.

— Oh.

— Do you know who Tom Cruise is?

— No who is he?

— Do you know who Cher is?

— No who is he?

We continue walking the promenade. There is something aimless about the three of us, perhaps because the trip is winnowing down to the final full day tomorrow. Gerry is preoccupied with school. Zach is already talking about returning to work at the law firm and the grocery store. I am distracted, thinking of when the boys were truly little boys with one on the left of me and one on the right as we ambled, fingers locked into fingers in the divine illusion of permanence. The long shadows of my mother and father follow us since we all walked the promenade together in that long-ago time of 2000. It is hard to think they are not here, except that they're not. But the picture Zach carried with him for over three thousand miles helps me visualize them now.

We navigate toward Ocean Drive, past the Travelodge and the Pacific Sands and the Ivy restaurant, where the rich and famous have their permanent tables far enough from the sidewalk so as to not be accosted but close enough to earn the excited whisper of recognition.

We head for the Santa Monica Pier. We go through a piss-scented tunnel. We set foot on the pier and are hit with the scent of creosote and suntan lotion and funnel cakes and sausages pinging and popping on greasy grills. There is a flow of a breeze. We stop and take the breeze in, as we lean against the pier railings out over the water. The view stuns me because I never ever associate Los Angeles with the ocean. I forget it is there like you tend to forget that most of Los Angeles is there. People move through the sand with surprising lightness and agility playing volleyball. Others stretch themselves out to the anatomical limit to sunbathe, their own torture rack. Others walk along the edge of the beach in sundresses to immerse their toes in undulating waves creased with soft silver. They look incredibly happy, kind of like Bette Davis at the end of *Whatever Happened to Baby Jane?* after she has buried her sister in the sand. It is still California.

Down an incline of the pier is a small amusement arcade called Pacific Park. There is a roller coaster in a spaghetti of tracks in faded yellow. There is a Ferris wheel. There is a green contraption called the Sea Dragon that rocks back and forth faster and faster until it reaches its apex and then plummets down and repeats the motion. A store called the Bubba Gump Shrimp Company sells crappy T-shirts in uneven piles that have thoroughly been picked through. A mesh basket is filled with cheap basketballs. Stuffed animals hang like carcasses. The smell of creosote thickens.

I have a sudden memory of when I was a little boy in a sixties summer of Nantucket, and the carnival came to town, all the equipment offloaded from the ferry in tractor-trailers and pieced together into rickety, momentary magic. I can feel a ten-dollar bill slipped into my hand by my father as we ride in a green jeep to the field behind the high school where he drops off my sister and me and says he will be back in two hours. The freedom is the most I have ever felt in my life to that point, the barkers barking their preprogrammed deliveries. We follow the same ritual the next night, only my father goes with us. He spends a good hour trying to knock down all the bowling pins to win a stuffed animal. Then we ride the Ferris wheel together until it gets stuck, and he clutches me around the shoulder as he so often did.

I remember riding my bike to the field the very next morning to find everything packed up and gone, already on the ferry to what seemed like some distant port, Hyannis maybe or New Bedford or Fall River. I remember the ache in my heart staring at that empty field, wondering to myself why it all had to disappear so quickly, not just the rides but also my father. Perhaps all sons feel that way about their fathers, and all fathers feel that way about their sons.

Gerry and Zach walk side by side and wait in line for the Sea Dragon. I stand near the mesh container of cheap basketballs and wave to them. Gerry whispers something into Zach's ear, and they both laugh.

I watch as they take their places on the yellow plastic seats, and Gerry protectively pulls the safety bar over them. Gerry is wearing a red T-shirt and Zach a blue one. Gerry is unshaven with a small but knowing smile across his lips. Zach is shaven — it is always important to look good at amusement parks — and steely-eyed as he braces himself for liftoff. The Sea Dragon begins to rock back and forth, slowly at first, then faster and faster and higher and higher. I shade my eyes against the hazy sun. The Sea Dragon is at its peak now, then swinging down with speed and thrust. I hear screams and yells. I cannot find the boys, lost in the blur of the downward force. But then I see them. Zach's arm is extended and clutching Gerry's hand. His eyes are welded shut, but he is alive with laughter as the Sea Dragon plunges. Gerry is laughing even harder, his mouth a sweetened oval.

There are my twins, born so beaten and bloody on a sweltering Saturday afternoon a quarter century ago, now merged into one. Three minutes does define a life, but never in the way I had always imagined. So many times I never thought I would get there. But we are a family, all different, sometimes divided, sometimes in pain, but unconquerable.

Father's Day.

Chapter 19

Reality Bites

ZACH AND I DRIVE to LAX two days later on Monday morning. We land in Philadelphia about 8:00 P.M. He is staying at my house tonight so I can drive him to work in the morning. On the way, he calls his mom, who has already scheduled at least a dozen social activities for him over the next month. She starts listing them over the phone. She is loading up his life, making sure he is never idle. His mom and I could never have stayed married, but I sometimes wonder what life would be like if we had, and I could have been with the boys without the stop-and-start.

On Tuesday I take Zach to the law firm. He is in the passenger seat, just as he was for the last two weeks. But it isn't the same without the minivan, the shaking of the steering wheel at anything over sixty miles an hour, the spilling of hot coffee from the cup holders in fitful spasms, the sweet-sour fragrance of rental car deodorizer. The freedom of being on the road is always an illusion, since even at the height of escape you eventually have to go back to where you started. But you still lose yourself in that exact moment of where you are. Until you come home.

The drive from my house to his office shows the best of Philadelphia — the wind of Kelly Drive along the Schuylkill River with a rower dipping his oar into water drizzled with morning light, the smooth dolomite limestone of the Art Museum, the marble and granite of City Hall that was once the world's tallest habitable building and over time became the world's most uninhabitable habitable building, a boon for cats in the basement catching rats.

Merely seeing it brings the discomfort of familiarity, back into the utilitarian rote of a thousand trips on this route and a thousand more. Zach is still and silent, preparing himself for work and going over his mental checklist — not too much chitchat with the partners, focus on the tasks at hand, no more requests to pat a bald head no matter how much it beckons. He seems miles away from me, immersed in the immutable definitions of his environment. I feel like we are attached by little more than a thin piece of string at the wrists, and it is about to break. I always feel this way when I drop him off — the divorced parent's lament — but I feel it more acutely than ever now, as I face the finality of something that became sacred. At least to me.

— You know I love you, right?

How many times am I going to say that?

Forever I guess.

— Yeah.

— I just don't like that I don't see you as much when we get back here.

— Yeah.

— Your mom makes good plans for you. She wants your life to be busy and full. But you have to remember you have a father, right? I make good plans for you too when I see you each week.

— Yeah.

— Sometimes you forget that because you get so busy.

— Sometimes I forget but I know you're my dad.

— I wish I had more time with you.

— Yeah but I don't have any friends my age who are in Philly the last time I remember I had friends here was when I was nine at Jenks like that guy Michael Lepore he came over a couple of times I remember I had friends in Milwaukee like the Carter boys I felt like in those days I had those friends.

It is true. He has no friends where I live.

I honk at another car. There is no reason to honk. I am beginning to fill with the fallback of anger when distressed. I fight it off. He has seen it too many times. He has work to do. Zach keeps looking nervously at his watch.

— You'll be on time.

— I'm always on time I went in late that one day when Grandma Laine was here that Thursday June 21 of '07 I had breakfast with her I had breakfast that morning I told them I was going to be a little late they were okay with it they were okay with it then because I wanted to say goodbye to Grandma Laine before she was going so they were okay.

The car stops on the sidewalk in front of his office building. Zach gathers his things. He says something to me he never said during our journey.

— I love you Dad we had a fun trip.

The words fill me up, what I so hoped for with Zach and was never quite sure we had achieved until now.

— Yes, we did.

— Bye Dad.

— Bye, sweetie. Give me a kiss.

He bends his neck into mine. I kiss him on the top of the head. Every time I do this I think back to when he was born and what he went through. How could anyone have such strength as he does?

I watch as he gets out of the car and walks in his Chaplinesque style with a green bag draped over his shoulder. He does not turn around and wave or come back to the car just to say one more time how great it all was. I didn't think he would.

Now Zach is stooped low and running as if he is dodging tacklers. He hurries through a revolving door. I capture a final glimpse of him, mostly of the green shoulder bag, before he disappears. He is gone, vanished, swallowed up into the building that is his life for today. A feeling comes over me, one I thought I would never ever have: I need Zach more than he needs me. He has reached that point of self-assurance.

I saw it unfold during the trip, all the times he asserted himself by wanting to be with someone else besides me or venture further and further into the discovery of his own self. He was gentle about it. He is always gentle. But I should have seen it coming. Zach gave me fair warning. When he decided he wanted to spend the night with the Chavez family in Odessa, he gave a brilliant closing argument on what it was like to stay in hotels with only me for company:

It's not much fun.

I sit in the car outside his office. I wonder what Zach is doing at this very moment, which elevator button he has pushed, what supplies he needs to stock, what people have welcomed him back, whether he has told them anything about the trip. I think of all the observations he made and all the empathy he gave, seeing and feeling more than I ever thought possible because I had summarily dismissed so much of him — his perfect summation of the Peggy Lee song, his hand on my shoulder when I lost the camera bag, how he spotted the row of ducklings in Oklahoma City, how resolutely he guided me out of the interstate torture of Chicago and Phoenix and Los Angeles, his conclusions that love is love and life is life.

What I think about the most, ironically perhaps, is the disaster of Vegas, as we were waiting for dinner and I probed him with questions until he stopped me with a voice that was not strident but firm.

The reason I don't like when you ask the questions is that sometimes I don't know how to really answer them.

So much of his life had been spent in captivity — me, his mother, his teachers, other adults — to corral his behavior within acceptable bounds. To declare himself, to protect himself and stand up for himself in front of his father, took courage. It was also his way of signifying his separation from me.

We normally associate success with intellect and riches and status — an Ivy League education, a fat-assed salary, a house twice as big as we need, a membership in a golf club with a long waiting list, gold-embossed party invitations to ten-thousand-dollar-a-pop political fundraisers we attend in order to say we attended them. Up until this trip, that was my own definition.

We assume that people like Zach have no interior, that they're embalmed in their concrete, working rudimentary jobs. They just exist in the tiny Gaza Strip that is given over to the different and the disabled, shunted away behind the psychic fence that we Normals have erected out of unease or disdain. Zach is truly loved by many. He is lucky to have an extended family of hundreds all over the planet. But he is forever different and difference causes fear whether conscious or unconscious.

Zach *has* an interior life. So do many — most — of the others we relegate to that Gaza Strip. He thinks, he feels, he intuits, he sees life through his own idiosyncratic design. It is not a design of abstraction or interpretation. He takes puzzle pieces that do not fit and works like hell to make them fit. In our minds, the way he has assembled the world looks like a piece from over here and a piece from over there jammed together in some impossible pattern. But in his mind they all fit, each word he hears connecting to a moment and a memory. Somebody mentions an amusement park. He has been there and off he goes, reciting all the rides he went on and then listing all the other amusement parks he has been to. It's the same with the mention of a restaurant. Or asking someone if he knows anybody at the law firm where he works, only a matter of time before he will recognize a name and then another and then another one.

"Every day he wakes up with broken wings," Lisa once said. "And every day he learns how to fly." It is a beautiful statement. But after driving across the country with him, I am not sure it is entirely true. I no longer think his wings are broken. He may skim perilously close to the ground. He may bump up and bump down and bruise himself. The landing may require a mayday. But he can fly. And sometimes he soars, leaving all of us down below to watch as he seizes every skill within him to skim the clouds.

If I learned anything about Zach during the trip, perhaps it is simply this:

Never doubt his sense of direction. He knows where he wants to go, whether on the grid of a map or anywhere else in life. He knows what he needs to do to get there. He will figure most of it out.

Like everyone else, I will one day become too old and sick for my own good or anyone else's. I think it's a pretty good guess I will be a cranky son of a bitch. Lisa has told me several times that she is determined to die first to avoid the misery of taking care of me. Like my father before me, I will be terrified. Like my father before me, I will know that I am dying. Like my father before me, I will lie awake thinking about what I did in my life and think about the terrible mistakes I made. But unlike my father, I will also think about what will forever reside in my heart. It won't be the sweet but ephemeral irrelevance of the Pulitzer and *Friday Night Lights*. It will be the times I broke through to a place I never knew existed. My beautiful Gerry and Caleb will be with me. So will my beautiful Zach. He will take my hand in his. His grip will be gentle. Neither of us will ever want to let go. We will both recall.

   — Remember the time Dad you and me drove cross-country I remember that.

   — Of course I remember it. I will never forget it.

   — Did you have fun?

   — I had the best fun ever, Zach. What about you?

   — I had fun I liked it.

   — What did you like the best?

   — Because it was just the two of us that's what I liked.

   — I love you, Zach.

   — I know.

   — How do you know?

   — You have to love me because you're my dad.

   — I love you because you're my son.

   — Yeah.

   — So let's do it again right now. We'll just go.

   — I'll think about it.

— *What do you mean think about it? Let's go. Let's go. Let's get out of here!*

— *Maybe.*

— *Come on, Zach. You know we'll have a blast!*

— *Only if we fly.*

Epilogue

MY TRIP ACROSS the country with Zach took place in the summer of 2007. Since this is a book I had thought about for two decades, I believed the words would flow easily, take at most a year to complete with publication in 2009 or 2010. But the process was difficult and painful. Writing about the personal is fraught with fear, a vastly different fear than I ever have experienced before as an author.

I felt the need to get every word right, to capture my son Zach and my relationship with him without understatement or overstatement. I also decided that this book must be completely candid no matter how difficult at times, to get at the truth of my heart. That meant confessing my own faults. It meant confessing my feelings about having a severely disabled son, so complex and contradictory, because love always has limits.

I also had to be completely honest about Zach, the amazing strengths I discovered during our journey as well as the considerable debilities that will never change. I also bore the million-pound weight of knowing that Zach, even if he read *Father's Day,* would not understand it. That gave me incredible license, as well as incredible responsibility.

With all these emotions to juggle and worry about and agonize over, a one-year project became a four-year one. I needed that time; the book could not have been written without it. Had I rushed, *Father's*

Day at best would have been careless and exaggerated, nowhere close to the truth. Whatever exactly that is.

In the year 2011, Zach's comprehension is still limited. Any abstract interaction is still difficult for him. When asked emotionally based questions about why he likes something, or what it feels like to do something, he almost always answers with a one-word "yes" or "no." He still fires away with his tracer-bullet questions of where are you working and what are you wearing and when is your birthday. He continues to often speak in disparate rambles. But he is teaching himself to enter conversations gently instead of crash-landing into them. His vocabulary continues to expand because of his habit of silently soaking in every word and phrase he hears and later trying them on for size.

Two and a half years ago Lisa took an administrative job at New York University in Abu Dhabi. After much agonized discussion, we decided she could not turn down this opportunity, the stimulation of being surrounded by brilliant people, the once-in-a-lifetime chance to be on the inside of starting up an unprecedented institution.

She is now a consultant to the university assigned to special projects. She still spends long stretches in Abu Dhabi, but her role gives her much more time in Philadelphia. The house becomes alive when she is here, filling up with her impromptu singing, her vivaciousness and humor.

When Lisa first left for Abu Dhabi, I was in shock. It seemed surreal given the bond between us and all the challenges we'd shared: the deaths of my parents, her struggle with breast cancer, the death of her father, and my mild but ever-present bipolarity. Without her, the house became ghostly, just myself and the dog.

Several days after she left, I picked up Zach at the nearby train station. We drove home without a word. I pulled the car into the garage. Zach looked at me and broke the somber silence.

— Well just a couple of empty-nesters.

He had heard the term from his mother. I don't think he quite knew what it meant. It didn't matter. It was said of Zach during the trip that he has a sixth sense for sincerity. But he also possesses a seventh sense of saying the right words at the right time even if he doesn't know they are the right words.

I laughed for the first time since Lisa had left.

It is Christmas of 2011. I have given Zach a map of South Africa so he can see where his brother Caleb will be spending the spring semester as an exchange student at the University of Cape Town. It is also a way of including him, without actually including him, in the trip the rest of the family — Lisa and Gerry and myself — will take this April to visit Caleb. Given Zach's continued propensity to fidget and gasp and talk aloud to himself when confined for hours with nothing to do, I don't think he can possibly survive the twenty-hour trip to Cape Town. The family has taken other trips overseas, and I have always asked Zach to come. But it has been mere lip service because he's never shown any interest in going. I make the same pro forma gesture toward South Africa.

— Zach, would you like to come?

— Is Gerry going?

— Gerry is going.

— I'd like to go.

It is not the answer I expected.

He will hate the flight. He will end up glued to the ceiling somewhere. Or somehow work his way into the cockpit in a pocket of severe turbulence and ask the captain if he always wears a hat to work. Or go up and down the aisles asking all the passengers their birthdays.

— It's twenty hours, Zach.

— That's okay.

— I'm worried it will be very hard for you.

— I'll be good.

— Plus you won't know anyone in South Africa.

— I'll know Caleb.

— Can you really sit still for that long?

— I'll sit still I promise.

He no longer wants to be left behind. He is part of the family, and he doesn't want to be excluded from anything we do because of his disabilities. It is important to him. I can tell from the tone of his voice, a quiet yearning to be further liberated from the assumptions I have so often made about him.

When we go to South Africa this April, Zach will be with us. It will not be easy. I have talked with him about ways to handle the first leg in particular, sixteen hours to Johannesburg: sleep for as long as he can since the plane leaves at night; play Angry Birds, which he has recently discovered, on my iPad; bring along his favorite film, *Pee-wee's Big Adventure,* to watch on my computer. I will also call his doctor and try to get enough Ambien to lull a herd of elephants to sleep.

Gerry will sit next to him in coach and help him when he struggles. It is a reflection of his protectiveness over Zach and his ability to cut off his brother's penchant for pestering when he becomes antsy.

It is also a reflection of the career path Gerry has chosen after getting his master's in education from Penn: being a full-time elementary school teacher in the Haddonfield school system teaching fourth grade, as well as going nights to Temple University for his PhD in educational administration to fulfill the goal of being a principal.

So I don't actually worry about the effect of the travel on Zach. But if Gerry thought two weeks with Zach in a car traversing from east to west would be a very long time, wait until he sits next to him for twenty hours.

Zach excitedly tells people he is going to South Africa to "see my brother Caleb and some animals." Which is also his way of saying that he is ready to make a gigantic leap beyond the borders of the familiar. When we drove to Los Angeles, the familiar excited him the most. His eagerness to loosen his grip on the repeated rituals of his life, to face the unknown in a place unknown to him, is the best Christmas present I have ever received.

He has also made strides in his work life. He still has his part-time job at the supermarket bagging groceries. I have yet to watch him in the actual process because I know I could never bear it. But Gerry recently saw him at work and came back excited to report that his brother is amazingly fast and focused. Much like he learned to play Super Mario Brothers by memorizing all the moves.

Zach left the part-time gig at the law firm. Much of what he did there was outsourced. The powers that be were kind and decent to still keep him on, but he was consigned to the basement with little to do.

Nine months ago he began working two days a week at the *Philadelphia Daily News* as an office clerk. He delivers interoffice mail and stocks supplies and changes the water cooler. He knew just about everyone at the paper beforehand because of his long history with the *Daily News* and the *Inquirer*. I was concerned that the job would be a dip back into too much of an old shoe for Zach and turn into a social event. But he works with head-down diligence. The very bald head of the executive editor, Larry Platt, remains untouched. He doesn't dawdle at the desks of the reporters and editors, except to wish someone a happy birthday.

When Zach worked at the law firm, he always said the job was fine, no matter how much or how little he was actually occupied. He never showed any initiative to do more because of his fear of novelty.

The opposite is true at the *Daily News*. He recently expressed interest in answering the phones when somebody calls the main number in the newsroom. It will be a complicated task for Zach because of the mechanics of transferring calls as well as the intricacies of directing the caller to the right department. But given the eternal gruffness of newsrooms, a reporter friend pointed out, "he couldn't possibly do worse than it already is."

Just as he showed on the trip, Zach still seizes life with joy, the promise of good things to come. Nor has he lost his innocence.

The night before Christmas, he made sure a glass of milk and a plate of cookies were left by the fireplace for Santa Claus. Zach is twenty-eight now, and I grilled him about whether he really believes there is a Santa who stuffs himself down the chimney with presents. I tried from every angle. He still clung to his conviction, although I did stump him.

— How come sometimes when you go to the mall you see two Santas?

— Maybe they're brothers.

Touché.

I wonder if Zach really thinks there is a Santa Claus but believes more in what the myth represents, the power of possibility in life and the thirst to transform it into reality. It is the credo by which he lives.

With each passing year, Zach becomes more perceptive. His social grace has exceeded my every expectation. A marriage counselor — and trust me, there have been many — once told me that the best barometer of future history is past history. But Zach tears up his history every day.

He came into the world covered in all that glistening blood, unable to breathe, kept alive by the metallic machines and monitors of medicine. But those tiny brown eyes were open, and if you looked into those eyes, you could see even then the steel of his soul, the belief in the possible.

There is no rose-colored ending to any of this. There is no pretty little package with a tidy bow. He will never drive a car. He will never marry. He will never have children. I still fear for his future. I still think of him sitting alone one day under a naked bulb in the freezing light. He is not the child I wanted. But he is no longer a child anyway. He is a man, the most fearless I have ever known, friendly, funny, freaky, unfathomable, forgiving, fantastic, restoring the faith of a father in all that can be.

Zach's Acknowledgments

(As dictated to his father)

Well I am thankful for all the people in the world who have done so much for me.

Family okay so you Buzz Bissinger Paul Nussbaum Molly Nussbaum Matt Nussbaum Gerry Bissinger because he's my twin brother Lisa Smith Caleb Bissinger oh my mom Deb Nussbaum because she's done so much for me like she arranges all my activities how about Mark and Annie and Sarah Grandma Laine okay Uncle Mike and Susan and Barrett and Nick and David oh and Alexander and even though I'll never see him again Grandpa Stone because he married his dead wife's nurse uh trying to think Goggie and Ellie they died Uncle Bobo because he's been great to me I've known him since I was born he had me to his pool Winkie and Peggy because Winkie is very funny he hates the dog and I do want Muff and Sally and Larry.

Friends whom I am thankful for Shanna and Christy and Maria and Michelle Joan Clark and Marvin oh and Amy Cooper I like a lot and Neal Hinshillwood and Carolyn Beulah she drives me to ShopRite.

Okay let's put from the paper Larry Platt Greg Osberg um Gar Joseph Lorenzo Signe Wilkinson Stu Bykofsky you know who else Molly Eichel and Ellen Gray because I see those people yeah Denise Gallo Dan Rodgers Rob Copes who I used to work with.

At the *Inquirer* there is Allison Steele Andy Maykuth Tony Auth Rick Nichols Mike Vitez and Maureen Fitzgerald Martha Woodall Dan Rubin Karen Heller I like Mike Leary Vernon Loeb I like all the wonderful things he's done like take me for car rides and had me over-night to his house October 4 of '09 Linda Lloyd oh yeah Bill Marimow I like Bill Marimow because he e-mails with me Brian Tierney because remember that time he took me up to his office it was on his birthday twenty-first of February '07 Paul Davies because he would ride the train with me you know who also I like Walter Naedele because he would ride the train with me.

I am thankful for these other friends okay Fen Montaigne Steve Lopez Lymans the Chavezes I'm trying to think of who else Patty Loeb the Eichels yeah Joey Logan Steve Stecklow yup Larry Ceisler and Lina yup well what makes them such special friends Larry has been great to me he's had me to his office party I've been up to his office a lot the Cardamones and the Hirshorns and the Hasses and the Hankins be-cause Art took me flying in his plane Sarah Neil Oxman Kevin Feeley Arthur Makadon because he was so great to me he bought me that blazer for my twenty-fifth birthday August 21 of '08 another person we should put in there is Lois Blinkhorn Dave Taylor Doug Robinson and Arlene Nancy Cooney the Bonettes and the O'Donnells the Manochis the Beltons the Weinsteins and the Potts who used to live in Haddon-field and Bill Getman he's the pastor at First Presbyterian where I'm a deacon and Mister Claus I remember Dad talked to his class he did it twice December 13 2004 and September 20 '05 Dave Payne that's it for now.

Buzz's Acknowledgments

First and foremost comes my editor at Houghton Mifflin Harcourt, Eamon Dolan. We have now worked on three books together. *Father's Day* was by far the most challenging because it was such a departure from my usual work. I needed help, quite desperately at times. With Eamon as fastidious editor and wordsmith and conceptualist (some chapters had more of his comments than they did my own words), what began as an earnest but rudderless first draft became a book. I loved Eamon. I hated him when he disagreed with me even though he was ultimately right. Frustrated at the pace of my writing, I tried to bait him into fights. He never bit but on several occasions he gently and firmly told me to grow the hell up.

The rest of the Houghton team shepherding the book, Executive Director of Publicity Lori Glazer, Senior Publicity Manager Megan Wilson, and Marketing Director Carla Gray, were wholly dedicated, hard-working, and fun in an industry not known much anymore for its *joie de vivre.* They restored my faith that publishing, while facing radical change like all creative forms, is hardly moribund.

My film agent, Ari Emanuel, is the biggest pain in the ass I have ever met. He makes the Ari Gold character in *Entourage,* based upon him, seem gentle and considerate. But every month for four years until the book was completed, he called to make sure I was not letting go of it (his words were slightly more pungent). I think what spurred me to finally finish was the peace and quiet of Ari not yelling at me. I also do not think I ever would have completed it without him. My literary agent, Eric Siminoff, was equally devoted to the book. Pete Berg, the brother I never had, also gave me great support. So did my therapist, Penny Stark. I must also include Steve Fried and the amazing Beth Kephart.

My wife, Lisa, was a staunch advocate. My son Gerry was a prince, giving of his time and forthright. He understood completely when I told him I did not want him to read the book until it was finished so as not to censor my heart. He too is a beautiful person inside and out, and I am more than proud of him. My son Caleb, despite being just twenty, may be the wisest person I know. We shared many conversations about the book and his instincts were sharp and insightful. He had no problem telling me to "chill out" when I was going off the rails, a recurrent theme in my life. I also must thank my sister, Annie, for her strength and absolute dedication as we both watched our parents die back to back. We had our moments because of the indescribable pain and stress. But Annie never quit and never wavered. She was literally side by side with my mother at the end and made her final months as happy and serene as they could possibly be. So did the saintly Albertha.

I am also indebted to Debra Nussbaum and her husband, Paul. Deb is a marvel; every day she works to make Zach's world as rich and rewarding as possible, and she has succeeded. The role of stepfather is never easy, but Paul has embraced the twins with love while treating my relationship with them with respect and dignity.

Then comes Zach. There is little I can say I have not already said. Except thank you. I do not know how much of *Father's Day* he will read or comprehend. He granted me his absolute trust. I can only hope and pray I have honored the wonder of his life.